HOW TO BE A SUCCESSFUL INVESTOR

HOW TO BE A SUCCESSFUL INVESTOR

Bailard, Biehl & Kaiser, Inc.

Dow Jones-Irwin
Homewood, Illinois 60430

Project editor: Gladys True
Production manager: Ann Cassady
Cover design: Image House
Cover illustration: David Lesh
Designer: Tara Bazata
Compositor: Eastern Graphics
Typeface: 10/12 Souvenir
Printer: Arcata Graphics/Kingsport

Library of Congress Cataloging-in-Publication Data

How to be a successful investor.

Includes index.
1. Investments. 2. Finance, Personal. I. Bailard,
Biehl & Kaiser.
HG4521.H784 1989   332.6'78   88-33401
ISBN 1-55623-135-0

Printed in the United States of America

1 2 3 4 5 6 7 8 9 0 K 6 5 4 3 2 1 0 9

PREFACE

In today's fast-paced, complex financial world many people fail to reach goals that are within their means simply because they lack organization and focus. It is possible to "take charge" of your financial affairs without becoming a full-time investment professional. In this book, and others in the *One Hour Guide* series, you will find new ways to increase your personal wealth, control financial risks, and boost your cash flow. This series will help you achieve the kind of personal satisfaction that comes only from mastering an important aspect of life: your financial affairs.

The information in this book and others in the series has been developed during our years of experience as financial advisors. We have helped hundreds of clients achieve their goals using the methods we describe in these pages. These goals have been as varied as the people themselves. They might include achieving financial independence or traveling the world, or paying for higher education, or providing for a family's financial security in retirement years, to name only a few.

Our popular seminars on personal money management have helped thousands of people from small business owners to corporate managers; from recent college graduates to retirees, become true *money managers*. They learned the importance of moving beyond being mere money makers and money spenders in order to achieve their life's goals.

Our college textbook, *Personal Money Management* (published by Science Research Associates and now in its fifth edition) is the leading text in its field. Hundreds of thousands of university and continuing education students have learned the fundamentals of personal finance through the book. Our own entrepreneurial experience, from our days together at Stanford Graduate School of Business to the top management of our own diversified corporation, has convinced us *personally* of the wisdom of these techniques. *We neither offer advice nor suggest any course of action that we have not applied successfully ourselves.*

For many years this hard-won expertise has been available only to wealthy investors and institutional accounts who can afford our specialized services and who appreciate the value of objective financial advice. Clients like these demand not only successful track records but also a deeper understanding of the role of money in achieving career and life goals. It was from our desire to make such counsel available to more people that this book and series was born.

As you would expect, a book as important as this one could not have been written by any three people alone. In addition to the generous cooperation of our clients, without whose feedback and support this series would not have been possible, we especially wish to thank Jerrold D. Dickson, Shirley Sarris, and Brenda Locke for their suggestions, extensive research, and other invaluable input for the final writing and editing of this edition. Our appreciation also goes to Jay Wurtz for his contributions to the original development of this book, and to John V. O. Leary, Ph.D., for bolstering our experiences with professional insight and wisdom.

To these and many others who helped us create, prepare, and deliver this book, we express our sincerest gratitude. With them, we take great pride and pleasure in welcoming you to our growing family of clients.

Thomas E. Bailard
David L. Biehl
Ronald W. Kaiser

CONTENTS

CHAPTER 1

INTRODUCTION

Most of us were taught that hard work, education, and saving for a rainy day would make tomorrow turn out better than today. The world of investments was for the wealthy who could afford the risks.

But, as Bob Dylan said, the times they are a-changing. In the years since the Second World War, Americans experienced a great growth in personal wealth. Today, there are many more households earning $35,000, $50,000, and more, and far more millionaires than ever before.

The high inflation that we endured during the 1970s revealed how vitally important it is to protect and nurture what we have if we are to achieve our life's goals. Until then it seemed as though Social Security, pension plans, and savings would be enough to secure our future. But that future has become more expensive and much less certain. The need to be "financially fit" has become as essential an ingredient to the good life as to one's physical well being.

Investments have changed dramatically in the last 20 years. There are now more choices and more information than ever. How do you begin? What do you need to know? You've made an important first step by starting this book. By the time you finish, you will learn a method that works for taking control of your financial future.

THE CHANGING FINANCIAL WORLD

Not many years ago, preparing for your financial future was much simpler than it is today. People struggled to save; some managed to invest. Interest rates held fairly steady.

Since the 1950s, each Business Cycle has witnessed greater volatility in interest rates and inflation, leading to greater swings in the investment markets. Interest rates fluctuated more in a single month in the inflation-plagued late 1970s than they did in the entire decade of the 1950s!

The technological revolution has generated dramatic changes faster than most of us ever thought possible. Instantaneous communication has increased the interdependence of the world's economies. As a result, political and economic events in foreign countries affect your investments more quickly and dramatically than ever before.

You can now bank 24 hours a day through automated teller machines (ATMs). Your tax return can be prepared on a computer and filed directly across telephone lines. Personal computers can quickly access a mountain of information on just about any subject. Through your own PC you can access financial data that used to be available only to professional investors.

The financial industry has undergone massive alterations. Deregulation of much of the banking industry has blurred the line between savings institutions and vendors of investment products. You are just as likely to be solicited by your banker as by your stockbroker to buy a wide variety of financial products ranging from certificates of deposit (CDs) to mutual funds to annuities.

Financial products have proliferated at a dizzying pace. The range of investment vehicles, services, and opportunities has never been greater. But, at the same time, this wide variety of options presents greater risks for the uninformed. Each new product is inevitably touted as the best answer to your investment goals.

Only a few years ago your investment options were limited to stocks, bonds, real estate, and some agricultural commodities. But today new products are continually being introduced for public consumption. There are money market funds, CDs tied to the stock market, annuities, IRAs, Real Estate Investment Trusts (REITs), Government National Mortgage Association securities (Ginnie Maes), commercial bonds, tax-free municipal bonds, Federal National Mortgage Association debentures and notes (Fannie Maes), commodities futures, and currencies, gold bullion, coins and certificates, energy investments, research and development partnerships, master limited partnerships, foreign stocks and bonds, and many more.

Mutual funds, which pool investors' funds under professional management, are available for the full range of investment vehicles. Funds specialize in options, futures, foreign securities, precious metals, and real estate. Even stock funds are not so simple anymore. There are funds that specialize in "takeover" stocks, "turnaround" (e.g., Chapter Eleven) issues, small companies, large companies, stocks of a single country, or a single region in the world (e.g., the Pacific Rim), or of a single industry (e.g., technology), or gold mining.

However, sales of leveraged tax shelters (2:1 or greater tax writeoffs) have shriveled to a fraction of their pre-1984 level. Tax reform and stepped-up IRS prosecution of abusive shelters has curbed this once flourishing sector of the financial industry.

Professional financial planners who can help guide you through the investment jungle were, at one time, only a small part of the investment world. They now account for billions of dollars of financial product sales. The role of a financial planner has grown to encompass a broad range of advisory services, including, in some cases, managing clients' assets. Some planners charge only for their time and advice, basing their fees on an hourly rate or on the size of your portfolio. Others are compensated, at least in part, by commissions from the products they recommend. The former provide services that often make sense only for the wealthy. The latter are often salespeople in disguise, pushing specific offerings of insurance companies, banks, or brokerage houses.

This increasingly complex range of investment choices has effectively paralyzed many people into nonaction and caused many others to make unfortunate mistakes. Along with fluctuations in the economy and the many scandals, schemes, and frauds dominating the front pages, it's no wonder so many people are confused and skeptical.

The features of financial products are widely promoted, appealing to a number of psychological "buttons," such as fear, greed, or peace of mind. While purveyors whet your appetite with the opportunities to make and protect your money, to satisfy your needs, or to allay your fears, they also have to differentiate their offerings from all the rest. Too often, the hype results in forcing investors to focus on **what** is offered, rather than on **how** they can best meet their financial goals.

Our aim in this book is to provide you with an objective method of evaluating your alternatives and to help you choose those that meet your goals. We will demonstrate not only how to manage your money to achieve your desired results but also how to work with those who help manage your finances, such as bankers, brokers, and planners.

THE ROLE OF INVESTMENTS IN YOUR LONG-TERM FINANCIAL PLAN

Holding your money in passbook savings accounts may seem safe, but is it a wise choice? The reasons for putting money aside are varied. They include preparing for emergencies, saving enough to put your children through college, buying a home, taking a long vacation, purchasing a new car, or preparing for a comfortable retirement. You must ask yourself if your current approach will satisfy your goals.

We tend to have short memories when it comes to our financial affairs. Inflation, once the primary concern of American consumers, has moved off the front pages. After experiencing an inflation rate approaching 20 percent per year in the late 1970s, the consumer price index (CPI) climbed a mere

1.1 percent in 1986. But, has the back of inflation been broken permanently? Will you still have to consider the impact of inflation in your financial planning? Will building a savings nest egg cover your needs? Let's see.

In 1987 the CPI rose over 4 percent, the major variable being energy prices. Excluding energy (principally the price of oil), inflation was steady in the 4 percent to 5 percent range through the end of 1988. Compared to the 1970s, that's an improvement. Yet, *even at 5 percent inflation, the purchasing power of your money will still be halved in less than 15 years.*

What does that mean for those who keep all their savings in a 5.25 percent passbook account? To find out, first adjust the return for inflation. Even at the 4 percent rate that we've seen in recent years (and that is still considerably below the average for the past 20 years), that leaves only 1.25 percent **real** growth. And don't forget taxes (because you can rest assured the state and federal authorities won't!).

So, it's obvious that you have to do something with your money beyond passbook savings, if only to keep ahead of inflation. But it isn't enough to just put your money where it might earn more than in a savings bank. You have to be certain that your money is working for you, regardless of economic conditions. You have to adjust your approach in response to changes that take place. Making money is far different than *managing* it. Two examples will illustrate this point.

Just before the Great Depression, many people managed their money as though the speculative bubble would never burst. It did. And they lost all they had.

In the late 1970s, many people lost **real purchasing power** even though their bank account balances increased. Inflation exacted a very real and very substantial penalty. Passbook savings accounts, with their 5.25 percent yield, actually lost over 5 percent per annum when adjusted for inflation.

On the one hand, during the Great Depression a very conservative cash-oriented investment approach was the best approach. On the other hand, during the inflationary 70s, such a conservative approach proved disastrous for its practitioners.

We live in a complex and everchanging world. Financial affairs are no exception. An investment that worked well in the past may not perform as well in the future. Your financial well being is dependent on learning how best to deal with widely varying economic scenarios. To do so you need to become familiar with the world of investments.

Like it or not, you are an investor. You may not think of yourself in such terms, but it is, nonetheless, true. When you put your money into a savings account or a money market fund, you are making an investment decision. If you elect to spend your entire paycheck every month on current consumption, you are making an investment decision.

There is only one real test of investment success. Are you able to achieve the goals you have set for yourself? *Not*, Did you earn "x" percent? *Not*, Did you outperform the stock market? *Nor*, Did you stay ahead of inflation? The only measure of success is your answer to: **Did you meet your financial goals?**

Your decisions about money should be viewed in this light. Too many people think of investing as the purview of the highly sophisticated, wealthy, Wall Street speculators. Yet, all of us are investors. And there are far more of us than there are Wall Streeters.

Investments in all their diversity are meant to provide alternative uses for your money. Since people have differing wants and desires, investment vehicles are designed to meet certain of those ends. For example, most investors are seeking either current income or growth, or a combination of the two.

An investor in need of current income (e.g., a retired or disabled person) would seek investments that regularly pay higher than average interest or dividends. These vehicles may include (though are certainly not limited to) preferred stock, government or corporate bonds, or money market instruments.

Someone who has adequate income but needs asset growth to build a retirement nest egg (or to buy a yacht) would look for other types of investments. Growth-oriented investments include (but are not limited to) common stocks, real estate, foreign stocks, or more speculative alternatives, such as options or futures.

KNOWING YOURSELF

As you may have guessed by now, the real key to defining an investment plan for your unique situation is to **know yourself**. Investments are being marketed more aggressively every day. But, despite what a salesperson may tell you, every investment is not ideal for every person. Sometimes the one who benefits most from the sales of a particular product is the salesperson, not the client.

Through our daily work dealing with people and their finances, we have seen that individuals tend to fall into one of four financial categories, as determined by their mix of assets and income. Understanding your own financial physique will help you decide what investment plan will be best for you. Take a look at Figure 1–1 to find your financial physique.

The four "financial physiques" characterized in Figure 1–1 not only have varying incomes and assets, as you can see on the graph, they also have different attitudes and behaviors about dealing with money. You should be able to recognize yourself in one of the descriptions that follow.

FIGURE 1–1
The Four Financial Physiques

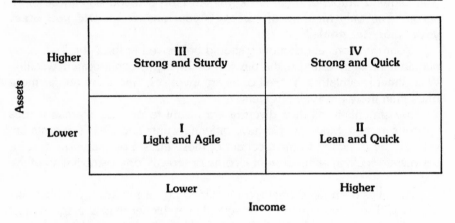

The Four Financial Physiques

TYPE I: Light and Agile
This financial figure has few assets and a modest income. A person in this category may be just starting a career or may simply not place a great value on money or the things that money can buy.

TYPE II: Lean and Quick
Enjoying a significant income, this physique has few assets. It lacks the staying power of true financial fitness. Lean and Quicksters often have great money-making talents but are usually enthusiastic money spenders as well.

TYPE III: Strong and Sturdy
These solid "money muscle" people have numerous assets but may be short of ready cash. Due to inherited or acquired wealth, Strong and Sturdy types can make the long haul financially. But, many of them are muscle-bound by their possessions, keeping too great a portion of their wealth in illiquid assets, such as collectibles, real estate, or low-risk/low-return investments.

TYPE IV: Strong and Quick
Although Strong and Quicks seem to have "arrived" financially, most seek more satisfying ways to apply their wealth and income. To ensure that those

well-developed money muscles don't wither before or during retirement, these physiques are usually as concerned about preserving their resources as adding to them.

Knowing your financial physique will be helpful in understanding the examples and worksheets as you progress through the book. We've designed the following questionnaire, Taking Stock Number 1, to help you identify your own financial physique and gain some clues about where your individualized Personal Profit Plan should take you. Take the time to complete it now, and then evaluate your results.

Taking Stock Number 1

Knowing Your Financial Physique

For each of the incomplete sentences below, circle the letter of the answer that best reflects your *current* financial attitudes and circumstances.

1. My salary (or income) is . . .
    a. barely adequate for, or doesn't meet, my needs.
    b. adequate for my needs.
    c. adequate for my needs but less than I would like.
    d. more than adequate for my current needs and desires.

2. Financially, I . . .
    a. often struggle to make ends meet.
    b. can meet my current expenses but have trouble saving for the future.
    c. am sometimes short of cash, but I have my share of possessions.
    d. can do almost anything I want to do.

3. In terms of material possessions, I . . .
    a. own very little.
    b. have fewer possessions than most people with my income.
    c. have a good deal of real and personal property.
    d. have most of the material things I want.

4. When I think about *making* money, I . . .
    a. first think about what I'd have to give up to get it.
    b. think about *spending* money, too.
    c. think about the tangible things it can buy.
    d. feel a sense of accomplishment and satisfaction.

5. When I think about *losing* money, I . . .
    a. am not too worried because I don't have that much to lose.

Knowing Your Financial Physique (*concluded*)

---

    b.   don't worry because I know I can make it back again.
    c.   am fearful because it threatens what I have already gained.
    d.   don't worry too much because there's more where that came from.

6. When I think of *spending* money, my thoughts turn to . . .
    a.   watching every nickel.
    b.   buying what I can right now.
    c.   buying something substantial or an investment that will grow.
    d.   attaining important goals.

7. If people envy me, it is probably because . . .
    a.   I'm not preoccupied with money.
    b.   I earn a good salary.
    c.   they would like to have the things I own.
    d.   they think I have everything I want.

8. If I had just a *little* more money, I would . . .
    a.   be a *lot* better off.
    b.   probably spend it as fast as I got it.
    c.   invest it in something substantial.
    d.   use it where it would do the most good.

9. When I think about *debt*, I . . .
    a.   worry about mine a great deal.
    b.   know I can pay mine off as I go along.
    c.   know I could get a loan because of the property I own.
    d.   think more about *lending* than borrowing.

10. Money is . . .
    a.   a worrisome topic.
    b.   an *easy* come, *easy* go proposition.
    c.   valuable because of the tangible things it can buy.
    d.   a potential source of personal fulfillment.

Taking Stock of Your Financial Fitness

The questionnaire you've just completed measures the money-related attitudes and circumstances we have found to be most closely associated with the four basic financial physiques. To score your choices, count separately the *(a)*, *(b)*, *(c)*, and *(d)* answers and record the totals under the heading marked "*Current*".

Desired		Current
_____	Total number of (*a*)s:	_____
_____	Total number of (*b*)s:	_5_
_____	Total number of (*c*)s:	_3_
_10_	Total number of (*d*)s:	_2_

Finding Your Current Financial Physique

If you have more *(a)* answers than any other, you tend toward Type I, a Light and Agile financial figure. Both your income and assets are relatively modest, which may be a source of discomfort in your life. Most people in this category, even if they are nonmaterialistic, would find their lives enhanced by a more robust financial physique. If you are like most Light and Agiles, you want a financial cushion to fall back on as well as more disposable income to spend on the things that really matter.

If you have more *(b)* answers, you tend toward a Type II, Lean and Quick financial physique. You are long on income but short on accumulated wealth. You lack the asset foundation necessary to gain investment income or buffer you against economic adversity.

If you have more *(c)* answers, you tend toward the Strong and Sturdy financial figure, Type III. Your values or circumstances have left you with more *things* than cash. You may have less financial flexibility than you would like.

If your *(d)* answers outnumbered the others, you are probably a Strong and Quick financial type. You may have already mastered many important skills of money management. Neither income nor wealth is a particular problem for you; but you may, nevertheless, be seeking to improve your financial well being.

Now go back to the questionnaire and put a check beside each answer that best reflects how you would like to see yourself in the future. When you're done, compute your new score for each letter as you did before and enter the results under the left-hand column. The letter with the highest count is your *desired* financial physique. You may discover that your current situation suits you or, as is often the case, that a new financial physique will provide a better vehicle for fulfilling your wants and needs. Bear your *current* and your *desired* financial physique in mind throughout the book. You will learn disciplined money-management strategies that will support the program best suited to *you*. Within the parameters determined by your financial physique, you are probably ready to begin building wealth and alternative income sources through wise investments.

Fit Your Investments to You

Many of the most heavily advertised investments are simply not suitable for most people. They were designed to meet specific needs in the marketplace. Many salespeople will try to sell you an investment vehicle without first taking the time to learn about your needs and abilities. You will be very lucky, indeed, if the product is appropriate for you. In the next two chapters you will learn about your *personality* as an investor, which, when taken into account, will help you make your financial decisions.

Too often, investors find themselves trying to fit their personalities to a lucrative-sounding investment. "I'm a conservative investor but my broker (or friend, or co-worker) tells me how much money can be made buying options. I think I'll give it a try."

If you have used the book as directed, you will be much better prepared to know whether you should give options (or any other unfamiliar investment) a try. Does it fit **your Investment Personality?** If not, it should be avoided.

We've learned through the years that discipline is a key difference between those who succeed and those who fail as investors.

THE GOALS OF THIS BOOK

Many books provide readers with a compendium of investment definitions. Our goal is much more ambitious. Not only do we want to introduce you to the major elements of the investment scene but we want to provide you with the tools to blend those elements into a successful investment program.

Specifically, we'll help you:

1. Find out who you are as an investor (Chapter 3). Your portfolio is as individual as your clothes, your car, or your home. If you don't mind "wearing" just any old thing, you'll be happy to shop randomly for financial products. But, you'll wind up buying those products your salesperson most wants to get rid of. However, if you want to take control as your own Personal Profit Planner, you will want only investments that fit you best. You will want to feel comfortable with them. The only way you will know which ones to buy is to know yourself. That's what this book is all about.

2. Diversify your financial assets safely and effectively (Chapters 4, 5, and 6). Remember the many different economic environments we mentioned above. Unfortunately there is no one single investment that is suitable for all potential scenarios. Proper *diversification* of your investments will enable you to preserve your asset base while earning a good return, regardless of the economic climate. Knowing how to allocate your resources is a key lesson in this book.

3. Identify which investments will most effectively help you achieve your financial goals (Chapter 5). The book is designed to go from the general to the more specific. First, you will learn how to allocate your investable resources into the five major asset classes. Next, you will learn about specific investment vehicles in each class that will help you attain your objectives. These details will help you sort through the many investments available to find those which suit your Financial Physique and fit your Investment Personality.

When you have finished, you will know how, what, and where to invest to achieve your financial goals. We don't know of any other financial book that offers the tools and experience necessary to guide you through this process.

Who Is Bailard, Biehl & Kaiser?

As financial advisors to some of the wealthiest individuals and most prestigious institutions in the country, we have assembled winning portfolios of diversified investments. During our many years of experience, we have developed an investment strategy that has not only survived but prospered—in virtually every economic climate.

We have coached thousands of individual *money-makers* like yourself in how to *manage* their money and gain higher investment returns with safer asset allocating. But, most important of all, we have used these techniques *ourselves*—in our personal investments and in managing the successful, diversified corporation that has borne our name since 1969.

How do you make investments work for you? We think the answer is straightforward: **Take control of your financial life.** Learn about yourself and what you need. Write down your goals. Devise a game plan that takes advantage of diversification and stick to it.

The Book's Structure

We have designed *How to Be a Successful Investor* to provide you with practical, usable advice. The exercises are meant to focus your thinking on the important variables you will have to contend with among the maze of alternatives out there.

In Chapter 2 we take a survey look at the world of investments. We discuss how to make sense of the economic news. We cover the impact of people's varied expectations on their investment posture. We look at the problems that the rapidly changing investment arena poses for investors. Finally, we introduce the five asset classes that form the basis of our diversified investment approach.

In Chapter 3 the focus is on **you**. You will discover your Investor Personality. How well do you handle risk? You may be surprised to find that you are more conservative (or more speculative) than you thought. We also discuss how couples can reconcile their different investor personalities. You will learn an overall strategy that all types of investors can use to their advantage.

In Chapter 4 you will begin to build your investment portfolio. The first step is always hardest. We discuss what information to gather to make intelligent choices for the future. You'll discover the numerous ways to use diversification to your benefit.

Chapter 5 helps you to put it all together. You will be introduced to the BB&K Rosetta Stone—a tool that deciphers financial doubletalk and prescribes the investments you need for your Personal Profit Plan. You will set the groundwork for your own Personal Profit portfolio.

In Chapter 6 you will learn just what kind of portfolio manager you are. We describe two basic styles of portfolio management: a *fixed* mix, where you maintain your predetermined percentage allocation among your chosen asset classes by adjustments made at specific intervals, and a *variable* or *dynamic* mix, in which you decide what percentage to allocate among the asset classes in your portfolio, based on your analysis and forecast of economic trends and probability of action. We show you how to revise your allocations to make certain your investments keep pace with changing conditions. You will see how market forecasts can add value to your portfolio.

Chapter 7 explains how you can make the best use of mutual funds. The dramatic growth in the mutual fund industry has led to changes that may offer you opportunities to take advantage of professional management without prohibitive cost. We describe various kinds of mutual funds in terms of their investment objectives. You will also read about sources of information that will help you make your decisions.

Finally, in Chapter 8, we provide concise yet complete descriptions of various investment vehicles within the five asset classes.

If you take the time to complete the Taking Stock questionnaires and Action Papers as they come up, you will come away from this book with a personal investment plan that is at least as good—and far more personal—than those prepared by most professional financial planners. You will have more confidence in yourself as an investor. You will feel better about the financial condition of your household. And you will see that it is possible to enhance the likelihood of achieving your financial goals.

Remember, you already possess valuable skills as a money maker. We will help you utilize those skills to make you a successful *money manager*. The rewards of successful money management await your efforts!

WHAT DO I KNOW ABOUT INVESTING?

Before you begin Chapter 2, take a few moments to complete the following Taking Stock questionnaire.

Taking Stock Number 2

What Do I Know About Investing?

Many people start their careers as money-managers with built-in biases about the investment process. To judge your investment assumptions against investment realities, indicate your agree- ment or disagreement with the following statements by circling T (for true) or F (for false). When you (and your partner, if you have one) have finished, read the evaluation that follows the questionnaire.

	Partner A	Partner B
1. If I make enough high-risk investments, I will eventually "hit a home run" and make a bundle of money.	T F	T F
2. If I'm going to be an investor, I'd better be prepared to spend several hours every week monitoring my holdings.	T F	T F
3. "Luck" is the name of the game in successful investing.	T F	T F
4. Without an honest, well-informed broker to guide me, I can never make reliable investment decisions.	T F	T F
5. A small sum of money can never amount to anything as an investment.	T F	T F
6. If I don't have the resources of a big organization, with its power and research capacity behind me, I can't really make it big in investments.	T F	T F
7. A diversified portfolio involves a lot of record-keeping.	T F	T F
8. With frightening government deficits and unpredictable infla- tion, real estate is the only safe investment.	T F	T F

What Do I Know About Investing? (*concluded*)

	Partner A	Partner B
9. With high interest rates, the place to put money is in certificates of deposit (CDs) or Treasury bills (T-bills).	T F	T F
10. The best way to make money is to be where the action is: in the most popular investments.	T F	T F
11. If I turn my money over to someone else to manage, I lose control of it.	T F	T F

Now read the evaluation and discussions of your answers.

Evaluating What I Know about Investments

The Taking Stock questionnaire measured your attitudes and beliefs about making money work for you—your *suitability* for and *readiness* to make investments. Because life (or your own initiative) has put you into a position to make investments work for you, there is no scoring for this questionnaire. Rather, we hope you'll compare your answers to ours and be ready to *amend those preconceptions* you may have about investing, *with an eye to increasing your personal profit.*

Item 1.   True. Time works in favor of investment gamblers, but you may pay out more than you win!

A dice player in a casino might eventually make a hundred, or a thousand, consecutive passes—but it may take more than one lifetime to do it. By definition, *long odds* are a high risk, meaning that the probability of failure is greater than the probability of success. But, that's not the same as *impossibility*. Someone might visit the same casino, put a silver dollar in the slots, and win the million-dollar jackpot on the very first pull of the handle. Another person may play the same machine year after year, knowing (quite correctly, from a mathematical point of view) that persistence will eventually pay off. Unfortunately, by the time the million-dollar jackpot is won, that player may have had to invest $20 million in the machine—hardly a winning proposition for gamblers—or investors.

Item 2.   True and False. It all depends on your personality.

Do you prefer to watch a game, or would you rather play in it? Perhaps you're the person who stands on the sidelines coaching the players? You can look at money-management the same way. If you want to watch, you can hire others to choose and manage your investments, providing you're willing to pay for the service. Or, if you have the time and the inclination, you could put it together and manage it yourself. Some people spend a lot of time on a daily basis managing their own small to sizable portfolios, while others (often the very wealthy) spend only a few hours a month being briefed by a portfolio manager whom they have learned to trust. Some people have settled on a middle ground, making their own choices and keeping their eyes on what's going on, but relying on professionals to manage at least some aspects of their portfolios. How you handle it is up to you. You can be successful either way.

Item 3. True, but only if you depend on luck for results.

If we had perfect knowledge of the future, we could make our investment decisions with perfect certainty. Putting your money in a passbook savings account at a trustworthy bank comes close to this model. There's a high degree of assurance that the bank will be able to pay your 5 percent or 6 percent interest at the end of a year. But, as you extend your choices through the range of investment instruments you'll learn about in this book, the knowledge of the outcome and, indeed, the likelihood of success, will become less certain. However, the potential for returns will exceed that 5 percent or 6 percent several times over. Balancing the forces of safety (risk) and of return (reward) to meet your goals is what Personal Profit Planning is all about.

Item 4. False. Brokers are commissioned salespeople, not impartial counselors.

You can't expect a broker, whose livelihood depends on transactions, to talk you out of a potential buy or sell decision. The best you can hope for is that the broker will have a financial product on the shelf that happens to fit your needs. By learning the BB&K method of Personal Profit Planning, you will reduce your dependence upon such financial salespeople and be more responsible for your own money-management success.

Item 5. True and False. It depends on what you decide to do with it.

Suppose you took the $2,000 allowed by the IRS for an individual retirement account (IRA) and put it under your mattress. At the end of 20 years, you would still have your $2,000 in cash; but, at 5 percent annual inflation, you would need $5,300 to buy then what that $2,000 buys today. Alternately, if you put the $2,000 in an account paying 8 percent simple interest, you would have $5,200 at the end of 20 years. That's better, but not nearly as good as if that account *compounded* your returns. If your $2,000 was deposited at 8 percent compounded, it would have grown to $9,322— almost four and a half times its initial value. (Now suppose you earn not only 8 percent compounded interest on your $2,000 but you *add* an additional $2,000 to your principal sum each year—that's the way a *small* investment really grows!)

Item 6.   False. It doesn't take a big resourceful organization to earn big returns.

It will humble many financial journalists and commissioned brokers to learn that, over the past 10 years, the majority of professionally managed stock portfolios *underperformed* the market indices against which their success was measured. There's no correlation between long-term success and costly analytical resources. On the contrary, many fabulously successful investment advisors have earned their reputations as lone eagle practitioners. With a little help, and the right perspective, you can do at *least* as well as the market averages, even with a modest portfolio.

Item 7.   True. But, you don't have to do it personally unless you want to.

Years ago, if you wanted a diversified investment portfolio, you had to go through a technical and tedious process yourself. But, as a result of two enterprising advances, it's much easier now. First, cooperative investment programs called *mutual funds* were created, with an experienced investment advisor who manages the assets you invest in the fund. The other was the development of personal computers and software, which allow you to manage your assets yourself, without having to perform laborious and repetitive calculations. Of course, a full-service brokerage firm will provide you with a computerized statement of your investment transactions, as long as they handle *all* your transactions. In any case, a diversified portfolio can be developed by anyone who can make the minimum investment, sometimes as little as $1,000.

Item 8.   False. Diversification, not concentration, is the wise investor's hedge against adversity.

In the 1920s, when postwar inflation was rampant, many people concentrated their assets in commercial real estate, only to lose most of the dollars they invested. By the middle of that decade, real estate prices had begun to decline as part of a general inflation. By the time the economy went "over the edge" in 1930, real estate could do little more than follow suit. If those same people had diversified their portfolios into high-grade, fixed-income bonds (particularly government issues), they not only would have saved their principal, they would have made a tidy profit besides. You can never tell with certainty what economic news is around the corner, so you'll come out ahead in the long run by diversifying your investments over a variety of asset classes.

Item 9.   True. But, only to a certain extent.

At a time when interest rates are high, inflation is low, and your goals are only a few years away, you would be foolish not to lock into a superior rate of return from an essentially risk-free investment. But some people take that logic to extremes. Instead of seeing such opportunities as a one-time good thing, they view them as a permanent condition which, as history shows, is clearly not the case. Over the last half century, T-bill returns have kept pace with inflation, but rarely exceeded it. Thus, investors desiring a *real* return on their money (i.e., increased purchasing power) would have been disappointed by not putting a portion into stocks and real estate. You should take advantage of the whole spectrum of investment markets and vehicles, rather than just one or two, to keep your Personal Profit Plan on track.

Item 10. False. Unless you were there before those investments became popular.

One of the penalties of following the herd into anything is that all the good grazing will be gone by the time you get there. The classic example of this was in the 1960s when mutual funds were the "in" thing to buy. Naturally, as the value of the stocks that those funds purchased increased, the price of mutual fund shares became more expensive, until the market bears came to Wall Street and took their profits, lowering stock prices and badly depleting the honeycomb for everyone else. Those who had not diversified into other investments lost a good bit of cash when those mutual fund shares fell, reinforcing our belief that it's good to be where the action is, only if you get there first.

Item 11. True. So, it makes sense to find a good money manager, or do things yourself.

Let's face it, few of us like the idea of putting ourselves completely at someone else's mercy. If you design your own diversified portfolio according to the rules in this book, you will be in a better position to so manage those who manage your money that they won't steer you wrong in your investments. Of course, if you allocate and invest your funds according to our guidelines, you'll have nobody but yourself to blame (or thank) for your success. Once the mystique of money management has been lifted from your investments, you'll be surprised what you, as a conscientious Personal Profit Planner, can do.

CHAPTER 2

THE INVESTMENT MARKETS: WHAT THEY ARE

ECONOMICS AND EXPECTATIONS: THE FOUNDATIONS OF INVESTING

The economy is a stage on which investors are the actors. And, as in the theater, the props and sets on the stage, indeed, the play itself, are subject to change. In this chapter you will gain an understanding of the key economic concepts that affect the investor's environment and why they are important to you. Good investment decisions are aided by understanding some fundamental factors in the economy. Economics is neither as dismal nor as abstract as is often thought. The huge investment world can be narrowed into five asset classes that each play a distinct role in a portfolio designed to weather a variety of economic environments.

First: A Warning about the Monthly Economic Numbers

When the media report economic news, there's a tendency to become numbers-fixated. Government statistics are reported regularly for a wide variety of areas. You have probably read reports on such matters as durable goods orders, construction spending, consumer spending, income, unemployment, machine tool orders, industrial production, auto sales, and many others. All are reported with solemn appraisals by government spokespeople and independent analysts.

When the data are recounted, they are compared to the previous month (or to the previous reporting period). The month-to-month comparisons don't really tell you much of significance. Yet some long-term investors tend to overreact to monthly reports, because of the short-term orientation of the media reporting the news.

There are two things to keep in mind when you read or hear the latest economic news flashes. First, government statistics are prone to substantial revisions later. The revisions, which are even more important, receive much less fanfare.

Second, there is a lag between the time when the data for a particular report are gathered and when they are reported. So what you are hearing is how things were two, three, or even four months ago. Investment markets, though, anticipate the future. For example, at important stock market bottoms, the economic data typically seem very gloomy. Only after the market has begun to rise will the economic data begin to confirm a better environment.

We mention these caveats because far too many investors become so wrapped up with the "trees" (the mass of economic minutiae) that they fail to see the "forest" (the important long-term economic trends that move investments decisively).

Some Common Terms and What They Mean to You

GNP

The single most widely watched indicator of the health of the U.S. economy is GNP (gross national product), which is the total value of goods and services created in the economy. GNP is made up of consumer and government purchases, private domestic and foreign investment in the United States, and the total value of exports. *Real GNP* is reported quarterly on an inflation-adjusted basis. There are normally at least one, and often two or three, revisions of the preliminary figures. That's another reason to stand back and keep your long-term perspective.

Over the long-term (decades), GNP has tended to rise at an annual rate of about 3 percent per year. However, there have been significant short-term fluctuations in the GNP's growth rate. The Business Cycle is defined by these swings (see below).

Inflation

Inflation is commonly defined as a rise in the price of goods and services. From an investor's standpoint, inflation means that "things" are more valuable than the paper dollars that purchase them. For example, in the late 1970s the price of such tangible goods as gold, silver, diamonds, art, rare coins, and other collectibles rose rapidly as people chose to own them, rather than to hold paper dollars. They felt that the purchasing power of their paper money was decreasing rapidly. But, when investors perceived a turn in inflation in 1982, they chose to hold dollar-denominated assets, rather than intangibles. Gold, silver, and collectible prices fell sharply while "financial assets," such as stocks and bonds, rose dramatically.

You should also be familiar with the terms *nominal* and *real* prices.

Nominal prices are those stated or listed for an item. When prices have been adjusted for inflation, they are real.

In times of high inflation the difference between nominal and real returns is important. An investment that returns a nominal ten percent when inflation is ten percent is a wash. To increase your purchasing power, the investment must appreciate more than the underlying inflation rate. Otherwise, you have gained nothing.

Another important aspect of inflation for investors is that *borrowers* are better off than *lenders*. Borrowers are people who use someone else's money to buy things. While they pay their lenders a *fee* (usually interest), under inflation they are able to repay their loans with future devalued dollars.

The most widely accepted measure of inflation is the *consumer price index* (CPI). The CPI reflects change in consumer prices as determined by a survey of the Bureau of Labor Statistics that is reported monthly. Most references to the "rate of inflation" are based on the CPI.

The Leading Economic Indicators

The government's primary economic forecasting tool is the Commerce Department's *Index of Leading Economic Indicators*. This index is made up of 11 separate components that have been judged to have value in predicting the direction of the economy.

While the index has been accurate in calling the economy's ups and downs, it is far from exact. The lead times from signals to economic follow-through vary substantially. However, the index can be useful, because it helps investors to know whether the economy is in an expansion or contraction phase.

The Budget and Trade Deficits

The "twin deficit" problem has played an increasingly important role in the investment markets in recent years.

Many economists believe that the single greatest obstacle to recession-free growth for the U.S. economy is the large and growing federal budget deficit. The deficit is, simply stated, the difference between the government's revenues and its expenditures. If you ran a deficit in your household budget for any length of time, outside constraints would eventually be imposed to prevent it from growing ever larger. But the federal government is able to continue running a deficit because (1) it is able to borrow with the best credit rating possible and (2) through the Federal Reserve, it has the ability to create money to fund its growing debt.

Even though the federal government has substantial advantages when it comes to handling its debt, both foreign and domestic investors know that the rising debt load will impose restrictions on the government's flexibility.

For example, during recessions, government spending normally expands to provide a stimulus to the economy. The huge deficits may limit the government's future options for the economy.

The federal government plays a very large role in the bond markets, because it sells so many Treasury bonds to finance government activities. How the government copes with the deficit is an important consideration for bond investors.

Concern over the huge budget deficits has led investors to focus on the "trade deficit," which is the difference between the value of imports minus the value of exports. The trade deficit most directly affects the dollar's status. Investors need to be aware of how the dollar fares, because it affects American businesses and, ultimately, the state of the economy.

When the dollar was strong in the early 1980s, the demand for foreign goods weakened American industry, causing some companies to fail. As more products are purchased that are made overseas, domestic employment is hurt. As companies fail and unemployment rises, fears about the prospects for the U.S. economy mount.

In a fearful environment, investors are more cautious. They shy away from investments, such as stocks, which depend on the strength of the economy. Instead, they invest in vehicles with guaranteed returns, such as bonds. They give up the potential of more growth for the safety of a set return. Without investment, capital business will suffer even more.

This vicious circle feeds on itself, hurting the economy. The trade deficit can be viewed as a sign of the vitality of the U.S. economy. If imports exceed exports for too long a period, however, employment and business begin to falter.

When the dollar is "strong," foreign goods are cheaper on a relative basis. This condition existed from 1982 to the end of 1986. When the dollar is "weak," foreign products become more expensive. Rising foreign prices create inflationary pressures. American manufacturers are able to raise prices, because their price competition from foreign goods is lightened.

Investor Alert. Investors should keep a close watch on the trend for both the budget and trade deficits. An "increasing" budget deficit may warn of revived inflation and higher interest rates. A "declining" budget deficit would free the government's hands to act if the economy turned down.

The direction of the trade deficit also yields valuable clues for investors. A rising deficit would signal increased inflation, higher interest rates, and stagnant economic growth. If the deficit shrinks (not too many years ago there actually was a surplus!), it signals recovering business for export-oriented companies. A declining deficit would also help stabilize the dollar, leading to lower interest rates and a strengthening economy.

Our investment approach requires minimal forecasting acumen. As you will learn in Chapters 4 and 6, familiarity with long-term trends may help you fine tune your portfolio, but it is not critical to success. The risk-averse, conservative diversified approach is far more important than economic forecasts.

The Federal Reserve

The Federal Reserve Bank (the Fed) is the central bank for the United States. The Federal Reserve system consists of 12 regional banks across the country. The Fed monitors banks to ensure compliance with regulations.

The Fed is also the "lender of last resort" for the banking system. This means that, if member banks need an infusion of money to meet legitimate needs (e.g., a sudden demand by depositors to withdraw their money), they can borrow from the Fed. The *discount rate* is the interest rate that the Fed charges member banks for the money they borrow.

The most important and visible function of the Fed is its control over the nation's money supply. Money makes possible today's complex economic transactions. The Fed attempts to regulate the money supply to facilitate economic growth.

While it all seems simple in theory, there are many conflicting forces for the Fed to contend with. Encouraging economic growth by lowering interest rates or by creating more money must be balanced against the risk of increased inflation. If too many dollars are created it would lessen the value of each existing dollar.

As you can see, the Fed must walk a fine line. Money that is "too tight" will cause an economic slowdown. If money is "too loose" inflation will pick up.

Investor Alert.   The financial media makes frequent mention of the Fed adopting an "easy" or a "tight" money policy. An easy money policy means the Fed is injecting money into the financial system. Initially, more money pushes interest rates lower (more supply will lower the price or interest rate of money). An easy money policy stimulates the economy.

If an easy money policy were a cure-all it would be permanent policy. But too much money leads to inflation, and inflation leads to higher interest rates. Higher interest rates stunt economic growth.

A tight money policy was credited with breaking inflation's back in the early 1980s. The initial effect was to raise interest rates. With limited credit available, the least creditworthy borrowers were forced out of the market. That resulted in a sharp recession as businesses were forced to retrench.

Eventually, though, the lower inflation rate led to lower interest rates. Lenders no longer had to tack such a large "inflation premium" on their loans.

Market reaction to Fed policy is not always constant. When inflation fears are high, a turn to easy money may immediately trigger higher interest rates. If inflation is not a primary concern, however, interest rates will usually turn lower with the initial flush of easy money.

The Fed is not always able to accomplish exactly what it wants. Don't make the mistake of assuming an infallible Fed. No one can know or control the future with certainty. This is why it is important to have an investment approach that can weather a variety of economic conditions and government blunders.

The Economy: How It Relates to Your Investments

It is not necessary to understand the fine nuances of economic developments to succeed as an investor. In fact, there is no evidence that economists are superior investors. However, it is important to understand that the periodic fluctuations in the economy have important affects on investments.

Different investments exist because people don't share their expectations about the future. These expectations are dynamic; they change as the economy changes. For example, when the economy is expanding, employment opportunities are improving, income is rising, and the general confidence level is high. Investments that tap this growth and good feeling will perform the best. Buying stock in companies with good business prospects makes sense. Real estate values will rise in regions of the country where business is booming.

During a recession, unemployment rises, income shrinks, and business failures increase. Confidence dips as consumers become more cautious. Investors tend to take a less-aggressive approach. They may trade the uncertain prospect of growth offered by common stocks for the guaranteed interest of a bond. Gold is considered by many investors to be a hedge against bad times. Likewise, buoyant foreign economies may offer growth opportunities not found in the domestic economy.

It would be great if we could all forecast economic changes with precision. We would know exactly when the economy is just beginning to come out of a recession and what is the perfect time to buy stocks. We would know when to buy and sell gold, real estate, and foreign securities to maximize our profits.

Unfortunately, not even professional economists can predict the future. The economic profession is perennially split over the economy's prospects. A quick perusal of the financial press every January will show you just how diverse their opinions are. Some predict a boom, others forecast an impending recession, and others project more of the same (whatever *that* is !).

They do agree on one thing, though. The economy is always under-

FIGURE 2–1
The Business Cycle Roller Coaster

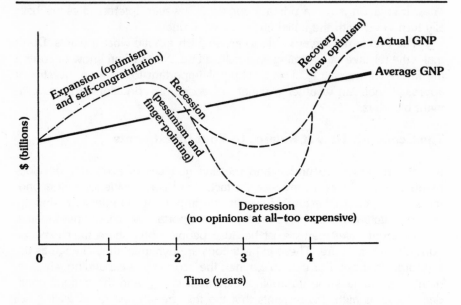

going change. The one sure bet you can make about the economy is that it *will* change. That is the basis of our investment approach.

The economy always has, and probably always will, go through periodic phases of expansion (the "good times") and contraction (recession, or, even worse, depression). This periodic rise and fall is called the *Business Cycle.* Figure 2–1 illustrates this roller coaster action.

You can see that, as an investor, it is important to have an idea *where* the economy is in the cycle. An expanding economy (rising GNP) requires new money to facilitate business. Common stocks generally do well in this phase. A contracting economy tends to favor investments that don't depend on growth for their returns. Bonds are one investment that would be favored in this environment.

THE FIVE ASSET CLASSES

Because people are different, they require different things from their investments. Such a wide diversity of wants, needs, and goals has led to a great variety of investment vehicles. This vast array of options can be divided into five broad *asset classes*: cash equivalents, fixed-income investments, common stocks, international securities, and real estate/inflation hedges. From these five basic areas of investment, described below, you will choose the vehicles you need for your Personal Profit Portfolio.

Cash Equivalents

Cash equivalents are short-term investments that mature within one year. This class would include passbook savings accounts, time deposit accounts, and short-term debt instruments, such as commercial paper issued by corporations, or short-term notes issued by governments, such as Treasury bills or municipal bonds.

Money market mutual funds have grown to be a major factor in the cash equivalent market. These funds pool investor money to invest in short-term debt instruments that require large sums beyond the reach of most individuals.

Cash equivalents provide a liquid haven for funds in uncertain times. They provide **some** protection against inflation, because of their short-term nature. As the general level of interest rates moves higher, you are able to obtain higher yields when your instruments expire. During low inflation, or when prices are falling, cash equivalents do well. They do not depend on an expanding economy for their returns.

Because they are short-term, cash equivalents do not offer high returns. They should be thought of as a liquid reserve for money you may need quickly, or while you are waiting for better opportunities to develop in other asset classes.

Fixed-Income Investments

Fixed-income investments are debt instruments with a maturity of more than one year. When you lend your money to an institution by buying its bonds, you receive a promise from it to repay your principal amount (the amount you lend) plus a guaranteed profit (the interest rate) for the term of the loan.

Some examples of fixed-income investments include corporate bonds, federal, state, or local government bonds, or mortgage instruments, such as Ginnie Mae (Government National Mortgage Association). The fastest-growing sector of the mutual fund industry in recent years has been bond funds, which cover the gamut from diversified holdings, to Treasury issues only, to high-risk *junk bonds*, to mortgage bonds. Liquidity—the ability to convert your investment to cash quickly—is an important consideration in evaluating investments. Treasury bonds are among the most liquid investments in the world. Bonds issued by most major corporations and state and local governments are fairly liquid most of the time.

Since the health of the economy can change substantially from the time you buy a bond (loan your money to the borrowing institution) and the time it matures or you sell it, the market value can change significantly. For example, if long-term interest rates go up, the value of bonds purchased when interest rates were lower will be less than your purchase price if you elect to sell. On the other hand, if interest rates go down, bonds purchased when rates were higher will appreciate in value.

So you see, fixed-income investments, while not normally thought of as affording growth, can be an effective hedge against deflation (falling prices) or a sluggish economy.

Finally, you should realize that all bonds are not created equal. Since they represent debt—a promise to pay—the creditworthiness of the issuing organization is very important. If affects not only your prospects for getting your full return but also the trading liquidity of the bonds.

Corporate and municipal bonds are rated by independent organizations. The two largest rating services are Standard & Poor's and Moody's Investors Service. Their ratings reflect their analysis of the borrower's ability to pay promised obligations (principal and interest) even in times of economic adversity.

Standard & Poor's highest rating (lowest risk) is AAA. Moody's equivalent is Aaa. When you buy an AAA rated bond, you pay a premium for this rating by receiving a slightly lower return than weaker (lower rated, higher risk) issuers pay.

Government bonds offer a tax advantage over corporate issues. The interest you receive from most municipal issues is exempt from federal taxes. If you buy municipal bonds from jurisdictions where you live, the interest is usually also exempt from local taxes. The interest paid by Treasury bonds is exempt from state taxes, but it is fully taxable on the federal level.

Common Stocks

Shares of *common stock* represent ownership in a company. Unlike bonds or other interest-bearing, fixed-dollar investments, stock values are as elastic as the economy itself. They offer you the chance for virtually unlimited growth, but they carry the risk of substantial loss.

As a stockholder, you are entitled to participate in many of the benefits of ownership. These include the right to share in profits through *dividends*. Normally, you also have the right to vote for the company's board of directors.

The biggest benefit of owning stock in a successful company is the chance to share in the appreciation of the value of your stock. This appreciation of your stock's price is called *growth*. The biggest risk to owning stock is the chance of losing part or all of your investment if the company fails.

Stock ownership represents a greater risk to your principal than either cash equivalents or fixed-income instruments. Common stocks depend on the health of the U.S. economy for their returns. The greater potential reward is balanced with the risk of greater losses for poor investment decisions.

International Securities

Substantial interest in international securities came about after the crash of 1929. But the romance was short-lived. It wasn't long before advisors thought foreign securities were too volatile or specialized for most investors. However, the higher economic return experienced outside the United States, the volatility of the dollar, and the inflation of the 1970s changed the views of many experts. Investors in international markets are no longer solely dependent on the prospects of the U.S. economy. International stock and bond markets are growing dramatically.

As foreign markets began to grow in size and sophistication, investors in the United States began to seek the higher returns that some of these markets offered. This interest was intensified as the international currency markets became increasingly volatile.

When the high inflation of the 1970s ravaged the purchasing power of the U.S. dollar for Americans, foreign markets became a secure haven for many investors. Experienced investors sought to capitalize on the diversification benefits that international investing offered. By including international securities in broadly diversified portfolios, money-managers were able to achieve more stable returns.

By 1987 over 50 percent of the total value of all stocks in the world were traded on foreign exchanges. At that time, the Tokyo market surpassed New York as the single largest equity market in the world. International fixed-income markets have grown sharply, also, as markets razed by inflation in years past regain stability and, hence, credibility with investors.

Since the economic fortunes of other countries tend to lag (or lead) the United States, it is possible to diversify your stock and bond portfolios to ride out the ripple effect of economic change in the United States by investing in stocks in many countries. That way your portfolio is protected from overreliance on a single country's economic fortunes.

But international markets pose unique risks over and above the risks incurred when buying U.S. stocks and bonds. Foreign securities are denominated in each country's currency. Fluctuations in relative currency values will affect your return in U.S. dollars. However, they can add stability while enhancing your opportunities for growth in your portfolio.

Real Estate/Inflation Hedge

Many American fortunes have been built on *real estate*. After all, land is any nation's original limited resource. While tax reform has changed many of the tax advantages of investing in real estate, there are still significant benefits for homeowners.

You are undoubtedly familiar with the tax advantages of residential real estate if you are a homeowner. The 1986 Tax Reform Act actually enhanced the tax benefits of home ownership by eliminating the deductibility of virtually all consumer credit, except mortgage loans.

For many Americans, their home represents their single largest and most successful investment. Their personal net worth grew through the appreciation of their homes.

As we stated in our discussion about inflation, people who *own things* do better in times of inflation than those who have *financial assets*. Real estate—because of its limited quantity and substantial intrinsic worth—is a traditional hedge against inflation.

More middle-class homeowners became "inflation millionaires" during the inflationary spiral in the 1970s than at any other time in history. The rising value of their real estate holdings played the biggest part in this phenomenon.

Real estate tends to be less sensitive to the economic forces that affect the prices of stocks and bonds. For example, when inflation moves into double digits, fixed-income investments drop in value. Historically, real estate appreciates even faster than inflation rises, paying a substantial *real* return over and above the inflation-related return.

As with all investments, there are drawbacks to real estate. Foremost is the lack of liquidity. There is no central auction place to provide a continuous market for the sale of real estate like there is for stocks and bonds. It may take weeks or even months for a seller to find a buyer. Even then, the problems do not end, because of the complexities of financing.

Once you have purchased a property, you must still hold the property for some time to experience a capital gain. In addition to illiquidity, real estate investing is a long-term proposition.

How to Recognize a Risk When You See One

All investors have a need to know about risk and how to protect their investments. But it's not just a question of guarding against risk. We don't want to become so risk-averse that we're afraid to take any chances at all. We want to be able to handle risk in such a way that we can reduce our exposure yet maximize our investments.

Here's a cross section of the investment risks we think any savvy investor can do something about.

1 The Risk of Inflation

Inflation is the erosion of your dollars' purchasing power due to a rise in the level of overall prices. Naturally, if the rate of return on your investment is less than the rate of inflation, and you have "locked in" that return by investing, say, in a low-interest bond, you will experience an actual *loss* in purchasing power when your investment matures. If you limit the duration of these fixed-return investments (i.e., "roll over" your certificates of deposit, bonds, and similar instruments to take advantage of gradual interest rate increases), you can offset this creeping menace. Better still, you could also invest in vehicles whose intrinsic worth automatically outpaces the general rise in overall prices—in such investments as gold, common stocks, or real estate.

2 The Risk of Deflation

If the overall level of prices declines, deflation is occurring, and these same fixed-return investments mentioned above become safe havens for your dollars. It's been a long time since deflation has occurred in our economy (even the Great Depression of the 1930s saw only a modest rate of deflation), but periodic *dis*inflation—the sudden reduction in the rate of inflation's increase—may be a permanent part of future economic cycles. This can make bonds and CDs and other fixed-return investments a good foundation for your portfolio.

3 The Risk of Business Failure

Any commercial enterprise runs its own peculiar risks of bad fortune—from shoe manufacturers who fail to foresee a leather shortage to potato farmers who fall victim to a plague of insects. If the company in which you own stock happens to be outguessed by a more aggressive competitor, you may lose dollars when the market price of your stock adjusts itself to that competitor's higher earnings.

4 The Risk of Interest Rate Changes

If you buy a long-term bond with a fixed rate of return of x percent, that bond will drop in value as soon as *new* bonds go on the market at a higher $(x + 0.25$ percent) interest. Similarly, if you borrow money to secure an asset (such as real estate) and the interest rates and rate of inflation

How to Recognize a Risk When You See One (*continued*)

go down, you may be saddled with a debt that's larger than the value of the asset it secured.

5   The Risk of Asset Price Fluctuations

Like the movements of a seismograph in an earthquake, the prices of some assets fluctuate wildly in the marketplace. This *price volatility*, as it's known, is the measure of an asset's price stability and predictability over time. If the long-term rate of change is in an upward direction, as it is with many investments, short-term volatility would be of no concern. But when you draw out your money to buy a goal, you might just catch a volatile investment at the bottom of its price cycle and come out with less than you put in.

The only way we know to offset price volatility in any one investment is to so spread your investments over *many* markets that the downward trends of one may be offset by the upward gains or constant value of another. In this way your portfolio is assured of a generally upward motion, and funds will be there when you need all or part of it for goal-related spending.

6   The Risk of Illiquidity

Each of us knows someone who has had to sell a house or car in a hurry. The classifieds are filled with ads from people who are selling assets, because of adversity, a transfer out of town, or some other life emergency.

The *liquidity* of an investment is its convertibility into cash without a substantial loss in market value. Obviously, someone who must sell a house because of economic pressure is willing to settle for a lower price than someone who has time to make a deal. So it's smart money management to hold a portion of your assets in cash or in near-money instruments. Illiquidity risk is run by those who believe that financial emergencies only happen to the other guy.

Obviously, these risks can sneak up on you in varying degrees and in various combinations, although few of them can occur simultaneously. For example, in times of recession, business risk and illiquidity risk are far more dangerous than the risk of losses through inflation. In a period of economic expansion, alternatively, inflation and interest risks can slip in on you before you know they're here, their symptoms masked behind the euphoria of full employment and positive economic headlines. Fortunately, investment volatility varies between markets and within various instruments within those markets, so you can reliably assess how much the prices of your assets should fluctuate before you buy them. The smartest plan of all is to design your portfolio to rest on a base of stable investments while your more volatile holdings are free to boil and bubble, reaching for (if sometimes losing) those higher returns. Table 2–1 shows you the effect of the six components of investment risk, which we've just discussed, on a variety of investments.

How to Recognize a Risk When You See One (*concluded*)

Conventional wisdom suggests that risk and return go hand in hand, as in betting on a horse. If you bet on the favorite, your chances of winning may be good but, because the odds are lower, you'll make less on your bet. If the long shot comes in first, you will have experienced a statistically rare event; but, the handicappers will have made a bundle from the pot built up by the more conservative wagers.

Of course, you can inoculate yourself against many of these risks, reducing (but never quite eliminating) the possibility that one of them will impact your portfolio. If you invest in the stock market, for example, your portfolio's overall volatility risk will be higher than if you keep it exclusively in bonds, although your inflation and interest-rate risk will be lower than if you leave your money in nothing but fixed-return investments. As you'll see, the risk/return characteristics of different asset classes all have a role to play in reducing the risks and increasing the returns of your portfolio.

WRAPPING UP

In this chapter you've learned that *people*, not numbers, are the key ingredients determining economic trends. It's because people differ in their abilities, their needs, and their expectations that so many investment opportunities have developed. When you invest, you are placing your bets on the future today.

To invest successfully you have to recognize certain unalterable facts of life. The most important of these is that things change. The economy affects your investments, and it is an everchanging process that goes through periodic up and down cycles. No one knows for sure what tomorrow will bring. This uncertainty makes it impossible for one investment to suit all needs. In the absence of the perfect single investment, you should diversify over a variety of asset classes—to protect yourself from devastating losses resulting from economic cycles—while affording you the chance to accumulate wealth.

As an investor, you have two options for your money. You can be a *lender* or an *owner*. Each alternative has its strengths and weaknesses. Lenders are guaranteed a set return for their money. In exchange for the more secure return, they forgo the chance for greater returns through growth.

An owner trades the security of a set return for the potential of even greater growth. That greater growth carries with it greater risk.

TABLE 2–1
Six Components of Investment Risk

Investment Medium	Inflation Risk	Deflation Risk	Business Risk	Interest Rate Risk	Market Volatility Risk	Illiquidity Risk
Savings accounts and money market funds	Moderate	§	Very low	Very low	Very low	Very low
Insurance and annuities	Moderate	§	Low	Very low	Very low	Low
Bonds:						
Investment grade ...	High	§	Low	High	Moderate	Low
Speculative	High	Moderate*	High*	High	High	Moderate
Common stocks	High	High	Moderate*	High	High*	Low
Common stock mutual funds	High	High	Low	High	High	Low
Your home	†	Moderate‡	Very low	Low	Low	Moderate
Real estate:						
Your own	†	Moderate-high‡	Moderate-high*	Moderate	Moderate	Moderate
Syndicates	†	Moderate-high‡	Moderate-high*	Moderate	Moderate	High

* Risk may be reduced through diversification among several different investments. † Because these investments increase in value with inflation, they offer an offset to the inflation risks of the other investments. ‡ The risk increases as the size of the mortgage payments increases relative to income. § Because fixed-dollar investments and bonds become worth more in terms of purchasing power, they offer an offset to the deflation risks of other investments.

MEASURING YOUR OWN FINANCIAL FOUNDATION

Using the following worksheets as your guide, complete your own Action Paper No. 1 (see the Appendix). Review your current mix of assets and classify them according to the categories on the form. When you are finished, you will have the foundation to begin building an effective Personal Profit Portfolio by restructuring your assets.

Light and Agile

Figure 2–2 is a typical asset mix of a Light and Agile investor. As you can see, there has either been little time to accumulate assets (a young person or couple), or, perhaps, no desire to do more than live from paycheck to paycheck.

The small portfolio of stocks was acquired through a heavily marketed tax-advantaged IRA. But, early in your career you will normally have higher priority items than the retirement provided for by IRAs. You might be planning to buy a home or to start a family.

Considering the different hopes for the future of the typical Light and Agile investor, there will be other alternatives to consider for getting "from here to there." We will be detailing some appropriate options later in this book for Light and Agile investors (and for you, too, if this is your present financial position).

Lean and Quick

Figure 2–3 lists the asset mix of a typical Lean and Quick couple. They have had success in achieving higher incomes, but they have not concentrated on putting their assets to work in a consistent manner to achieve their objectives.

The diversification over three asset classes (cash, fixed income, and stocks) is a good first step. However, it's equally important to select wisely *within* each asset class. Do the specific holdings within each asset class support their goals of keeping more of what they earn?

Throughout the book, we will use the Lean and Quick investor as a model for our discussions. In Chapters 4 and 5 we show you how Lean and Quick investors could focus on blending disparate investments to meet their goals.

Strong and Quick

Figure 2–4 shows how a mature, experienced couple—Strong and Quick— may put its assets into three of our asset classes. But, on closer examination,

FIGURE 2–2
Light and Agile's Current Asset Mix

Action Paper No. 1

Your Current Asset Mix

Name(s) *Light and Agile*

Date *October*

Asset Class and Name	Market Value or Amount ($)	Totals ($)	% of Total Investable Assets
Cash Equivalents: *N/A*	– 0 –	– 0 –	0%
Fixed Income: *N/A*	– 0 –	– 0 –	0%
Domestic Equities: Clystron Corp. (COMMON stock)	$4,000	$4,000	100%
International Equities: *N/A*	– 0 –	– 0 –	– 0 –
Real Estate and Inflation Hedges: *N/A*	– 0 –	– 0 –	– 0 –
Total Portfolio Value:		$4,000	100%

FIGURE 2–3
Lean and Quick's Current Asset Mix

Action Paper No. 1

Your Current Asset Mix

Name(s) _Lean and Quick_

Date _December_

Asset Class and Name	Market Value or Amount ($)	Totals ($)	% of Total Investable Assets
Cash Equivalents:			
Savings Acct.,	10,000		
Checking Acct.,	2,000	12,000	34%
Fixed Income:			
Bingo Bango Bond Fund	8,000		
		8,000	23%
Domestic Equities:			
Phaser Industries, (common stock)	15,000		
		15,000	43%
International Equities:			
—	—		
		0	0%
Real Estate and Inflation Hedges:			
—	—		
		0	0%
Total Portfolio Value:		35,000	100%

FIGURE 2–4
Strong and Quick's Current Asset Mix

┌───┐
│   **Action Paper No. 1**   │
└───┘

Your Current Asset Mix

Name(s) *Strong and Quick*

Date *December*

Asset Class and Name	Market Value or Amount ($)	Totals ($)	% of Total Investable Assets
Cash Equivalents:			
Passbook Savings	*32,400*		
Jodwell Bank			
		32,400	*27%*
Fixed Income:			
Argyle Corp. AAA Bond	*20,000*		
Hollywood Drug Co. AAA Bond	*20,000*		
Buffalo Bill Chip Co. BBB Bond	*2,000*	*42,000*	*35%*
Domestic Equities:			
Profit Sharing Plan MF	*45,600*		
Seese & Desiste			
Law Partners		*45,600*	*38%*
International Equities:			
—	*0*		
		0	*0*
Real Estate and Inflation Hedges:			
	0		
		0	*0*
Total Portfolio Value:		*120,000*	*100%*

there does not seem to be any consistency among the various investments. Buying on cocktail party "tips" is a common approach. But is it wise? As your peak earning years begin to wane, it becomes even more important to protect what you have.

What seems to be a conservative diversified portfolio on the surface has problems. The couple's profit-sharing plan is the largest single holding and offers the best chance for growth; but, the track record of this fund is a below-average 4 percent per year. Their passbook savings account is sizeable. This couple should look to increase the interest it receives without increasing risk.

It is not enough to just diversify. Setting your goals and planning carefully how to get more of what you want out of your income and assets is covered in Chapters 4 through 6.

Strong and Sturdy

Figure 2-5 depicts the asset allocation of a Strong and Sturdy investor whose portfolio, at first glance, appears to be well diversified, with investments in all five asset classes. But, after a closer look, we can see that the portfolio is not as strong as it might be.

It is heavily weighted to fixed income, rather than growth (even the utility under equities trades like a fixed income). The investments are conservative and fairly secure, although there is some exposure with the XYZ bonds, rated only BBB. The portfolio is also at risk, because it is so heavily oriented to stable interest and a declining inflation rate. The investment in international equities offers some hedge against some risks, but it is quite low. The only true inflation hedge is a modest investment of $7,500 in gold coins.

While this Strong and Sturdy investor may not want to sacrifice safety for greater income, if interest rates go up the portfolio would be exposed. This investor should investigate what other vehicles might help attain the desired goals while offering protection from inflation and volatility in the economy. The inflation hedge portion of the portfolio should be increased. Real estate (REITs) and international bonds could offer some opportunities.

This investor should reevaluate the investment allocated to each asset category and look at the nature of the investments within the categories. Remember, you want to diversify *within* as well as *among* the asset classes.

FIGURE 2–5
Strong and Sturdy's Current Asset Mix

Action Paper No. 1

Your Current Asset Mix

Name(s) *Strong and Sturdy*

Date *December*

Asset Class and Name	Market Value or Amount ($)	Totals ($)	% of Total Investable Assets
Cash Equivalents:			
Passbook savings	10,400		
CDs	22,000	32,400	17.6%
Fixed Income:			
T-Bond	25,000		
XYZ corp – BBB bond	34,000		
ABC bond	16,000	75,000	40.8%
Domestic Equities:			
Pension Plan	55,600		
Gas & Electric Utility stock	8,000	63,600	34.6%
International Equities:			
International fund	5,000	5,000	2.7%
Real Estate and Inflation Hedges			
Gold coins	7,500	7,500	4.0%
Total Portfolio Value:		183,500	100%

CHAPTER 3

LEARNING YOUR INVESTMENT PERSONALITY

You can tell how much the money you have invested will earn at a specific rate over a specific time by using a calculator and straightforward mathematics. But, investing is much more than mathematic calculations. You have to first determine what your needs are. It may be as simple as saving enough to buy that new car you have always wanted. Or your planning may call for investing so you can put your children through college in 10 or 15 years. Even though the goals are different, your financial needs can be determined objectively.

However, another essential element goes into financial decision making: your individual investment personality. What is right for one person is not necessarily right for another. Just think of your circle of friends. Even if you don't talk about investments with some of them, they all exhibit widely varying personalities. Some are more aggressive than others. Some go through life with a "What, me worry?" outlook. Others worry themselves into a frazzle about every little detail. It shouldn't surprise you that personality traits affect how financial decisions are made.

Your emotional makeup—specifically your money-related feelings—may help or hinder you in achieving your financial goals. In this chapter you will learn about your own unique investment personality. Knowing yourself and how you react to economic concerns, such as risk, is the basis for long-term success.

It's important not only to make money with your investments but to *feel comfortable* in the process. If you are uneasy with your Personal Profit Portfolio, you will pay an emotional price—stress—that can be costly. Profit is as much an *emotional* achievement as a financial one.

There is no one best investment personality. Knowing the strengths and weaknesses of your personality in the investment arena is critical to achieving consistent success in your own comfort zone.

Couples have the additional task of recognizing and reconciling differences between partners. Working together requires that you acknowledge differences, but doing so pays dividends. We offer you proven guidelines for maximizing the results of such teamwork.

And finally, we give you BB&K's seven rules for designing a diversified portfolio that will help you cut a path through the wilderness of investment vehicles.

IT IS MORE THAN MONEY

The way we feel about money—and other important areas in our lives—is an extension of our personalities. There are people who feel better with their money under a mattress than chancing the volatility of the stock or bond markets. However, there are people who relish new adventures, new experiences, new risks. You may know (or be one yourself) an analytical type who must examine all the facts before making any decisions. Then there are the spur-of-the-moment impulsive sorts for whom laborious fact-gathering seems a waste of time.

All in all, we can infer a great deal about how such people will probably make, spend, and invest their money, based on the way they think about, and react to, the world around them. You, too, have certain attitudes and habits that can affect your investment decisions. Take a few moments now to complete the Taking Stock questionnaire, "Discovering Your Investor Personality."

EVALUATING YOUR INVESTMENT PERSONALITY

We have found that investors tend to fall in one of five categories, based on their attitudes and behavior, when it comes to making investment decisions. The questionnaire you just completed measures attitudes and feelings about money that we have found to be important in making, and living with, investment decisions. They form what we call your *Investor Personality*, and you will need to understand it thoroughly if you want to design the Personal Profit Portfolio that's right for you (and your partner).

THE INVESTOR PERSONALITY GRID

The maximum score in any column is 30. The column where you scored highest identifies your investor personality. If your score is in the mid-range for all four categories, then you fall into a fifth category, which we call *Straight Arrow*.

Taking Stock Number 3

Discovering Your Investor Personality

This brief questionnaire will help you understand your attitudes about, and general approach to, making investment decisions. After reading each statement, choose the number in the following scale that best reflects how well that statement describes you.

Bear in mind, there are no personalities that are better than the others.

Not at all like me 1	Seldom like me 2	Occasionally like me 3	Often like me 4	Very like me 5

	Partner A	Partner B
Example: I read the financial pages of the newspaper every day.		

If you really read the financial pages every day, you would put a "5" in the space for *Partner A*. Don't put a 5 in this space if you only *intend* to read the financial pages or feel that you *should*. If you only read them occasionally (perhaps only on Sunday), you might put a "3" in the space. If you read them only when there's some extraordinary economic news, you would probably answer with a "2" or even a "1."

Remember, there are no right or wrong answers to these questions, only different responses to commonly encountered investment situations. When you have completed the questionnaire, have your spouse or partner (if you have one) complete the spaces marked *Partner B*, then read the evaluation and discussion that follows.

	Partner A	Partner B
1. I prefer investment opportunities with potentially large returns, even if they are more risky.	2	
2. I don't usually worry about my investment decisions once they are made.	3 / 5	
3. I wish I knew what the best investments are right now.		
4. Before making an investment decision, I like to know all the facts.	3	
5. If an investment catches my eye, it doesn't take me long to decide to jump in.	1	
6. I tend to rely on the advice of others in making my investment decisions.	2	

Discovering Your Investor Personality (*concluded*)

	Partner A	Partner B
7. I feel more comfortable with an investment decision I have made myself than one made for me by an expert.	3	
8. It is hard for me to resist investing in something that is new and exciting.	1	
9. I keep records of my finances so I know where my money is at all times.	3	
10. I have been making my own investment decisions for some time.	4	
11. Deciding in what to invest my money makes me anxious.	2	
12. I don't believe in investing in something just because everyone else is doing it.	4	

To determine your score, put your number next to the item under each category and then total that column:

Guardian	Enthusiast	Individualist	Adventurer
#3 ____	#1 ____	#2 ____	#1 ____
#4 ____	#3 ____	#4 ____	#2 ____
#6 ____	#5 ____	#7 ____	#5 ____
#9 ____	#6 ____	#9 ____	#7 ____
#11 ____	#8 ____	#10 ____	#8 ____
#12 ____	#11 ____	#12 ____	#10 ____
Total 17	Total 13	Total 20	Total 14

To confirm that you did, indeed, score appropriately, we ask that you look at Figure 3–1, the Investor Personality Grid, to locate your *feelings* about solving financial problems on the axis from anxious to confident and your *behavior* in dealing with money and investments on the axis from careful to impetuous. Be as honest as you can in your self-assessment.

You and your partner can each pinpoint yourselves on the scale on your anxiety versus confidence attitudes and on your impetuous versus careful behavior. To figure your confidence level, think about how much you trust your own judgment in making an investment decision. Do you worry about it? Do you trust others more?

To determine your carefulness level, think about how you act, regard-

FIGURE 3–1
The Investor Personality Grid

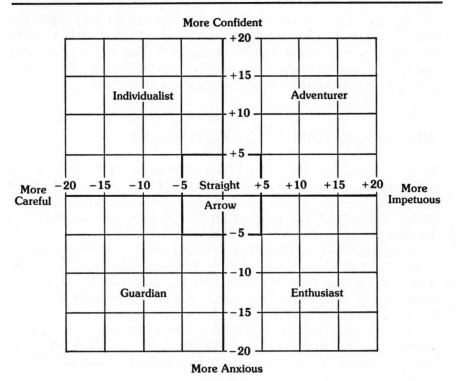

less of whether you trust yourself. Do you make quick decisions? Do you deliberate about financial matters? Do you do what someone else recommends?

For example, let's say that on this scale of minus 20 to plus 20, you feel you are about minus 10 in confidence/anxiety. On the behavior scale, you think you are just a bit impetuous, about plus 5. Where plus 5 in behavior and minus 10 in attitude cross, you would find your investor personality, Enthusiast. This category should match the column in which you scored highest on your questionnaire. If you are a Straight Arrow, you should find yourself in the middle of the grid and in the mid-range on all four columns on your questionnaire.

Now, draw a heavy dot at the point where your attitude and behavior intersect on the grid and label it with your initials. The sector in which your dot falls is labeled with the name of your investor personality.

If you are making your investment decisions with another person, have your partner repeat the process until you have each identified your investment personality on the grid.

Figure 3–1 shows how the elements of carefulness versus impetuousness in investment analysis relate to your overall feelings of confidence versus anxiety about making investment decisions. The way in which they combine for you determines your investor personality. You will use it to guide your portfolio building throughout the rest of this book.

DISCOVERING YOUR INVESTOR PERSONALITY

As you can see, the combination of factors measured in the questionnaire and confirmed on the grid has placed you in one of the sectors defining the five investor personalities that we have encountered during our years as financial advisors. Naturally, the more extreme your position is on either scale the more pronounced are your tendencies on that scale.

People whose scores in all categories are about the same, somewhere between 13 and 17, and whose dots fall between 0 and 5 on both dimensions of the grid, are called *Straight Arrows*. Straight Arrows tend to take the middle ground in risk-related decisions. They exhibit moderate confidence in solving investment problems.

If your result falls close to the result of another category, you may show some of the characteristics of that personality. You will want to read about both your primary and your secondary personality in the discussions below.

The Individualist

Characteristics
If you are an Individualist investor, you are careful and confident. How careful and confident you are tells us how strongly you fit this category. If you are careful but on the anxious side, then you probably are somewhat of a Guardian. If you are confident but somewhat impetuous in your decisions, then you have a little Adventurer in you.

You want to have all the facts before making a money-related decision. Numbers and details don't intimidate you. In fact, you prefer using them to get a solid understanding of your investments. Although you are interested in the opinions of investment experts, you tend to use those opinions only as a source of additional information to make your own decisions. You are not easily swayed by financial journalists or analysts, regardless of their credentials, unless they explain their reasoning and substantiate their claims.

Finally, with all that care and confidence, you tend to stick with your decisions, even when others around you are changing their minds.

Drawbacks

Your biggest shortcoming as an investor is probably your tendency to trust your own judgment beyond its level of competence. That's an occupational hazard for most independent thinkers.

Another danger you face is "paralysis by analysis"—the tendency to put off decisions until you have "just a little more data." You will have to learn that, in some cases, the extra bit of information just won't be available and you will have to trust your instincts.

Investment Preferences

Individualists tend to favor diversified portfolios. They look for investments with demonstrated track records, since these tend to show up best in detailed analyses. They are neither risk-averse nor risk-tolerant. They take a balanced view of risk and reward, judging each opportunity on its own merits.

Investment Types

Among professional money-managers, Individualists are often seen as "contrarian" investors—those whose principal philosophy is to go against the grain of popular investment opinion.

The Adventurer

Characteristics

If you are an Adventurer you are likely to lead an exciting financial life. Confident and impetuous, you are sometimes tempted to take major investment risks. Unlike other risk-takers, though, you usually understand the long odds against you in high-risk situations; but you are often willing to take the risk, anyway. Sometimes the results are startlingly successful. But, certainly, not always!

Adventurers are energized by the thought of exploring new financial territories. They just know that riches are there for the taking.

If you are less than 100 percent confident, you might share some characteristics of the Enthusiast. If you tend to take a bit more care in your decisions, you probably have something in common with the Individualist.

Drawbacks

Your adventurous spirit is not without its drawbacks as an investor. Adventurers sometimes suffer boom and bust finances. Often they need all their investment skill (and a touch of luck) just to recover money they've lost in their latest speculative plunge.

Investment Preferences

If you are an Adventurer investor, you tend to favor a few high-potential and aggressive growth investments. You are liable to resist advice to diversify into less-colorful investments. Learning to control your impulsiveness while maintaining your optimism and energy will be your major challenge—and this book's major accomplishment.

Investment Types

Adventurers are most often "market timers" who play the markets on a short-term basis. They include commodity futures traders, options players, and other short-term speculators.

The Guardian

Characteristics

If you are a Guardian investor, you are cautious with your money—perhaps more than you need to be. Many Guardians are excellent investment analysts, because of their careful, detail-oriented nature. The more confidence you have, the more you might share some traits with the Individualist. As it is, your anxiety about money gives you something in common with the Enthusiast, who is more impetuous but equally anxious about investment decisions.

Experience or training (or, in some cases, an active imagination) has made you slightly anxious about the world of investing. As a result, you generally want to minimize your chances for losses.

Drawbacks

Your very cautious nature helps you keep your wealth intact, but it can sometimes lead you to jeopardize your goals. Concentrating your assets in safe but low-performing investments may not provide you with enough opportunity to achieve reasonable targets. Sometimes an overcautious approach prevents a Guardian from making any new investment decisions at all.

Investment Preferences

Guardian investors favor blue-chip, mature growth and income-oriented stocks, stable real estate investments, certificates of deposit, and government bonds—whether they need the tax benefits or not.

Helping you reach beyond these limiting investments while keeping your portfolio safe will be the major focus for Guardians in the balance of this book.

Investment Types

Guardians do well as institutional investors, pension fund executives, and financial officers for organizations where a premium is placed on preservation, as well as on expansion of assets.

The Enthusiast

Characteristics

If you are an Enthusiast investor, you share the Guardian's insecurity about money; however, you differ significantly in your approach. You are more intuitive than analytical. If you have some degree of confidence, you might have some characteristics of the Adventurer.

As an Enthusiast investor, you are among the most receptive to new information. You will seldom let a good opportunity go by unexamined.

Drawbacks

An Enthusiast investor often operates under the assumption that it's probably better to do *something* even if it's wrong. Enthusiasts frequently follow the crowd into widely publicized, trendy investments. Too often they act before knowing what potential risks and rewards could result.

As a crowd-follower, an Enthusiast often shifts investments *following* economic changes, rather than leading them. That puts Enthusiasts at the end of the line for their investment profits. Investing is a business of *anticipation*.

Finding ways to make these popular investments work for you first—to be a trend-setter, rather than a trend-follower—will be an important goal for Enthusiasts who use this book.

Investment Preferences

Enthusiast investors tend to assemble eclectic portfolios that are not diversified in the technical sense, but, rather, are random collections of good deals from here and there. Often their portfolios will be overconcentrated in that latest hot investment idea. One year they may invest heavily in real estate, because it's the place to be. The next year they might be buying high-tech stocks.

Investment Types

Enthusiast investors often include financial journalists, investment broadcasters, and, most certainly, sales-oriented brokers.

The Straight Arrow

Characteristics

You found yourself right in the middle, not firmly into any of the other categories. As a Straight Arrow investor you have a balanced view of risk and reward. You have an equal appreciation for logical and intuitive methods. You are moderately confident in your money-management abilities.

You probably have something in common with all the other investor types, but you're not as anxious as either the Enthusiast or the Guardian, and not as confident as the Adventurer or the Individualist. Your decisions are not as impetuous as the Adventurer or the Enthusiast, nor as careful as the Individualist or the Guardian.

Straight Arrows have a lot going for them as investors. Because they have no one dominant viewpoint or prejudice to overcome, they can be very flexible investors. They are natural diversifiers. They sense, intuitively, that a little bit of a lot of things may be better than a whole lot of one thing, just in case that one thing might go sour.

Drawbacks

Even middle-of-the-roaders have some problems. The more cautious Straight Arrows (those favoring the careful side of the grid) sometimes find it hard to make a decision. They feel as though they just never have enough data to account for all the factors they see.

The more impetuous Straight Arrows tend to talk themselves into investments they really shouldn't make. Their analytical side rationalizes (rather than objectively analyzing) the decision that has the greatest emotional appeal.

Learning to utilize your natural instinct for diversification, while tempering your drawbacks, will be the focus for Straight Arrow investors for the balance of this book.

Investment Preferences

Straight Arrow investors tend to assemble portfolios diversified over a broad range of investments. They should be careful to focus on the relationships between elements in their portfolio. Too many small investments with haphazard correlations[1] among them may offer too little chance for growth.

---

[1]Investments that are correlated behave in the same manner toward the same incidents, although not necessarily to the same degree. Those that are inversely correlated behave differently to a given incident, one going up while the other declines, again not necessarily to the same degree. Still others are not correlated at all. There's a greater discussion on correlated assets in Chapter 6.

Investment Types

Straight Arrow investors are often found among professional brokers who have been trained to take a balanced view of the investment world to put themselves in a better position to sell a full range of financial products.

COUPLES: RECONCILING DIFFERENT INVESTOR PERSONALITIES

As you can see from the discussion above, your basic approach to investment decisions is affected by:

1. Your confident versus anxious feelings about money.
2. Your desire to emphasize the careful versus the impulsive aspects of these decisions.

Naturally, people don't always pair up with partners of exactly the same investor personality. Sometimes those personalities—like other aspects of your personal makeup—are complementary, sometimes contradictory, or sometimes fall somewhere in between.

If you and your partner both completed "Discovering Your Investor Personality" and began to question the compatibility of your attitudes toward investing—don't worry. That was what we intended. There are many ways to help partners of all investor personalities form a successful goal-getting team.

Congruent Investor Personalities

In geometry, *congruent* figures are those that go together perfectly. They match exactly in form and fit. If you and your spouse or partner are both Straight Arrows, Guardians, or the Straight Arrow/Guardian combination, you are probably about as close to a perfect match in your instinctive approach to investment decisions as you are going to get. This is because both of you tend to be risk-averse. You both use a balanced approach between the rational and intuitive in your decision-making processes.

Individualists and Straight Arrows are often congruent investors, too. The Straight Arrow usually appreciates the Individualist's careful, logical methods. At the other extreme, Adventurers and Enthusiasts are often compatible investors. Both are moved by impetuous natures. The Enthusiast's willingness to follow melds well with the Adventurer's desire to lead.

Unfortunately, these congruencies do not always lead to investment success—only to fewer fights along the way! Two Guardians may trap themselves in a portfolio that is simply too conservative. Although it appeals to their mutual need for safety, it can yield disappointing results. That, in turn, may endanger their ability to achieve their goals. Similarly, the Adventurer/ Enthusiast combination can be overly impetuous. They often mistake the need to invest quickly for a license to invest without thinking.

Occasional Incongruent Investor Personalities

Imagine the potential for conflict between two Individualists. Both are careful, confident, and deliberate in their decision making. But their focus on details and statistics may lead to disagreements and problems, since such matters can often be interpreted differently. Just because their approach is the same doesn't mean their interpretations will be.

Similarly, two Adventurers may be more likely to agree on how quickly they should act, rather than on how they should act. Two Enthusiasts, who might otherwise agree that action is necessary, will sometimes disagree about *which* course of action will meet their needs to reduce anxiety AND keep up with the crowd.

Surprisingly, Guardians and Enthusiasts have a good chance for congruency as an investment decision-making team, despite their obvious differences. They share a common tendency to worry about their money. The Guardian's aversion to risk, combined with the Enthusiast's instinct for following the crowd, are often motivated by the same desire: to avoid mistakes.

Frequent Incongruent Investor Personalities

Not surprisingly, two people at polar ends of the careful/impetuous or confident/anxious scales may have real problems in making their investment decisions. Independent-thinking Individualists often have marked difficulty dealing with a crowd-following Enthusiast. Individualists place their trust in a logical, often numbers-oriented, approach. They tend to dismiss out of hand the intuitive, qualitative factors that are most important to Enthusiasts.

Similarly, Adventurers and Guardians have essentially opposite views of investment life. Adventurers are motivated by the desire to *maximize rewards*. A Guardian's strongest motivation is to *minimize potential regret*. Adventurers see the silver lining in every risky situation. Guardians, though, tend to focus on the risk itself and want to avoid any chance of loss.

Individualists and Adventurers may also wind up in conflict over time. Though Individualists take calculated risks occasionally, they will eventually become uneasy with too many impetuous investment "adventures" proposed by their partners. Adventurers temper their enthusiasms sometimes;

but action, rather than reflection, is their trademark. They will become frustrated with the lower returns that satisfy an Individualist. They yearn for the home run opportunity.

COUPLES: COPING WITH DIFFERENCES IN YOUR INVESTMENT DECISIONS

The key to smoothing out even the strongest differences between partners is for both to recognize that, through cooperation, the best features of each type can be brought to bear on the challenging task of investing. Manipulative win/lose (one person must lose if the other is to win) attitudes aggravate financial problems. Remember, there is no one best investment personality. Each has strengths and weaknesses. By taking a win/win (if one person wins, then both win) attitude, you can maximize your enjoyment as well as your success in the investment arena.

The ideas we have listed below are suitable for resolving all your financial differences, not just your investment decisions.

Talk Things over by Focusing on Mutual Goals

It helps to approach problems as a team. What are the drawbacks and potential rewards for *each partner*? Admittedly, this works best with partners who are confident and have strong views. Individualists and Adventurers, our last example of incongruent personalities, have that initial advantage.

Use our personality descriptions to help focus your discussion on the main sticking point at any one time. Has one or the other partner made a strong emotional or analytical commitment to one side of the issue? It is important to talk through misconceptions about motives, objectives, or intent.

Focusing on your *mutual goals*, rather than on your individual needs or desires, will afford a greater chance for amicable resolution of the dispute. Keep in mind that there are a number of correct approaches for solving problems.

Agree to Delegate

Sometimes an investment issue involves a recurring decision that both partners know will cause disputes. In such cases it is often helpful to delegate responsibility and authority for the decision to the partner who is most qualified, able, and willing to assume it.

For example, a Guardian/Adventurer couple will recognize that each's natural approach to investment decisions will be poles apart. It may be simpler to agree *ahead of time* on who will make the investment decisions in various areas. This helps avoid negotiating *every* decision, ranging from those as simple as what bank to work with to the more complex, such as which new investments to undertake.

The delegation decision should not be taken lightly. You have to determine whose interests or responsibilities are most closely associated with each decision area. For example, the partner who is in charge of paying bills would be most appropriate for decisions relating to bank services, like check-writing and savings.

The most important concept here is that *delegation of authority* is not the same as *denial of responsibility*. Delegation works only as long as both partners continue to deal in good faith according to their mutually agreed ground rules. Naturally, either partner can review the basis for delegation at any time, if things are not working out.

These periodic reevaluations should be welcomed as another opportunity to bring partners closer by solving important problems *together*.

Use an Independent Third Party

Sometimes differences are so great that solutions cannot be successfully negotiated or amicably delegated. If you and your partner face such a problem, consider obtaining the advice of a neutral third party. It may even be best to leave certain investment decisions to a hired advisor or pre-established system.

Consider the problems faced by an Enthusiast/Guardian couple. Fixed-income investment decisions may bring out their sharp differences. An Enthusiast would tend to want to buy junk bonds, because of their high yields and high trendy profile in recent years. High-risk bonds would certainly grate on a Guardian's emotions! A Guardian would much prefer very safe, established AAA-rated bonds.

There are a number of ways to resolve the dispute while keeping the couple together. One way is to take advantage of the wide variety of mutual funds that invest solely in bonds. This couple could select a mutual fund that invests in a broadly diversified bond portfolio. By using a third party (the mutual fund) the Enthusiast/Guardian couple could both be happy, because their financial objectives could still be met without having an emotional discomfort for either party.

Sharing Investment Decisions

While the above methods—negotiation, delegation, or using a neutral third party—can work in some situations, there is an even better method: *shared decisions*, or decision making by true consensus. The following are some important points to keep in mind about this alternative.

When made properly, consensus-based decisions do not come about from one partner winning and the other losing. The win/lose syndrome is injurious to a healthy working partnership. Decisions should be based on a complete and candid airing of all sides to the question. Focus the discussion on your mutual financial goals. The idea is to enhance, not hurt, your mutual trust and respect of each other's ideas and input.

Shared decisions should include every member of the family who may be affected by the decisions. It is important to head off future recriminations after an important decision has been made.

Finally, shared decisions encourage and reward openness, self-awareness, and mutual trust. These are values we believe will lead to better, higher-quality decisions for all investment teams.

THE BB&K APPROACH TO INVESTING

Buttressed with your new knowledge of the economic environment, the risks and human factors that affect investments, and your awareness of your own investor personality, you are ready to learn the details of portfolio building—the BB&K way.

To get you started, we are pleased to introduce the principles of sound investing that we have learned through years of managing money. Used in conjunction with what you've learned about investor personalities, you will be well on your way in devising your own Personal Profit Plan.

Rule 1. Diversification Pays

Conventional wisdom holds that, to achieve high returns, you must take large risks. But, actual practice shows that it is possible to realize high returns with a low-risk portfolio. The secret is to spread your investments over the five asset classes we detailed in Chapter 2 (cash equivalents, fixed income, stocks, international securities, and real estate/inflation hedges). But, it is important to carry it one step further: vary your holdings within these classes as well.

Diversification is simple in concept and powerful in result. But, it must be done correctly. Proper portfolio diversification does not mean randomly spreading your money into a variety of investment vehicles. It is vital to approach diversification with a consistent plan. In Chapters 4, 5, and 6 we go into specific rules for diversifying the BB&K way.

Rule 2. **Patience Is an Overlooked Investment Virtue**

In Chapter 2 you learned the importance of time for investment decisions. If you invest so time is working for you, you will be ahead of the game in the long run. To clarify what we mean, let's take a look at two of our investor personalities to see how time affects their portfolios.

John and Gene were brothers who inherited $10,000 each from their father. John, a chemist, was an Individualist investor. He trusted his own good judgment in science, but recognized that economics and the world of investments was in the realm of the social sciences. He put his money into a diversified portfolio of common stocks, municipal bonds, and real estate.

Gene was a producer for network television. An Adventurer, his experience led him to believe that success in life came from taking risks. He chose to concentrate his inheritance in a few aggressive growth stocks recommended by his broker.

After the first year, John's portfolio was up 12 percent. But, a slow economy had depressed the stock market and Gene's portfolio was down 6 percent. The following year, the stock market embarked on a strong up-move and Gene's portfolio jumped 17 percent. John's also grew nicely, finishing the year up 18 percent.

By the third year the economy had slipped into a recession. John's return dropped to 10 percent, while Gene's plummeted to a loss of 24 percent. This up and down cycle continued for the next five years, as summarized in Figure 3–2.

As you can see, John's earnings never exceeded the 18 percent he earned in the second year. However, he managed to avoid any down years (net losses) with his diversified portfolio. Gene, though, had a few very successful years, earning 21 percent, 34 percent, and 50 percent. By the ninth year, Gene's aggressive approach had netted him a 14 percent average annual return, despite his three down years. John's portfolio showed a slightly lower 12 percent average annual return.

Was Gene's concentration on a single-asset class really the better strategy for long-term investing than John's diversified approach? It pays to examine the numbers in some detail to learn what they reveal.

Since Gene had to make up for his down years, it was necessary for him to achieve sharply higher returns to stay ahead of the game. He had "built in" the necessity for almost superhuman expertise, good timing, or luck to balance out the losing years. By losing 6 percent, 24 percent, and 15 percent, he had to gain 21 percent, 34 percent, and 50 percent to make up the difference and attain the return he did. Before congratulating Gene on his results, you must ask yourself, How often can anyone—let alone an amateur investor—accomplish that?

FIGURE 3-2
Slow and Steady vs. Aggressive Approaches to Investing

Strategy	Annual Returns (percent)								Average Return (percent)	Compound Annual Return (percent)
	Year	1	2	3	4	5	6	7	8		
Slow and steady		+12	+18	+10	+17	+12	+8	+10	+9	12	11.9
Aggressive		−6	+17	−24	+35	−15	+21	+34	+50	14	11.2

But, as you may have guessed, we left out an important consideration. *Compounding* is the effect of one year's gains being added back onto the principal to increase the amount of next year's earnings. When you factor the effect of compounding into the two sample accounts, John actually came out ahead. His portfolio returned 11.9 percent on a total return basis ($21,969). Gene's portfolio, even after the spectacular gains of the last three years, returned 11.2 percent on a total return basis ($21,024).

There is one other cost to consider. John's steady performance meant he did not have to work hard on trading stocks. Nor did he spend sleepless nights to achieve his return! Monetary gain is not the only important consideration in handling your financial affairs. For many people, stability and peace of mind must be factored into their investment approach.

Rule 3. Diversify over All Five Asset Classes

The five asset classes we described in Chapter 2 were not chosen arbitrarily. They represent groups of investments and markets that have important characteristics in common. When taken together, they have offsetting characteristics that are vital to the building of an effective portfolio. By investing in assets that react differently to economic stimuli, your portfolio is protected from market crashes in one type of asset.

For example, on October 19, 1987, the stock market fell over 500 points for the largest single-day crash in history. Investors who had concentrated their investments in the stock market gave back a year or more worth of profits in one day. But, on that same day, the bond market staged a very strong rally. If you had taken this simple one-step diversification, your stock market losses would have been at least partially offset by gains in your bonds.

Figure 3-3 shows how another simple two-asset portfolio gives you

FIGURE 3–3
The Benefits of Diversification

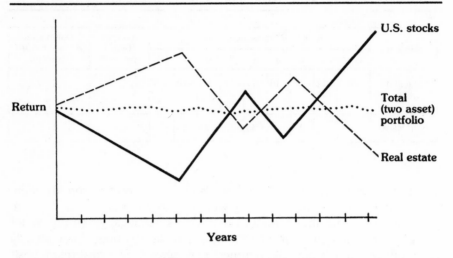

considerably higher, more stable returns over the long-term than concentrating on a single asset.

As you learned in Chapter 2, the one constant in the financial world is change. As the economy goes through changes, each asset class will be affected differently. No single ratio of cash equivalents to fixed income to common stocks will be the optimum balance at all times.

By diversifying your portfolio over the five asset classes that we recommend, you will be able to preserve and "grow" your capital, putting in as little or as much time and energy to manage your Personal Profit Plan as suits you. Following our guidelines, you will develop a portfolio that suits your financial physique and investment personality and also accommodates your management style.

If you don't have the time or inclination to manage your investments on a regular basis, your diversified "fixed-mix" portfolio can be designed for minimal maintenance. If, conversely, you are a "hands-on" investor, you will rebalance the assets in your diversified "dynamic-mix" portfolio to take advantage of the economic environments. Both approaches are discussed in detail in Chapter 6.

Rule 4. Intuition Can Be Very Helpful

Successful investing for most is more than just cold quantitative analysis. Investors quickly learn that, while the past does, indeed, repeat, it never does so exactly. Relationships change between asset classes. Declining interest rates are sometimes positive for the stock market. At other times, declining rates reflect an underlying economic malaise that will hurt stocks.

Your intuition can play a central role in helping you decide how the respective allocations in your portfolio will further your objectives. How will each asset perform in a changing economy? It would all be very easy if each Business Cycle unfolded just like the previous one. That doesn't happen.

It would be simple if each bull (rising) market in stocks unfolded in exactly the same manner. Unfortunately, that doesn't happen either. The stock groups that were top performers in the last bull market may be laggards this time around.

Your intuition, braced with the background knowledge from this book, can help you ferret out the inevitable differences in each cycle. If you ignore the intuitive component in your decision-making process (and many people have tried), you do so at your peril. Here's an example of what we mean.

Computers have been called *the perfect thinking machine.* If that is so, then computers should make the best portfolio managers. Computer science professor Joseph Meizenbaum of MIT spent years investigating the ability of computers to accept, store, rearrange, combine, and deliver vast amounts of symbolic information. He then asked how that information could be used by the computer to make judgments about how to deal with human situations—such as managing investments.

In his book, *Computer Power and Human Reason*, he summarized his findings: "The individual human being, like any other organism, is defined by the problems he confronts. He must necessarily confront problems that arise from his unique biological and emotional needs . . . no other organism, and certainly no computer, can be made to confront genuine human problems in human terms."[2]

In other words, if one of the fathers or mothers of artificial intelligence won't depend on perfect machinelike thinking to solve his or her human problems—neither should you. Remember, economics is a *social* science.

Investment decisions cannot be made effectively by using only quantitative data. There are *qualitative* nuances in any economic decision that can be addressed only by the human beings involved. In managing our clients' portfolios, we make extensive use of computers at BB&K; but, we would never leave the ultimate decision making to them. A machine might be very good at pointing out alternatives and consequences, but it can never choose between them. A computer cannot make your desired future happen all by itself.

---

[2]Joseph Meizenbaum, *Computer Power and Human Reason: From Judgement to Calculation* (New York: W.H. Freeman, 1976).

Rule 5.   Mistakes Are Going to Happen

When you decided to investigate the world of investments, you could have hired an investment professional to handle it for you. Your decision to buy and read this book indicates a willingness to do most, or at least some, of the work yourself. This being the case, you should be prepared for a fact of investment life—you will make mistakes.

Education is only the first step in learning the investment business. As in other endeavors, experience is the best teacher. Any investor who will not admit his or her mistakes certainly has not learned from them. And most professional advisors will tell you that learning from your mistakes is the single most important element in your education as an investor.

We consider this lesson to be very important—because experience unexamined is as useless as no experience at all. Too many investors blame bad luck, rather than bad planning for their losses. We prefer the view of Benjamin Franklin: "Diligence alone is the mother of good luck."

Rule 6.   Investing Isn't Just for the Rich

Far too many people talk themselves into a Catch 22 situation when it comes to investing. They say: "I can't invest now because I don't have enough money to make it worthwhile." Then, once they've earned enough money, they rationalize: "Well, if I'm such a good money-maker, why should I bother learning new skills?"

It's natural to feel a little nervous before any new endeavor. That anxiety level is raised considerably when it comes to financial matters for most people. But developing the self-discipline to accomplish your goals has its own built-in reward. Some people find it easier to invest by paying something into savings every paycheck until the account reaches a certain level, at which point they move it to their investment. Some find it easier to invest by establishing mini-rewards for themselves, allowing themselves certain pleasures or treats when a desired amount is reached. Whatever your system for getting you to put the money aside, self-discipline is a key ingredient in achieving success as an investor.

Rule 7.   Let the IRS Help You Save

The 1986 Tax Reform Act eliminated the deductibility of individual retirement account (IRA) contributions for many people. However, IRAs still offer most investors an outlet for sheltering the gains they make on contributions of up to $2,000 per year (after-tax dollars). You won't be taxed on the proceeds of your investment until you start to withdraw your money.

This has a twofold advantage. You can benefit from the effect of the compounding of your earnings. And, second, you will get into the routine of regular annual contributions. Let the government be a partner in your savings plans.

Rule 8. Beware the Dangers of Windfalls

Paradoxically, windfalls, such as an inheritance, a larger-than-expected tax refund, or a bonus from work, often wind up hurting your financial future. Too often, sudden windfalls are spent as down payments for new cars, second homes, or other luxuries that tend to add costs for the buyers.

These gifts "that keep on costing" have a way of siphoning funds from future years in the form of maintenance costs, interest payments, and other financial responsibilities. Your blessing may turn out to be an expensive burden.

If such a windfall comes your way, apply as much of it as you can toward your own financial future. Unless you must use the funds for some emergency problems, set aside a significant portion as part of your investable resources.

Rule 9. Don't Forget the Incredible Power of Compounding

The principle of compound interest is formidable in any investment calculation. Instead of withdrawing the money you've made (e.g., the interest paid by a bank on your savings account), that profit is added back onto your principal for the next computation of interest. For example, $1,000 deposited in a 10 percent interest-bearing account and left to compound for 10 years will grow to $2,594. That's a net return of almost 160 percent!

Table 3–1 shows the effect of compounding on a $1,000 lump-sum investment at 6 percent, 10 percent, and 12 percent, over various time periods.

Of course, nothing prohibits you from contributing regularly to such investments. Building on our previous example, $100 contributed each month at a 6 percent rate of interest compounded annually, in 10 years will result in a nest egg of $16,766.

At 12 percent interest, that sum would be $23,586. If you continued your contributions to retirement (we'll say 40 years), that amount would grow to $196,857 at 6 percent interest, or $1,030,970 at 12 percent interest. Note that, even though the interest rate is only double (12 percent versus 6 percent), the net return is five times higher!

Here are the lessons you should learn from these brief examples:

TABLE 3–1
Effect of Compounding on a $1,000 Lump-sum Investment

	Return on Investment Compounded Annually		
Years	6%	10%	12%
10	$ 1,791	$ 2,594	$ 3,106
20	3,207	6,727	9,646
30	5,743	17,449	29,960
40	10,286	45,259	93,051

1. Start investing as soon as possible. It doesn't matter if it's only a few dollars a month. In time, you will have an amount with real goal-getting potential.

2. Choose the highest returns, consistent with the feelings of comfort you have. Obviously, your investment will grow faster at 12 percent than at 6 percent. But, if the chances of realizing that 12 percent over the long term are less certain, and the goal is very important, you may be better off with the lower rate.

3. Don't withdraw money from your investments until it's absolutely necessary. "Out of sight, out of mind" is a good motto for most beginning investors. If you can build a psychological wall between yourself and your fledgling investment, you will improve your chances of achieving your financial goals.

4. Try to contribute to your investments as regularly and as often as you can. To increase the size of the kitty on which the magic of compounding can work, it will pay you to make contributions to your nest egg whenever you can.

WRAPPING UP

In this chapter you've learned that the biggest obstacle people face in the hunt for investment profits is often their own personality. If you have completed the Action Papers and exercises, you have a good idea of your own investment personality, which will help you understand the balance of this book, when we get down to the nuts and bolts of building your own portfolio.

If you are married or working with a partner, it is important that you know each other's instinctive approach to money. Two heads can be better

The Rule of 72

Simple interest tables, compound interest tables, and interest tables with annual contributions are all a bit cumbersome to use if you want only a quick and dirty estimate of a lump sum's future value at a given rate of return.

The Rule of 72, long used by investment analysts, tells you quickly how long it will take to *double* your money at a given rate of return. To find this number, simply divide 72 by the quoted rate of interest. For example, at 1 percent rate of interest, it will take 72 divided by 1, or 72 years to double your money. At 6 percent interest, it will take 72 divided by 6, or 12 years; at 12 percent, 72 divided by 12, or 6 years; and so on. While this technique should not be used for detailed investment planning, it can help you see if the payoff of a contemplated investment will be enough for the goal you have in mind—*when* you want to have it.

than one, if you recognize that differences do not mean one partner is wrong. You learned that focusing on mutual goals is the key to working together.

And, finally, you learned some basic ground rules for successful investing regardless of your investment personality. It is important to start as soon as possible, even if you can only put away a few dollars at a time. If used correctly, time is your biggest ally. Don't worry about making a big killing. The power of compounding yields astounding results to those who are patient.

No one knows what the future holds in store. By diversifying your investments over the five asset classes that we have outlined, you will lower your overall risk while still being in position to earn returns sufficient to meet your goals. That is the true test of your investment program.

CHAPTER 4

BUILDING YOUR
INVESTMENT PORTFOLIO

LEARNING HOW TO ALLOCATE YOUR RESOURCES

In Chapters 2 and 3 you learned three very important lessons about the world of investing:

1. There are a great number of investment products to choose from that were devised to meet the diverse needs and desires of investors.
2. Economic trends and developments affect these investment products in varying ways. No two Business Cycles will influence the investment markets in exactly the same way; investors must deal with that element of uncertainty.
3. The critical first step in narrowing down the alternatives is knowing yourself.

Investment success is not just a matter of getting a big bank account, or luck, or even technical expertise. Rather, it results from a combination of factors that add up to one unique ingredient—*you*—as a happy, fulfilled individual.

We think this idea is so important we've reduced it to its essentials:

$$IS = K + E + E + P$$

Investment Success equals **Knowledge** plus **Experience** plus **Emotions** plus **Purpose**. "Knowledge" is the awareness of your—and your family's—financial physique and the economic factors that affect you as a money-maker and a money-manager. "Experience" is what you will gain by developing and applying the skills we teach you in this book. "Emotions," of course, relate to your investor personality and the more qualitative aspects of financial decision making. "Purpose" equals the goals you are hoping to achieve.

These are all necessary ingredients for fashioning success as an investor. Remember what we said in Chapter 2: the real test of investment success is whether you achieve *your* goals. Matching the return of the stock market or some other index is not going to tell you how satisfied you are with your financial affairs. "Success," as our formula stresses, consists of much more than numbers.

In this chapter we start the nuts and bolts work of building your investment portfolio. First, we will explain how to complete and use your Personal Balance Sheet and Personal Income Statement which, together, comprise your Personal Financial Statement. Next, we describe how to define and prioritize your goals and translate them into achievable financial objectives. We then show you how to fit these elements together. And, finally, we demonstrate how to allocate your resources over the five asset classes. When you have finished, you will have a detailed plan for investing your money, showing where to invest and how much, and designed to meet your short- and long-term goals.

USING YOUR PERSONAL FINANCIAL STATEMENTS

You cannot know where you are nor how well you are doing without keeping score. In personal finance, that scorecard is your *financial statement*. We've included sample forms[1] for your Personal Balance Sheet and your Personal Income Statement (see Action Papers 2 and 3 in the Appendix at the end of the book).

The forms are self-explanatory. Simply fill in the blanks with the numbers that you, alone, can know. Don't feel intimidated if you are able to fill in only a few of the lines. The skills you are learning here will enable you to so increase your net worth that your balance sheet in the future will be filled in more completely, the way it is in our Lean and Quick example.

Your Personal Balance Sheet: Assets versus Liabilities

Liabilities are claims that other people or institutions have against your assets. For example, when a bank loans you the money to buy a car, you are *liable* for the balance of the loan until it is paid in full. Short-term liabilities are those claims which have to be paid off quickly.

---

[1] A number of software programs run on a personal computer that collect similar data and offer the same "what if" capabilities as our forms. The computer can do the necessary calculations and frequent recalculations in a flash. Two of the best-selling programs are "Managing Your Money," and "Dollars and Sense."

There should be a general correspondence of short-term liabilities, such as credit card bills, with short-term assets, such as checking account balances. Long-term liabilities, such as a mortgage, should be balanced with long-term, or fixed, assets, such as the home for which the mortgage loan was used.

We have chosen the financial records of a Lean and Quick couple as the example to follow throughout this chapter. Figure 4–1 is the balance sheet for a typical Lean and Quick investor. As you can see, both the short-term and long-term assets and liabilities match up well.

In our example, short-term liabilities are only $6,500 versus liquid (monetary) assets of $35,000. This Lean and Quick investor's long-term picture is similar to many homeowners. The value of their home ($100,000) amply covers their long-term mortgage debt of $80,000. The amount over and above their mortgage balance represents the equity in their home.

As a result of the Tax Reform Act of 1986, that extra *home equity* has gained increased importance for homeowners. Prior to 1986, interest on consumer loans, such as credit cards and auto loans, was fully tax deductible. Only 40 percent of the interest from consumer loans was deductible in 1988, 20 percent in 1989, and 10 percent in 1990. As of 1991, interest on such consumer loans is no longer deductible at all. The only interest fully deductible at this time is that paid on mortgage loans. Homeowners whose homes are worth more than their mortgage balance can take out "home equity" loans, which are heavily touted by banks. The interest on these loans is still 100 percent deductible.

Our Lean and Quick couple's financial statement reflects good financial health ($88,500 more in assets than in liabilities). Although it might appear that they don't have a problem, nevertheless they still have to do some careful planning to achieve their goals.

As an investor, one of your main concerns in the planning process is to find out how much to commit to new goal-getting investments. (As we mentioned in Chapter 1, typical financial goals can include having enough resources to cover your children's college education, a trip around the world, or a comfortable retirement.) Since monetary assets are the most liquid, they are the easiest part of your portfolio to use.

Even with all the information you have from completing your own Personal Balance Sheet, you still have not addressed your ability to meet day-to-day living expenses or to contribute to an annual investment fund. To do this, you must complete Action Paper No. 3, Your Personal Income Statement, in the Appendix.

FIGURE 4–1
Lean and Quick's Balance Sheet

Action Paper No. 2

Your Personal Balance Sheet

Name *Lean and Quick*
Date *December*

ASSETS		LIABILITIES	
Monetary Assets		**Short-Term Liabilities**	
1. Cash and Equivalents			
		14. Unpaid Bills	
Cash/checking/savings	12,000	Taxes	
Money market funds	_____	Insurance premiums	
Certificates of Deposit	_____	Rent	
Bonds (< 1 yr. maturity)	_____	Utilities	
		Charge accounts	500
Total Cash and Equivalents	12,000	Credit cards	
		Other_____	
2. Notes Receivable	0		
		Total Unpaid Bills	500
3. Investments			
		15. Installment Loans	
Stocks	15,000	(balance due)	
Bonds (>1 yr. maturity)	8,000	Automobile	6,000
Real estate (REITs, partnerships)	_____	Other_____	
Cash value of life insurance	_____	Total Installment Loans	6,000
Cash value of annuities	_____	16. Total Short-Term Liabilities	6,500
Retirement plans	_____	(14 + 15)	
Total Investments	23,000		
		Long-Term Liabilities	
4. Total Monetary Assets (1 + 2 + 3)	35,000		
		17. Non-mortgage Loans	
Fixed Assets		(balance due)	
		Bank	_____
5. Home and property	100,000	Educational	_____
6. Automobiles/vehicles	15,000	Other_____	_____
7. Other personal property	25,000	Total Non-mortgage Loans	0
8. Total Personal Assets (5 + 6 + 7)	140,000	18. Mortgage Loans (bal. due) Home	80,000
		Other_____	
9. Other real estate	_____	Total Mortgage Loans	80,000
10. Ownership in small business	_____	19. Total Long-Term Liabilities (17 + 18)	80,000
11. Total Fixed Investment Assets (9 + 10)	0	20. Total Liabilities (16 + 19)	86,500
12. Total Fixed Assets (8 + 11)	140,000	21. Net Worth (13 minus 20)	88,500
13. Total Assets (4 + 12)	175,000	22. Balance (21 + 20)	175,000

Your Income Statement: Income versus Outgo

Most of us have, at one time or another, wondered "Where did our money go?" It seems to go out much faster than it comes in! It's as though your expenses grow right along with, or even faster than, your income. No matter how much you make, it still seems that you are just barely making ends meet.

The solution rests with closely examining the information requested in Action Paper No. 3. Your balance sheet tells you where you are. Your income statement will tell you where you are headed.

The magnitude of the dollars going into your worksheet is not what's important. Rather, the most significant number you will glean from this exercise is how many dollars you are left with when the tally is complete, item 8, "Amount Remaining for Savings and Investment."

The "Total Monetary Assets" (item 4) and "Total Fixed Investment Assets" (item 11) from your Personal Balance Sheet plus the "Amount Remaining for Savings and Investment" from your Personal Income Statement, are necessary components in identifying your *Investable Resources*.

Figure 4–2 is the income statement for our Lean and Quick investor. The first important number to look at is item 5, "Amount Remaining for Living Expenses, Savings, and Investments." In our example, that comes to $62,000.

Next, you will want to see the breakdown of expenses. Variable expenses are costs that are controllable in the short term, such as entertainment expenditures. Fixed expenses are long-term commitments, such as your mortgage, insurance, or car payments.

Our Lean and Quick investors showed $10,000 (item 8) available annually for investment *without* changing their current lifestyle. If you come up with an item 8 figure that is less than what you hoped for, don't jump to the conclusion that you must reduce your living standards to pay for your future goals. There may be times when that would be appropriate, but that's not the first solution. Your aim, after all, is to so organize your financial affairs that you keep more of what you earn to enhance your happiness, not to deprive you.

To trade today's tangible enjoyment (e.g., recreation, a vacation, or some new gadget) in exchange for some vague promise for tomorrow is a difficult bargain at best. This is one good reason that your goals should be *specifically* defined. Defining those goals takes more work than stating a simple desire to "retire comfortably," or "send my children through college," or "buy a bigger house."

If you have not already done so, take the time now to create your own

FIGURE 4–2
Lean and Quick's Income Statement

Action Paper No. 3

Your Personal Income Statement

Name *Lean and Quick*
For the Year Beginning January 1, 19_____ and ending December 31, 19_____

1. **Income**
   Spouse or Partner A   *48,000*
   Spouse or Partner B   *30,000*
   Total wages or salaries   *78,000*
   Dividends and interest   *1,800*
   Rents
   Other _____
2. **Total Income**   *79,800*
3. **Taxes**
   Personal income taxes   *15,000*
   Social Security and disability taxes   *2,800*
4. **Total Taxes**   *17,800*
5. **Amount Remaining for Living Expenses, Savings and Investments**   *62,000*

6. Living Expenses	Fixed	Variable
Housing		
Utilities		*2,400*
Repairs		*1,000*
Insurance	*400*	
Taxes	*1,000*	
Rent or mortgage payments	*15,000*	
Other _____		
Food		*7,200*
Clothing (including laundry, dry cleaning, repairs, and personal effects)		*4,500*
Transportation		
Gas, tolls, parking	*3,000*	
Repairs	*600*	
Licenses	*200*	
Insurance	*1,300*	
Auto payments or purchase	*4,800*	
Fares		*500*
Recreation, entertainment, and vacations		*5,000*
Medical		
Doctor	*200*	
Dentist	*200*	
Medicines	*100*	
Insurance	–	
Personal	*2,400*	
Life insurance (term)	*1,200*	
Outlays for fixed assets		*1,000*
Other expenses _____		–
Subtotal	*30,400*	*21,600*

7. **Total Annual Living Expenses**   *52,000*
8. **Amount Remaining for Savings and Investment**   *10,000*

Personal Financial Statement by completing Action Papers No. 2 and No. 3 in the Appendix at the end of the book.

DEFINING YOUR GOALS

Career and life goals, and the financial objectives that achieve them should be:

1. *Specific.* You should know *what* you want in as much detail as possible.
2. *Time-bounded.* You should know *when* you will want to achieve and pay for your goal.
3. *Quantified.* You should know *how much* the goal will cost **at the time you need to pay for it**.[2]
4. *Results-oriented.* Your goal should be stated as some desired future outcome or possession.
5. *Attainable.* Your goal should be reasonably matched to the resources you have to obtain it.

We realize that it is difficult to visualize the implications of these rules. We will walk through our Lean and Quick example to put the above concepts into concrete terms and to help you understand the theory behind their actions.

Your Investment Specifications

Action Paper No. 4, Your Investment Specifications (in the Appendix at the end of the book), is a worksheet that we designed to give you a trial-and-error format. You would be an unusually perceptive person if you were able to determine both your goals and how to achieve them at one pass.

While the form is clear, there is one concept we have not covered yet: *present value*. Just as you would correct your *future value* objectives to reflect the changes that inflation would bring about, it is important to understand the flip side. Present value is calculated by discounting the future value at a given investment rate.

For example, $100 that you will receive 10 years in the future has a

---

[2]The amount of money you will need to accomplish what you want at a later date is known as the *future value*. To figure the future value, adjust today's price at whatever rate you think inflation will be over the time period. Another way to get a price for the future may be to contact an expert in the field. For example, if you want to buy a car in five years, ask the dealer what the car you are interested in might cost five years hence.

FIGURE 4–3
Lean and Quick's Investment Specifications

Action Paper No. 4

Your Investment Specifications

Name _Lean and Quick_   Date _December_

Goals (in Priority)	Future Value (at 5%)	Year Needed	6% (High Priority, Near Term)	8%	10%	12% (High Priority, Long-Term)	14%	Present Value Sum (Final Investment Objectives)	Percent Return
① Emergency Reserve	6,500	2	.890/5,785	Group I		.799/5,180		5,785	6
② new car	19,000	5	.747/14,193			.567/10,773		10,773	12
③ Sons College	98,000	10	.558/54,684			.322/31,556 Group II		31,556	12
④ Daughters College	108,000	12	.497/53,676			.257/27,756		27,756	12
⑤ Retirement Fund	4,000/year	20	11.47/45,880			7.47/29,880		29,880	12

Present Value of Goals for Various After-Tax Rates of Return (factor from Table 4-1 or 4-2 Present Value Table)

	Low Priority, Near Term (6%)	12% (Low Priority, Long-Term)
(A) Total Present Value of Goals:	174,218	105,145
(B) Total Investment Resources PLUS Present Value of Projected Savings	149,700	109,700
(C) Final Goals Achievement Surplus (or Shortfall) (B) − (A) above:	(24,518)	4,555

Final Investment Objectives totals: 105,750   109,700   3,950

69

present value of $38.60 at a discount rate of 10 percent compounded annually. To get that figure, you have to use the Present Value Table, Table 4–1 (see pp. 72–73). Find the column headed by 10 percent, then look down that column to the 10-year row. The present value factor is 0.386 for $1. Multiply that by $100 to get $38.60.

The present value calculation is used to determine how much money should be invested today—at a given rate—to result in a specific amount at a future date. In Chapter 3 we showed you a compounded interest table. Present value tables are compounded interest tables in reverse!

Let's take one more example to make sure you understand this important concept. Say you had a goal to take a world cruise in four years. If you established the cost of that cruise would be $8,000 in four years (the future value), you have all the data (along with the Present Value Table) that you will need.

If you are reasonably sure you can make an investment that will yield 10 percent over the next four years, the Present Value Table will tell you how much you need to invest now to have that $8,000 when you need it. Find "4 years" and read across the columns until you get to the one titled "10%." The number is "0.683." This number means that 68 cents invested today at 10 percent would yield $1 in four years.

But, you want to know how much you need to invest today to have $8,000 in four years. Multiply $8,000 by the present value factor of 0.683. You need to invest $5,464 today at 10 percent compounded annually to get $8,000 in four years.

While this may seem a bit confusing at first, it will prove worthwhile to try a few exercises on your own. The heart of the goal-getting process involves taking the future value of your goal and establishing investment objectives in present terms.

Determining Goals: An Example

Now you know how to use the Present Value Table. This is where you will turn to get the numbers you need for Your Investment Specifications worksheet. Note that, in our Lean and Quick example, Figure 4–3, the first number under the "6%" column is the present value factor. The number after the slash ("/") is the present value.

Our Lean and Quick investors have targeted a $6,500 emergency reserve. Guardian personalities would probably want to target closer to twice their monthly income. More impetuous types would be satisfied with less. Whatever the exact amount, it should fit *you*. Are you comfortable with that emergency reserve? While there is no perfect number to satisfy everyone, every household should have an emergency reserve. It never makes sense to put off setting up an *emergency* reserve!

TABLE 4–1
Present Value Table

Present Value of $1

Years Hence	1%	2%	4%	6%	8%	10%	12%	14%	15%	16%	18%	20%	22%	24%	25%	26%	28%	30%	35%	40%	45%	50%
1	0.990	0.980	0.962	0.943	0.926	0.909	0.893	0.877	0.870	0.862	0.847	0.833	0.820	0.806	0.800	0.794	0.781	0.769	0.741	0.714	0.690	0.667
2	0.980	0.961	0.925	0.890	0.857	0.826	0.797	0.769	0.756	0.743	0.718	0.694	0.672	0.650	0.640	0.630	0.610	0.592	0.549	0.510	0.476	0.444
3	0.971	0.942	0.889	0.840	0.794	0.751	0.712	0.675	0.658	0.641	0.609	0.579	0.551	0.524	0.512	0.500	0.477	0.455	0.406	0.364	0.328	0.296
4	0.961	0.924	0.855	0.792	0.735	0.683	0.636	0.592	0.572	0.552	0.516	0.482	0.451	0.423	0.410	0.397	0.373	0.350	0.301	0.260	0.226	0.198
5	0.951	0.906	0.822	0.747	0.681	0.621	0.567	0.519	0.497	0.476	0.437	0.402	0.370	0.341	0.328	0.315	0.291	0.269	0.223	0.186	0.156	0.132
6	0.941	0.888	0.790	0.705	0.630	0.564	0.507	0.456	0.432	0.410	0.370	0.335	0.303	0.275	0.262	0.250	0.227	0.207	0.165	0.133	0.108	0.088
7	0.933	0.871	0.760	0.665	0.583	0.513	0.452	0.400	0.376	0.354	0.314	0.279	0.249	0.222	0.210	0.198	0.178	0.159	0.122	0.095	0.074	0.059
8	0.923	0.853	0.731	0.627	0.540	0.467	0.404	0.351	0.327	0.305	0.266	0.233	0.204	0.179	0.168	0.157	0.139	0.123	0.091	0.068	0.051	0.039
9	0.914	0.837	0.703	0.592	0.500	0.424	0.361	0.308	0.284	0.263	0.225	0.194	0.167	0.144	0.134	0.125	0.108	0.094	0.067	0.048	0.035	0.026
10	0.905	0.820	0.676	0.558	0.463	0.386	0.322	0.270	0.247	0.227	0.191	0.162	0.137	0.116	0.107	0.099	0.085	0.073	0.050	0.035	0.024	0.017
11	0.896	0.804	0.650	0.527	0.429	0.350	0.287	0.237	0.215	0.195	0.162	0.135	0.112	0.094	0.086	0.079	0.066	0.056	0.037	0.025	0.017	0.012
12	0.887	0.788	0.625	0.497	0.397	0.319	0.257	0.208	0.187	0.168	0.137	0.112	0.092	0.076	0.069	0.062	0.052	0.043	0.027	0.018	0.012	0.008
13	0.879	0.773	0.601	0.469	0.368	0.290	0.229	0.182	0.163	0.145	0.116	0.093	0.075	0.061	0.055	0.050	0.040	0.033	0.020	0.013	0.008	0.005
14	0.870	0.758	0.577	0.442	0.340	0.263	0.205	0.160	0.141	0.125	0.099	0.078	0.062	0.049	0.044	0.039	0.032	0.025	0.015	0.009	0.006	0.003
15	0.861	0.743	0.555	0.417	0.315	0.239	0.183	0.140	0.123	0.108	0.084	0.065	0.051	0.040	0.035	0.031	0.025	0.020	0.011	0.006	0.004	0.002
16	0.853	0.728	0.534	0.394	0.292	0.218	0.163	0.123	0.107	0.093	0.071	0.054	0.042	0.032	0.028	0.025	0.019	0.015	0.008	0.005	0.003	0.002
17	0.844	0.714	0.513	0.371	0.270	0.198	0.146	0.108	0.093	0.080	0.060	0.045	0.034	0.026	0.023	0.020	0.015	0.012	0.006	0.003	0.002	0.001
18	0.836	0.700	0.494	0.350	0.250	0.180	0.130	0.095	0.081	0.069	0.051	0.038	0.028	0.021	0.018	0.016	0.012	0.009	0.005	0.002	0.001	0.001
19	0.828	0.686	0.475	0.331	0.232	0.164	0.116	0.083	0.070	0.060	0.043	0.031	0.023	0.017	0.014	0.012	0.009	0.007	0.003	0.002	0.001	
20	0.820	0.673	0.456	0.312	0.215	0.149	0.104	0.073	0.061	0.051	0.037	0.026	0.019	0.014	0.012	0.010	0.007	0.005	0.002	0.001	0.001	
21	0.811	0.660	0.439	0.294	0.199	0.135	0.093	0.064	0.053	0.044	0.031	0.022	0.015	0.011	0.009	0.008	0.006	0.004	0.002	0.001		
22	0.803	0.647	0.422	0.278	0.184	0.123	0.083	0.056	0.046	0.038	0.026	0.018	0.013	0.009	0.007	0.006	0.004	0.003	0.001	0.001		
23	0.795	0.634	0.406	0.262	0.170	0.112	0.074	0.049	0.040	0.033	0.022	0.015	0.010	0.007	0.006	0.005	0.003	0.002	0.001			
24	0.788	0.622	0.390	0.247	0.158	0.102	0.066	0.043	0.035	0.028	0.019	0.013	0.008	0.006	0.005	0.004	0.003	0.002	0.001			
25	0.780	0.610	0.375	0.233	0.146	0.092	0.059	0.038	0.030	0.024	0.016	0.010	0.007	0.005	0.004	0.003	0.002	0.001	0.001			
26	0.772	0.598	0.361	0.220	0.135	0.084	0.053	0.033	0.026	0.021	0.014	0.009	0.006	0.004	0.003	0.002	0.002	0.001				
27	0.764	0.586	0.347	0.207	0.125	0.076	0.047	0.029	0.023	0.018	0.011	0.007	0.005	0.003	0.002	0.002	0.001	0.001				
28	0.757	0.574	0.333	0.196	0.116	0.069	0.042	0.026	0.020	0.016	0.010	0.006	0.004	0.002	0.002	0.002	0.001	0.001				
29	0.749	0.563	0.321	0.185	0.107	0.063	0.037	0.022	0.017	0.014	0.008	0.005	0.003	0.002	0.002	0.001	0.001	0.001				
30	0.742	0.552	0.308	0.174	0.099	0.057	0.033	0.020	0.015	0.012	0.007	0.004	0.003	0.002	0.001	0.001	0.001	0.001				
40	0.672	0.453	0.208	0.097	0.046	0.022	0.011	0.005	0.004	0.003	0.001											
50	0.608	0.372	0.141	0.054	0.021	0.009	0.003	0.001	0.001	0.001												

EXAMPLE: Suppose you need $20,000 ten years into the future How much must you invest today to achieve it assuming a 12% rate of return? First, enter the chart at "10 Years Hence". and move right until you intersect the column headed by the label "12%". The factor is .322. Multiplying $20,000 by .322, you will find that the present value of this amount (discounted at 12%) is $6,440.

TABLE 4–2
Present Value of an Annuity Table for Investments Made at End of Each Year

Length of Investment (Years)	Percentage Rate of Return or of Inflation								
	3%	4%	5%	6%	7%	8%	10%	12%	14%
1	0.9708	0.9615	0.9523	0.9433	0.9345	0.9315	0.9090	0.8923	0.8771
2	1.9134	1.8860	1.8594	1.8333	1.8080	1.7832	1.7355	1.6900	1.6466
3	2.8286	2.7750	2.7232	2.6730	2.6245	2.5770	2.4868	2.4018	2.3216
4	3.7170	3.6298	2.5459	3.4651	3.3872	3.3121	3.1693	3.0373	2.9137
5	4.5797	4.4518	4.3294	4.2123	4.1001	3.9927	3.7907	3.6047	3.4330
6	5.4171	5.2421	5.0756	4.9173	4.7665	4.6228	4.3552	4.1114	3.8886
7	6.2302	6.0020	5.7863	5.5823	5.3892	5.2063	4.8684	4.5637	4.2883
8	7.0196	6.7327	6.4632	6.2107	5.9712	5.7466	5.3349	4.9676	4.6388
9	7.7861	7.4353	7.1078	6.8016	6.5152	6.2468	5.7590	5.3282	4.9473
10	8.5302	8.1108	7.7217	7.3600	7.0235	6.7100	6.1445	5.6502	5.2161
11	9.2526	8.7604	8.3064	7.8868	7.4936	7.1389	6.4950	5.9877	5.4527
12	9.9540	9.3850	9.8632	8.3838	7.9426	7.5360	6.8136	6.1943	5.6602
13	10.6349	9.9856	9.3935	8.8526	8.3576	7.9037	7.1033	6.4235	5.8423
14	11.2960	10.5631	9.8986	9.2049	8.7454	8.2442	7.3666	6.6281	6.0020
15	11.9379	11.1183	10.3796	9.7122	9.1079	8.5594	7.6057	6.8108	6.1421
16	12.5611	11.6522	10.8377	10.1058	9.4466	8.8513	7.8237	6.9739	6.2650
17	13.1661	12.1656	11.2740	10.4772	9.7632	9.1216	8.0215	7.1196	6.3728
18	13.7535	12.6592	11.6895	10.8275	10.0590	9.3718	8.2014	7.2496	6.4674
19	14.3237	13.1339	12.0853	11.1581	10.3355	9.6035	8.3649	7.3657	6.5503
20	14.8774	13.5903	12.4622	11.4699	10.5940	9.8181	8.5135	7.4694	6.6231
21	15.4150	14.0291	12.8211	11.7640	10.8355	10.0168	8.6486	7.5620	6.6869
22	15.9369	14.4511	13.1630	12.0415	11.0612	10.2007	8.7715	7.6446	6.7429
23	16.4436	14.8568	13.4885	12.3033	11.2721	10.3710	8.8832	7.7184	6.7920
24	16.9355	15.2469	13.7986	12.5503	11.4693	10.5287	8.9847	7.7842	6.8351
25	17.4131	15.6220	14.0939	12.7833	11.6535	10.6747	9.0770	7.8431	6.8729
26	17.8768	15.9827	14.3751	13.0031	11.8257	10.8099	9.1609	7.8956	6.9060
27	18.3270	16.3295	14.6430	13.2105	11.9867	10.9351	9.2372	7.9425	6.9351
28	18.7641	16.6630	14.8981	13.4061	12.1371	11.0510	9.3065	7.9844	6.9606
29	19.1884	16.9837	15.1410	13.5907	12.2776	11.1584	9.3696	8.0218	6.9830
30	19.6004	17.2920	15.3724	13.7648	12.4090	11.2577	9.4269	8.0551	7.0026
31	20.0004	17.5884	15.5928	13.9290	12.5318	11.3497	9.4790	8.0849	7.0198
32	20.3887	17.8735	15.8026	14.0840	12.6465	11.4349	9.5263	8.1115	7.0349
33	20.7657	18.1476	16.0025	14.2302	12.7537	11.5133	9.5694	8.1353	7.0482
34	21.1318	18.4111	16.1929	14.3681	12.8540	11.5861	9.6085	8.1565	7.0598
35	21.4872	18.6646	16.3741	14.4982	12.9476	11.6545	9.6441	8.1755	7.0700
36	21.8322	18.9082	16.5468	14.6209	13.0352	11.7171	9.6765	8.1924	7.0789
37	22.1672	19.1425	16.7112	14.7367	13.1170	11.7751	9.7059	8.2075	7.0868
38	22.4924	19.3678	16.8678	14.8460	13.1924	11.8288	9.7326	8.2209	7.0937
39	22.8082	19.5844	17.0170	14.9490	13.2649	11.8785	9.7569	8.2330	7.0997
40	23.1147	19.7927	17.1590	15.0462	13.3317	11.9246	9.7790	8.2437	7.1050

EXAMPLE:
Suppose you plan on investing $1,000 at the end of every year for 5 years at a compound rate of return of 6%. What is the present value of the future sum you would earn? First, find the intersection of the 6% column and the 5 year row. This present value factor is 4.21. Multiply this number by your annual investment of $1,000. The present value of this investment plan, then, would be $4,210.

The emergency fund is a short-term goal and the Lean and Quicksters have indicated a target of two years for accomplishing it.

Transportation is a necessity for many families. Our Lean and Quick investors expect they will need a new car in five years. They figure a car to their liking in 5 years will cost $19,000.

The cost of college education is rising every year. Any family with college aspirations for their children **must** plan for this contingency early, or face an expensive surprise later! Our Lean and Quick investors project college costs for their two children, for 10 and 12 years from now. These future values are $98,000 and $108,000, respectively.

And, finally, planning for your own retirement should be an integral part of your goal-setting program. Even under the current tax laws, IRAs still provide a means for saving money on a tax-deferred basis.

The 1986 Tax Reform Act severely limited eligibility for tax-deductible IRAs. Basically, only those people who are not covered by another retirement plan are eligible to deduct their investment up to $2,000. However, money invested in IRAs (up to $2,000 per year per person) can still accrue interest and growth, tax free, until the proceeds are withdrawn from the IRA.

Our Lean and Quick investors plan to put aside $4,000 per year in an IRA for their retirement. This involves annual contributions, as well as compounding. To calculate the proper present value for this situation, you will need to refer to Table 4–2, the Present Value of an Annuity Table. This table is used only when you have a goal requiring regular annual contributions.

For this computation, multiply the annual contribution by the appropriate factor from the table. To find your factor, enter the table at the column of the percentage rate of return you are testing. Follow the column downward to where it intersects with the number of years until you plan to use your investment. The number found at this intersection is the one you want.

An example will clarify this. Our Lean and Quicksters will contribute $4,000 per year to their retirement fund for 20 years. They are testing the effects of a 6 percent annual rate of return. The factor found at the intersection of "6%" and "20 years" is 11.47; $4,000 times 11.47 equals $45,880— the present value of the goal amount needed in 20 years.

These goals, the estimated costs to achieve them (given a constant 5 percent annual rate of inflation), and the year in which they will be needed, are shown in the box at the left of the investment specifications worksheet.

Calculating How to Pay for Your Goals

Now it's time to apply our "attainable" test. How can you determine if your goals are realistically attainable? You will not want to take many chances with your most important near-term goals. However, you may choose to be a bit more speculative with your long-term goals, since even those with a high priority allow you more leeway to operate. You have more time to let your money work—even, perhaps, to make up losses that may occur.

We have labeled each column with various rates of return that you might expect, beginning with 6 percent and going to 14 percent. Since few people like to take more risk than is necessary, our Lean and Quick investors first calculated how far their resources would take them at the conservative 6 percent rate of return.

It's here that the concept of "present value" comes into play. At a 6 percent compounded annual rate for their highest priority item, the emergency reserve, our couple will need to invest $5,785. This figure was arrived at by taking the present value factor for two years at 6 percent (0.890), multiplied by the goal of $6,500.

If you perform the same calculation at the same 6 percent rate (don't forget to note the different time periods for each goal, as indicated in the column titled "Year Needed"), you will find that the couple must invest $174,218 today to achieve their goals.

To see if this is "do-able," you have to check their financial statement. The Lean and Quick's balance sheet shows $35,000 in investable assets (items 4 and 11). Their income statement discloses that they can save another $10,000 per year for their investment funds (item 8). But because their savings will be attained over a number of years, we need to once again present value the $10,000 income surplus that will be contributed to their investment funds each year. Using Table 4–2, we find that the present value factor for annual contributions earning 6 percent for 20 years is 11.47; $10,000 times 11.47 equals $114,700—the present value of their projected $10,000 per year savings. Now, add this $114,700 to their current investment assets of $35,000, to reach the total $149,700. This sum appears on Line (B) of the Investment Specifications Worksheet. Subtracting (B) from (A), you see they are left $24,518 short of the figure needed. Obviously, the conservative 6 percent return would be insufficient to meet their goals.

You can work through all the numbers to see how each step up improves their picture. Your computer would make quick work of these calculations. But, let's skip ahead to see how a 12 percent annual return would affect the figures. As you can see, the total Present Value Goals at 12 percent comes to $105,145. That's $4,555 less than the amount our Lean and Quick investors have available as investable funds resources.

Does this mean their investment planning is finished? Not yet. Remember, they have distinctly different priorities for their goals. Foremost is their emergency reserve. Simply stated, attaining a 12 percent rate of return is riskier than sticking with a 6 percent return. A two-year time period leaves little time for error.

A good approach in situations like this—which most investors will face—is to split your goals into two different groups. Group I is for high-priority, near-term goals. Group II covers the lower-priority, but important, and long-term goals.

We've cheated a little to show you how this dual priority system works. The first item in our Lean and Quick investor's goals is short term, or Group I priority. The remaining four items are Group II, or long term. Since Group I goals are to be achieved with minimal risk, they are calculated at the conservative 6 percent rate.

The Group II goals are to be accomplished in an ample time period, so our Lean and Quick investors are willing to take a bit more risk to achieve them. Group II goals have been figured at the more aggressive 12 percent rate. Keep in mind that the couple in our example is working within the constraints of staying at their current standard of living.

Using these new groupings, the total Present Value of Goals (item A) is $105,750. That is still $3,950 below their Total Investment Resources (item B).

Taking the time to set the priorities that make sense to you is a critical step in producing a plan that will work for you. Don't get too tied to our example. Your goals and resources will probably be far different. The *process* of getting from vague goals to a specific plan is the important lesson here.

Know your starting point (the balance sheet and the income statement). Identify your goals (emergency reserves, college, world travel, a new car, retirement, whatever). Ascertain costs. Set priorities, based on the time necessary to achieve your goals. Use the Present Value Factor Tables to do your calculations.

ALLOCATING YOUR INVESTABLE DOLLARS

You now have a complete set of investment objectives that will achieve your goals *when* you want to have them. You know *how much* to invest in today's dollars to achieve the amounts you need. You *even* know the approximate *rate of return* your investment vehicles will have to earn to make it possible for you to meet your goals.

But, one rather important piece is missing from the puzzle. Your plan does not tell you *where* to look for vehicles that will provide those returns. It does not tell you what *mix* of assets will assure those returns while affording you protection for your invested dollars.

So far you have learned a lot about different investor personalities but not much about how that knowledge can be applied to your specific case. Take a look at Table 4–3, BB&K's Target Mix for a Fully Invested Portfolio.

This table shows the percentages we recommend for each asset class,

TABLE 4–3
BB&K's Target Mix for a Fully Invested Portfolio*

	Light and Agile (percent)	Lean and Quick (percent)	Strong and Sturdy (percent)	Strong and Quick (percent)
Cash equivalents	5–20%	0–10%	5–15%	0–10%
Fixed income	10–40	10–30	15–45	10–40
U.S. stocks	10–40	20–40	20–45	20–50
International stocks	0–20	10–25	10–25	10–30
Inflation hedges/ Real Estate	5–25	15–45	10–30	15–50

* "Fully invested" means simply that you do not have to keep a larger than indicated percentage of resources in cash equivalents because of abnormally unstable markets.

based on the needs of each financial physique. For example, our Lean and Quick investors need a lower percentage of cash equivalents than, say, Light and Agile investors, because the Lean and Quick's higher income can quickly replenish their liquid reserves in case of emergency.

Strong and Sturdy investors need a bit more fixed-income allocation than Lean and Quick to help augment their sometimes inadequate cash flow. Take a moment to study the allocation recommendations that are appropriate to your own financial physique. This table will help you make difficult choices when it comes to making specific investments.

Allocating Your Fund to Short-Term/High Priority Goals

Action Paper No. 5, Your Group I Goal Allocations will be your worksheet for apportioning money for your near-term, highest-priority goals. A blank copy for your use is included in the Appendix. Think about how you would complete your own as we go through Lean and Quick's Group I Goal Allocations (Figure 4–4).

We've already touched on grouping your goals when you worked on Action Paper No. 4, Your Investment Specifications. Group I goals are a combination of "emergency reserves" and "other" goals that are to be achieved in less than five years. Since these goals will depend on approximately the same rate of return, they are viewed as part of one pool of cash for asset allocation purposes. Our Lean and Quick investors have a total Group I allocation of $6,500.

FIGURE 4–4
Lean and Quick's Group I Goal Allocations

Action Paper No. 5

Your Group I Goal Allocations

Name(s) *Lean and Quick*

Date *December*

Group I Allocation Costs:
(Short-Term [Less Than Five Years] Needs)

Emergency Reserve	*6,500*
Goal Costs, Next Five Years	+ *0*
Total Group I Allocation	*6,500*

Group I Allocation Targets

Asset Classes	BB&K Recommended Target Mix Range (percent)	Your Target Allocation Dollars	Percent
Cash Equivalents	20-80	*3,500*	*54*
Fixed Income	10-30	*1,500*	*23*
U.S. Stocks	10-30	*1,500*	*23*
International Stocks	0-10		
Real Estate/ Inflation Hedges	0-10 (REITs only)		
	Total	*6,500*	*100*

The target mix for Group I is heavily skewed to the most liquid of our asset classes, since this money will be spent in just a few years. As you can see from our example in Figure 4–4, our Lean and Quick investors have broken their short-term allocation targets into the three most-liquid asset classes. To complete your own goal allocations in Action Paper No. 5 (in the Appendix), you need to know that the *general range* of returns available from the chosen asset classes are high enough to meet your Group I goals. You should know the ballpark figure from Action Paper No. 4, Your Investment Specifications, where you tried different combinations of returns.

As a rule of thumb, you should invest more heavily in cash equivalents —the upper end of the suggested range—if your goal is due within the next two years. You will not want to risk losing principal on a bond (fixed income) by being forced to cash it in after interest rates have moved higher. Remember, if rates move up, the principal value of your bonds will fall. The full face value of the bond is guaranteed by the issuer only if held to maturity.

If your near-term goals tend to be grouped in the three- to five-year period, you can put more money into longer-term assets. *But don't exceed the upper limits indicated on the worksheet.*

The worksheet is designed to provide a quick double check of your calculations. Total the dollar amounts to ensure that they equal the dollar total for your Group I goals. Next, add the percentages to be sure they total 100 percent.

At this point, you won't have particular investment vehicles in mind. Before taking that step, it's important to give yourself a "roadmap" by first setting allocation targets. In the next chapter we will explore how to find the specific instruments in each asset class to meet your needs.

Allocating Your Funds for Long-Term Goals

Complete the blank Action Paper No. 6, Your Group II Goal Allocations, in the Appendix. You will use this form to allocate the balance of your investable assets that are targeted for the long term.

Our Lean and Quick investors completed their Action Paper No. 6, as seen in Figure 4–5. They transferred the BB&K Recommended Target Mix Ranges for their financial physique from Table 4–1 to their Action Paper No. 6. When completing your own Group II Asset Allocation form, be sure to transfer the correct figures for your own physique!

The Current Investable Resources figure of $45,000 comes from items 4 and 11 on the balance sheet and item 8 from the income statement. Here, we are not concerned with assets built over time, only assets that are available today. Subtract the total of their Group I needs from that balance,

FIGURE 4–5
Lean and Quick's Group II Goal Allocations

Action Paper No. 6

Your Group II Goal Allocations

Name(s) *Lean and Quick*   Date *December*

Current investable resources (Balance Sheet Items 4 + 11 PLUS Income Statement item 8)	45,000
Less Group I needs (From Action Paper No. 5)	– 6,500
Group II assets	38,500

Group II Allocation Targets
(Long-Term Needs)

Asset Classes	BB&K Recommended Target Mix Range (percent) (See Table 4–3 for Your Financial Physique)	Your Target Allocations Dollars	Percent
Cash Equivalents[1]	0 – 10	–	–
Fixed Income[2]	10 – 30	8,470	22
U.S. Stocks[3]	20 – 40	14,245	37
International Stocks[3]	10 – 25	–	–
Real Estate/ Inflation Hedges[4]	15 – 45	15,785	41
Totals		38,500	100

Footnotes:

1. If your Group I goals are equal to or greater than one third of your Group II goals, put no more than 5% of your Group II amounts in cash equivalents.

2. If you are an income-oriented investor, use the upper end of the fixed-income range.

3. Although U.S. and foreign stocks can follow different market cycles, you should consider them as a single equity class for the long term. Their total should not exceed 60-65% of your total Group II assets.

4. Precious metals tend to be very volatile. A mix between gold mining shares and gold bullion or coins offers greater stability than shares alone. In any case limit your precious metals position to 12% or less. Your gold investments should not exceed your real estate position.

which leaves Group II assets of $38,500 to be allocated over the five asset classes.

If your total Group I assets are one third or more of the present value for all your goals, you probably have already allocated enough to cash equivalents. In that case, no more than 5 percent of your Group II assets should be allocated to cash equivalents.

When you consider your long-term goal allocations, bear in mind that you will not want to tie up money in less-liquid investments that may have to be liquidated at inopportune times.

If you have a larger than normal portion of your investable resources earmarked for short-term goals, you will fall outside the normal asset mix pattern recommended in Table 4–3, BB&K's Target Mix for a Fully Invested Portfolio. *This is applicable to all financial physiques.*

The less-liquid asset classes are primarily intended to protect you from long-term financial adversity. Such conditions as extended high inflation or increasing tax rates are two examples of longer-term contingencies. If your goals are mainly short-term, your money would be spent before the adverse affects of these long-term factors would be felt in your portfolio!

Your next step is to divide your assets into specific dollar amounts for each asset class, based on the percentages selected from the target ranges. Because each target mix is expressed as a range, you must decide what percentage to use. We have delineated some guidelines to help each investor personality[3] make those decisions.

Guardians

If you are a Guardian investor, our experience suggests that you should try to allocate about 30 percent of your Group II investments to fixed-income vehicles, 30 percent to U.S. stocks, and 30 percent to real estate/inflation hedges. Put the remaining 10 percent into international securities.

We have stressed that it is important to *feel comfortable* with your investment decisions. As a Guardian you are probably willing to forego potentially higher returns from a more aggressive stance, if it means that the chances of suffering a large loss are smaller.

The Straight Arrow

As a Straight Arrow investor, you probably *want* to select the middle of each suggested range. You might have a problem deciding whether that arithmetic mean is the percentage you *ought* to take. If that arbitrary midpoint doesn't seem satisfactory to you, review the Taking Stock section in Chapter 3 to confirm your Straight Arrow alter ego. Remember, Straight Ar-

---

[3]Refer to the discussion about investor personalities in Chapter 3 for clarification of your traits.

rows tend to reflect elements of the other investor personalities. To find the personality that suits you, check the Investor Personality Grid. Which quadrant of the chart—Individualist, Adventurer, Guardian, or Enthusiast—do you favor? You probably will find that certain traits of the investor personality quadrant where you fell will feel right when it comes to making your allocation decisions. Once you have determined your investor alter ego, refer to the investor personality descriptions that follow. You will find suggestions that will probably make sense to you.

Individualists

Individualist investors should have few problems making a sound *initial* allocation among the asset classes. You tend to analyze each asset class to the fullest before picking your points in each range. Unfortunately, you often begin to question those allocations as soon as you have made them.

You will wonder whether your decisions are correct each time some change appears in the economic climate. That's all well and good, as long as you view further allocation changes as midcourse corrections. Individualists have a tendency to view the need for changes as signs of failure. That triggers a need to find a brand new strategy.

If you keep things in perspective, you should have few problems making and living with your decisions. After all, changes are a necessary part of any effective investment strategy.

Enthusiasts

As an Enthusiast, you probably are getting the most up-to-date advice on what is the latest thing favored by those in the know. Be careful to guard against investing too heavily in an asset class that may be headed for a fall.

The stock market was the hot item for those investors who wanted to be where the action was during most of 1987. But, in October of that year, those who had overinvested in stocks paid a heavy penalty. Few people saw the crash coming. Many prominent advisors were enthusiastic (many are probably Enthusiasts!) right up to the crash itself.

An Enthusiast is the most likely type of investor to go beyond the recommended target ranges. If you stay within the ranges, you will not suffer too much damage if a sharp reversal occurs in the current hot investment. *Resist* the urge to exceed the maximum allocation in a popular class.

Concurrently, be sure to avoid the tendency to underinvest in another asset class that is out of favor. Such vehicles usually offer good bargains when you take the long-term view.

Adventurers

If you are an Adventurer, your natural inclination is to put most of your money into the classes with the greatest potential for gain: U.S. and international stocks and some of the riskier inflation hedges, such as gold or silver. You won't get into too much trouble **if you observe the minimum allocations in the other, less-dynamic classes**.

High-flying Adventurers have to guard against the dangers of large losses occurring from their impetuous plunges. Keep in mind the advice of hang gliding instructors to their charges: "Never fly higher than you are willing to fall."

PUTTING TOGETHER YOUR
ASSET ALLOCATION PLAN

So far you have determined your financial starting point, your investment targets, and your financial goals. Action Paper No. 7, Your Asset Allocation Plan, is the final worksheet that you need to create your fully invested portfolio. Fill in the blank copy, which you will find in the Appendix. You will undoubtedly find it easier to complete your allocation planning by following along with our Lean and Quick example (see Figure 4–6).

You will need the other Action Papers that you have completed to this point. Enter your Group I and Group II Goals' Allocations for each asset class from Action Papers 5 and 6. Total the amounts for both Group I and II allocations to make sure they match the numbers from Action Papers 5 and 6.

Next add your Group I and II allocations and enter the dollar amounts under "Current Target Allocations." Calculate the dollar amounts as a percentage of your total portfolio and enter the percentages in the next column.

Your previously completed Action Paper No. 1, Your Current Asset Mix, will provide the necessary numbers to complete the "Current Holdings" columns (the total should match the total monetary assets plus fixed investment assets from your balance sheet). The *difference* between these current holdings and your new targets is the prescription for reallocating your portfolio *the BB&K way*.

If you have a problem completing your forms, follow the numbers from Action Paper No. 1 through Action Paper No. 6 for our Lean and Quick example. We've designed these worksheets to be modules in building an increasingly detailed picture of your financial situation. Each worksheet shows the source of previously computed numbers.

As you can see from our example, Lean and Quick are overinvested in cash equivalents. They are about on target with their fixed-income portion. Their stock portfolio and real estate/inflation hedge are underweight. Now that they have identified the changes to be made in their allocations, they

FIGURE 4–6
Lean and Quick's Asset Allocation Plan

Action Paper No. 7

Your Asset Allocation Plan

Name(s) _Lean and Quick_   Date _December_

Asset Classes	Group I Allocations (from Action Paper No. 5) Dollars	Group II Allocations (from Action Paper No. 6) Dollars	Current Target Allocations Dollars	Percent	Current Holdings Dollars	Percent	Current Adjustments Needed
Cash Equivalents	3,500	+ 0	= 3,500	8	12,000	34	move $8,500 to another asset class
Fixed Income	1,500	+ 8,470	= 9,970	22	8,000	23	need $1,970 from another asset class
U.S. Stocks	1,500	+ 14,245	= 15,745	35	15,000	43	add $745 from another asset class
International Stocks	0	+ 0	= 0	0	0	0	not really for this!
Real Estate/ Inflation Hedges	0	+ 15,785	= 15,785	35	0	0	invest what's available now; add during year
Totals	6,500	+ 33,500	= 45,000	100	35,000	100	

Future Adjustments Needed?

Year	Action
1	Add to real estate from surplus income. Gold?
2	Really opt for international securities?
3	Invest surplus income proportionately across the board?

Making Money Is Not the Same as Managing It

Even the most hard-headed money-maker sometimes sees the world through rose-colored glasses. This is true especially when it comes to preserving and investing the money he or she has already made. Often business people, who work hard to make a living, approach investing with unrealistic expectations. Making money *with your money* doesn't come easy. Just as business rewards come through hard work, so do investment profits.

To paraphrase a well-known quote: The price of investment profits is eternal vigilance. When reviewing your investment returns it is natural to focus on the successes and overlook the failures. But sloppy thinking can be costly.

For example, suppose you decide that the return on that stuffy money market fund is too low. Besides, it doesn't provide any fun. You take $10,000 out and buy a stock your broker has been touting as the hottest thing in years.

In six months your stock has gone up 50 percent. Your account is now worth $15,000. You manage to avoid serious injury patting yourself on the back, but now you *know* that this investment game is not so tough after all. Diversify? Why, all that money languishing in money markets and bonds is holding you back!

But what goes up will come down. Six months later you see that your stock has dropped 50 percent. You think maybe it is time to sell to break even. Think again.

When the stock fell 50 percent, your $15,000 stock balance dropped to $7,500, not $10,000. *Winning* by 50 percent then *losing* by 50 percent will *not* put you back where you began.

Your first priority should be *preserving* your capital. Making up losses is a difficult proposition. For example, if you start with a $10,000 account and lose 50 percent, you must earn *100 percent* just to get back to even.

Successful *money-makers* often look at the investment world through rose-colored glasses. If it were so much easier to make money investing than to make money in business, everyone would quit their jobs and invest for riches.

This doesn't mean that only professional money-managers can make investments work. It does mean that the principles of money management that you are learning in this book—such as diversification or the power of compounding—still count, even if you choose to ignore them. Remember, it's what you keep, not what you make, that counts.

will have to take the next step and shift their assets toward a new and better balance.

Once you've completed the math, it's important that you include detailed notes under the "Current Adjustments Needed" column. You will find that putting it in writing will not only highlight needed changes but will also provide perspective for you. Recognizing and making the modifications called for in this worksheet is your first task in assembling your Personal Profit Portfolio.

You should always be looking ahead to anticipated future adjustments. As in our Lean and Quick example, note those areas that will affect future allocation strategies early. These can always be changed later, but writing it down will help focus your investment discipline.

One other factor will affect your future allocation moves. As the market values of your investment change, so will their relative ranking as a percentage of your total portfolio. In Chapter 6 we detail how to approach the reallocation process. At this stage make notes about the assumptions you had when you formulated your allocations.

WRAPPING UP

In this chapter you have gained a detailed look at your financial picture. It is impossible to make usable future financial plans without knowing your starting point. The very exercise of completing a balance sheet and an income statement helps answer those nagging questions about where your money goes.

Financial goals can be expressed in dollars and cents. If you are sincere in your desire to reach your goals, you must move beyond the vague "someday I will" stage. What do you want? How much will it cost? When do you want it? These questions must be addressed specifically and the answers written down.

Once you have that basic information at your fingertips, making your investment plans is a fairly simple matter of putting your calculator to work. You learned the importance of "present value" (i.e., how much of today's money is needed to meet tomorrow's goals). The present value factor tables will become a dog-eared addition to your financial papers.

Finally, you took the first concrete step in designing your Personal Profit Portfolio. You know where you are, where you want to be, and what initial steps are necessary to get you there. In the balance of the book you will learn how to select specific investment vehicles and how to manage your portfolio in the days ahead.

CHAPTER 5

PUTTING IT ALL TOGETHER

FINDING THE RIGHT INVESTMENTS FOR *YOU*

In Chapter 4 you worked through the first steps in your portfolio building process: determining where you are, where you want to go, when you need to get there, and how to allocate your funds among the five asset classes to make it possible. But, even though you've come this far, the investment jungle can still be intimidating.

Finding investments is easy; new investment products are entering the market every day. Finding those that fit your investor personality, financial physique, and goal-getting needs, requires more effort. By following this book and completing the Action Papers, you have already exercised more discipline in identifying specific financial goals, their costs, and time frames than most investors ever will.

Exploring the financial world can be interesting and stimulating. Succeeding in your investment plan is that, and more—it's exciting and profitable!

If you remember your history lessons, you may recall how one of Napoleon's soldiers unearthed a remarkable stone tablet near the mouth of the Nile. The stone was carved with a decree of the Pharoah Ptolemy V in both Greek and the long-dead language of ancient Egypt. Now known as the Rosetta Stone, this tablet allowed 19th-century scholars, using their knowledge of Greek, to crack the riddle of Egyptian hieroglyphics.

In this chapter we introduce you to the *BB&K Rosetta Stone*, your key to deciphering the financial doubletalk you get from advertisements, newspapers, brokers, and other salespeople. It will narrow the range of investment options to those that are suitable for you. With the BB&K Rosetta Stone, and the detailed discussion that follows, you will be able to choose the vehicles that enhance your Personal Profit Portfolio.

This chapter shows you how to recognize the right investments when you see them. But individual investments, by themselves, will not answer your needs. Your *strategy* is as important as the amount of money you have to spend. Use the BB&K Rosetta Stone to track down the investments that fit within your overall strategy, being certain to employ the whole diversification approach.

USING THE BB&K ROSETTA STONE

Our Rosetta Stone is actually the familiar financial physique diagram, laid out for each of the five investor personalities. The grid created allows you to pinpoint the best investment strategy for your particular investor personality at the level of your financial physique.

Table 5–1 offers a broad sweep of the general types of vehicles that are best suited to each personality and financial physique. Look closely at the diagram and note, especially, that the range and complexity of the recommended investment vehicles *increase* as your income and assets increase. Likewise, your investment alternatives expand as your investor personality grows more confident, analytical, and tolerant of risk.

Look over all the recommendations for the various physiques. More than likely you will move through the various categories as your goals and resources evolve, opening additional investment options to you.

As you look at Table 5–1, you can readily see distinctions in personality types. For example, Guardian investors, regardless of income and asset levels, have fewer investment options than other personality types, because there are *fewer* vehicles that meet the Guardian's stringent safety criteria.

At the other end of the spectrum, Individualists and Adventurers tend to have *more* options than anyone else. The Individualist's independent nature and the Adventurer's risk-taking propensities allow for a wider range of choices.

On the following pages we have delineated our investment recommendations for each model personality. More detailed descriptions of the vehicles in each asset class are featured in Chapter 7 on mutual funds, and in Chapter 8, which concludes this book. If you come across a term that is new to you as you read the sections below, take the time to look it up in Chapter 8 before continuing.

Before you read the section that pertains to your investor personality, we want to introduce a concept that applies to all investors. At some time, you will have to decide whether it makes sense to buy taxable or tax-free funds and bonds. To help you make that decision, you can perform a simple calculation to compare the *after-tax* returns. The formula is:

TABLE 5–1
The BB&K Rosetta Stone Investment Key

Your Investor Personality	Your Financial Physique			
	Light and Agile	Lean and Quick	Strong and Sturdy	Strong and Quick
Guardian	Taxable group investments with emphasis on asset preservation.	Tax-free or sheltered group investments preferred, with risk-averse strategies	Taxable or tax-free group or individual investments with emphasis on income and security.	Tax-free or sheltered group or individual investments with emphasis on mature growth and asset preservation.
Straight Arrow	Taxable group investments with objectives limited only by limited resources.	Tax-free or sheltered group or individual investments with balanced risk/return strategies.	Taxable or tax-free group or individual investments with well-tailored risk/return strategies.	Tax-free or sheltered group or individual investments with wide range of growth and tax-saving vehicles.
Individualist	Taxable group investments with wide range of growth-oriented vehicles.	Tax-free or sheltered group or individual investments with wide range of vehicles.	Taxable or tax-free individual investments with wide range of income or growth vehicles.	Tax-free or sheltered individual investments preferred with widest possible range of growth or tax-saving vehicles.
Enthusiast	Taxable group investments with limited choice of popular vehicles.	Tax-free or sheltered group investments with controlled exposure to popular vehicles.	Taxable or tax-free group investments preferred, with well-qualified popular vehicles.	Tax-free or sheltered group investments preferred, with wide range of well-selected vehicles.
Adventurer	Taxable group investments with risk-tolerant, more aggressive growth vehicles.	Tax-free or sheltered group or individual investments with wide range of aggressive growth vehicles.	Taxable or tax-free individual investments with wide range of aggressive growth vehicles.	Tax-free or sheltered individual investments with widest possible range of risk-tolerant, tax-saving and growth vehicles.

Note: *How to use the BB&K Rosetta stone:* The box where your investor personality and financial physique intersect shows the *general traits* of the investments that are right for you.

$$TY \times (100\% - \text{Combined tax rate}^1) = ATY$$
$$TY = \text{Taxable yield of a money market fund or bond}$$
$$ATY = \text{After-tax rate}$$

For example, if taxable money market fund rates are 7 percent and your combined federal and state tax rate is 35 percent, the numbers would look like this:

$$7\% \times (100\% - 35\%) = 4.55\% \text{ After-tax yield or,}$$
$$0.07 \times (1.00 - 0.35) = 0.0455 \text{ or } 4.55\% \text{ ATY}$$

Compare this figure with the yield on tax-free funds or bonds to see which would yield more actual take home revenue. This formula will prove handy, repeatedly, as you make certain investment decisions. You will find reminders of it in the pertinent section of what follows.

The Guardian Investor

Table 5–2 is a detailed "Rosetta Stone Inscription" for Guardian investors. We suggest you scan *all* the recommendations, not just the entries for your own financial physique. As your career and life develop, you will undoubtedly find yourself in a different category. Your evolving goals and resources will provide the impetus to explore new and distinct investment options.

Cash Equivalents for the Guardian Investor

Cash equivalents, by definition, are very liquid investments, meaning that they are relatively safe from many of the risks associated with the other asset classes. But, some cash equivalents *are* riskier than others.

For example, Treasury bills are issued and guaranteed by the U.S. government, which makes them the safest money market instrument you can buy. Other money market vehicles, such as commercial paper, are issued by corporations. Despite their short maturities—usually less than one year—they bear a higher risk factor. Although there is a high degree of probability, there is no guarantee that corporations will meet their obligations. Guardians are, therefore, most comfortable with Treasury obligations.

For most investors, money market funds offer the best alternative among cash equivalents. These funds pool the money from individual investors to invest in various money market instruments. The advantages are twofold:

1. The amount of money needed to enter a fund is fairly modest. Most funds require initial deposits of $1,000 or less, whereas many sophis-

---

[1]This would be the value of the combination of your federal and state taxes.

TABLE 5–2
Investment Vehicles for the Guardian Investor

Guardian Financial Physiques

	III. Strong and Sturdy	**IV. Strong and Quick**
Higher	CE —taxable/tax-free money market funds, T-bills, bank CDs. FI —Treasury notes/bonds, AAA munis and corporate bonds, taxable/tax-free mutual bond fund and/or unit trusts. US —blue-chip stocks, income/growth mutual funds, income/growth stock portfolio, index fund. INT —mutual funds. I/RE—public income limited partnerships, equity REIT, own property, SAMs, gold/silver mutual funds and/or bullion and/or coins.	CE —taxable/tax-free market funds, T-bills, bank CDs. FI —Treasury notes/bonds, AAA munis/corporate bonds, taxable/tax-free mutual bond fund and/or unit trusts. US —blue-chip stocks, growth mutual funds, income/growth stock portfolio, index fund. INT —mutual funds. I/RE—public limited partnerships, mortgage/equity REITs, own property, SAMs, gold/silver mutual funds and/or bullion and/or coins.
Lower	**I. Light and Agile** CE —taxable money market funds. FI —Treasury notes/bonds, taxable mutual bond fund and/or unit trusts. US —income, growth, or balanced mutual funds or index funds. INT —mutual funds. I/RE—public income limited partnerships, income/growth REITs, gold/silver mutual funds and/or bullion and/or coins.	**II. Lean and Quick** CE —taxable/tax-free money market funds, T-bills. FI —Treasury notes/bonds, taxable/tax-free mutual bond fund and/or unit trusts. US —growth or balanced mutual funds or index funds. INT —mutual funds. I/RE—public income limited partnerships, growth REITs, gold/silver mutual funds and/or bullion and/or coins.

Assets (left axis)

Lower   *Higher*
Income

Key: CE = cash equivalents   US = U.S. equities   I/RE = inflation hedges/real estate
      FI = fixed income   INT = international securities   muni = municipal bond

ticated money market instruments require large minimum investments (even Treasury bills require a minimum of $10,000).
2. The funds offer a diversified portfolio, which lessens the damage
that a default could cause.

You can easily withdraw your money from a fund. Most money market
funds have check-writing privileges—typically the minimum check is $100.
Normally the funds render higher interest rates than those paid by passbook
or interest-bearing checking accounts. Most money market funds do not
charge commissions or front-end fees; however, they do charge a management fee, which can vary widely.

Money market funds, like money market instruments, differ in their relative risk. Guardian investors should seek those funds that invest in Treasury, municipal, or highly rated corporate issues.

Consideration also must be given to the tax consequences of each vehicle. For example, the interest earned on Treasury obligations is exempt
from local and state taxation. The interest paid by short-term municipal
notes issued by local and state authorities is usually exempt from federal income taxes. Since tax-related matters are subject to change, it is best to
check with your tax advisor for the latest developments before buying a tax-
advantaged investment.

Before you make the decision to invest in taxable or tax-free money
market funds, calculate which would provide the better after-tax yield. Use
the formula we described earlier; TY × (100% − Combined tax rate) =
ATY, or, the Taxable yield of the money market fund, multiplied by 100%
minus the Combined tax rate of your federal and state taxes, equals the
After-tax yield.

Compare the results against the yield on tax-free funds; but, remember,
tax-free money market funds are not as secure as funds that invest solely in
Treasury obligations.

As a Guardian investor, you may prefer to forego the slightly higher return of tax-free funds to ensure greater safety. As an alternative, you may
elect to buy both a taxable and a tax-free fund to maintain your "comfort
factor" at an acceptable level on your confidence/anxiety axis.

As your assets increase, you may want to invest directly in T-bills,
which require a minimum investment of $10,000, with $5,000 increments
thereafter. T-bills are the most liquid of all money market instruments.

Some Guardian investors feel a greater sense of security working with
their bank, since commercial bank accounts are insured by an agency of the
federal government up to $100,000. This insurance covers purchases of
jumbo CDs up to that limit.

Direct purchase of either of these vehicles saves you the management fees you would otherwise have to pay on a money market fund. It enables you to *lock in* a yield if you think rates may fall. The yields on money market funds fluctuate, because their portfolios are undergoing constant change, with some instruments maturing and others being purchased. If rates go down, so will the yield on your fund. Bear in mind, though, that direct purchase of either T-bills or CDs will not afford you some of the other features of a fund, such as check-writing privileges.

To reiterate what we said at the beginning: Money market funds are the best cash equivalent vehicle for most Guardians (as well as other investors) for most purposes.

Fixed-Income Vehicles for Guardian Investors

As a Guardian investor, you will feel most comfortable with Treasury notes and bonds. These Treasury instruments should be the cornerstone of the fixed-income portion of every Guardian's portfolio.

The practical minimum investment for bonds is $10,000. As with cash equivalents, the best alternative in fixed-income investments for most Guardians is mutual funds but, in this case, those which invest solely in bonds. Bond investors also have the option of buying bond unit trusts.

Bond funds are actively managed. This means the fund manager buys and sells various bonds in an attempt to maximize the fund's yield. *Unit trusts* are portfolios of bonds that are set as soon as the bonds have been purchased. A unit trust's portfolio does not change, except through bond maturing.

Asset-heavy Strong and Sturdy (or Strong and Quick) Guardians also may want to add the safest rated municipal or corporate bonds.

To determine whether you should buy taxable or tax-free bonds, use the after-tax formula to determine your after-tax yield[2] and compare the results. Keep in mind that the *security* offered by Treasury bonds makes them most appealing to Guardians, regardless of the tax treatment.

U.S. Equities for Guardian Investors

If you are a Guardian investor, you may have strong doubts about *any* stock market investments. It's important to overcome that prejudice if you want to build a strong, diversified portfolio.

Even Light and Agile Guardians can participate in common stock mutual funds, which is a good way to get acquainted with these more variable

---

[2]TY × (1 − Combined tax rate) = ATY, or, the Tax yield of the fund, multiplied by 100% less your Combined federal and state tax rate, equals your After-tax yield.

markets. *Index funds* are preferred by many Guardians as their exposure in the stock market. These funds are designed to reflect exactly the performance of the stock market, as measured by one of the most widely followed indexes.

The two most widely reported measures of stock market performance are the Dow Jones Industrial Average (an average of 30 leading industrial company stocks) and the Standard & Poor's 500 (a market-weighted index of 500 leading industrial company stocks). When you hear that the market is up or down 5 points, that usually refers to the DJIA. The S&P 500 is the index used to judge the performance of most professional money managers.

An index fund will parallel the movement of the overall stock market, making forecasting unnecessary. The management fees of an index fund are typically lower than the fees assessed by more "performance-oriented" funds.

If your assets are substantial (over $1 million), you may want to assemble your own portfolio of blue-chip, growth-oriented, or income stocks. This would be equivalent to the type of stocks that the more conservative mutual funds would be buying on your behalf. You would avoid the management fees assessed by a fund. But, make sure that you don't pay more in commissions than you would in fees.

International Securities for the Guardian Investor

International stocks should be viewed as a logical extension of your domestic stock portfolio. Similarly, international bonds should be viewed as an extension of your fixed-income portfolio. International investments are more complex, though, since they are subject to different risks at different times.

To satisfy your international allocation, we recommend that all Guardians should invest in an established mutual fund of both stocks and bonds, or buy a fund that specializes in stocks and one that specializes in bonds. Because the international bond market is still in its infancy, there are fewer funds investing in bonds than in stocks. International bond funds, therefore, have much shorter track records, in general.

The complications of investing directly in foreign issues, even those traded on the major international exchanges, boggles the mind. There are problems of foreign currency fluctuations, differing economic forecasting indicators, diverse regulatory environments, and so forth. In an international fund, the manager has the responsibility of attending to such matters.

Other, more sophisticated international vehicles are available, but most Guardians will be uncomfortable with the higher risk carried by these more exotic and less-diversified investments.

Real Estate and Inflation Hedges
for the Guardian Investor

The 1986 Tax Reform Act changed the way losses in real estate can be used to offset ordinary income. Losses from partnership investments are considered "passive" and can be used only to offset gains from passive income generated through similar investments. As a result, many of the more aggressive tax advantages of real estate limited partnerships have been eliminated, so most of them are now marketed for their income generating capabilities. Real estate limited partnerships are often called *PIGs*, for passive income generators.

Guardians should begin their allocations in this category with *equity* or *mortgage* real estate investment trusts (REITs). REITs are professionally managed group investments that trade like stocks. There are over 140 REITs traded, with many listed on the New York and American Stock Exchanges. The balance trade on the Over-the-Counter (OTC) market.

An equity REIT invests directly in real estate projects. Shareholders receive income from the rents paid on the properties, and they receive capital gains when buildings are sold at a profit. Mortgage REITs lend money to developers. They pass on interest income to shareholders (after taking fees, of course). Some REITs are combinations of these two basic types.

As your resources grow, other investments related to real estate can help protect you against inflation. Income-generating limited partnerships or wholly owned income properties should be considered.

The classic inflation hedge is gold. This volatile commodity does not fit well with conservative Guardian temperaments. Nonetheless, small positions in gold-oriented mutual funds or in gold and silver coins may be appropriate as a diversification with your real estate positions.

We have just briefly touched on specific investment vehicles here; detailed descriptions will be found in Chapter 8. After you review the pertinent descriptions that follow, skip to "Making Your Portfolio Work," where we discuss how you choose the specific investment vehicles you will want to investigate further.

The Middle-of-the-Road Straight Arrow Investor

Table 5–3 details the section of the BB&K Rosetta Stone that applies to Straight Arrow investors. If you are one of these well-balanced, optimistic (yet cautious) investors, scan the entire diagram before concentrating on the financial physique that applies to you. It will prove valuable as time goes by to have at least some familiarity with the options available to you in each situation.

Since Straight Arrow investors reflect some of the elements of the other

TABLE 5–3
Investment Vehicles for the Straight Arrow Investor

Straight Arrow Financial Physique

Assets

Higher

III. Strong and Sturdy

CE —taxable/tax-free money market funds, T-bills, commercial paper, S&L/bank CDs.

FI —Treasury notes/bonds, FNMA or GNMA bonds, AAA munis/corporate bonds, second mortgages, taxable/tax-free mutual bond funds and/or unit trusts.

US —blue-chip stocks, income/growth mutual fund, income/growth stocks.

INT —mutual funds, ADRs.

I/RE—public/private income limited partnerships, equity/mortgage REITs, own property, SAMs, gold/silver mutual funds and/or bullion and/or coins.

IV. Strong and Quick

CE —taxable/tax-free money market funds, T-bills, commercial paper, TANs, S&L/bank CDs.

FI —Treasury notes/bonds, AAA muni/corporate bonds, FNMA or GNMA bonds, second mortgages, taxable/tax-free mutual bond funds.

US —blue-chip stocks, growth mutual funds, income/growth stock portfolio, index fund.

INT —mutual funds, ADRs.

I/RE—public/private income limited partnerships, growth REITs, own property, SAMs, oil drilling, gold/silver mutual funds and/or bullion and/or coins.

Lower

I. Light and Agile

CE —taxable money market funds.

FI —Treasury notes/bonds, FNMA or GNMA bonds, taxable mutual bond fund and/or unit trusts.

US —income, growth, or balanced mutual funds, index funds.

INT —mutual funds.

I/RE—public income limited partnerships, income/growth REITs, gold/silver mutual funds and/or bullion and/or coins.

II. Lean and Quick

CE —taxable/tax-free money market funds, T-bills.

FI —Treasury notes/bonds, FNMA or GNMA bonds, taxable/tax-free mutual bond fund.

US —growth or balanced mutual funds or index funds.

INT —mutual funds.

I/RE—public income limited partnerships, growth REITs, gold/silver mutual funds and/or bullion and/or coins.

Lower   *Higher*
Income

Key: CE = cash equivalents   US = U.S. equities   I/RE = inflation hedges/real estate
        FI = fixed income   INT = international securities   muni = municipal bond

personality types, you should review the prescriptions for all the investors, especially those whose descriptions strike a responsive chord.[3]

Cash Equivalents for Straight Arrow Investors
We recommend money market mutual funds as the near-money foundation for every Straight Arrow's portfolio. Many banks offer accounts that, although called by other names, are very similar to money market funds and would also be appropriate for cash equivalent investments.

Money market funds are very liquid and typically offer check-writing privileges. There are both taxable and tax-free varieties. To ascertain which is right for you, use the following formula[4] to determine the relative *after-tax yield*: TY × (1 − Combined tax rate) = ATY, or the Tax yield of the fund, multiplied by 100% less your Combined federal and state tax rate, equals your After-tax yield.

When your assets increase, you may want to add Treasury bills, which are the safest and most liquid money market instrument, but paying the lowest return. The minimum investment for T-bills is $10,000.

Other vehicles to consider when you have accumulated substantial assets include commercial paper, commercial bank certificates of deposit (CDs), or the higher-yielding CDs issued by savings and loans. Commercial paper is simply another term for *short-term corporate notes*. Their relative safety depends on the financial condition of the issuing company.

Strong and Quick Straight Arrows also may be interested in tax anticipation notes (TANs) issued by municipal governments or in tax anticipation bills (TABs) issued by the federal government. These short-term instruments are issued by government authorities to even out their cash flow pending receipt of tax revenues.

Fixed-Income Vehicles for Straight Arrows
Safe and secure Treasury notes and bonds form the foundation of this asset class for all Straight Arrows. Other government-sponsored bonds will be suitable as your asset base grows.

Three government agencies package and sell mortgage-backed securities: the Federal Home Loan Bank (FHLB), the Federal National Mortgage Association (FNMA), and the Government National Mortgage Association

---

[3]See Chapter 3 for the questionnaire and discussion concerning "Discovering Your Investor Personality." Look at Figure 3–1 to see where in the chart you feel most comfortable. The quadrant that shows the levels of your anxiety/confidence attitudes and your careful/impetuous behavior will reveal what personality you lean towards.

[4]For a more thorough discussion of this formula, refer to page 89, just before the description of the Guardian investor.

(GNMA). The securities they issue are referred to as *Freddie Maes, Fannie Maes,* and *Ginnie Maes,* respectively. They are known as *pass-throughs,* because interest and principal payments of the underlying mortgages pass directly through to investors on a monthly basis.

Mutual bond funds and unit trusts offer diversified portfolios of bonds that would be suitable for Straight Arrow investors. The decision on whether to buy taxable or tax-free bonds should depend on the relative after-tax yield. Use the formula given earlier to help you compare results.[5]

Strong and Sturdy and Strong and Quick Straight Arrow investors may want to buy highly rated municipal or corporate bonds, or both, which offer competitive after-tax yields that still provide that important element of security for you.

U.S. Stocks for Straight Arrow Investors

Growth and income-oriented mutual funds form the base for Straight Arrows in this asset class. Like Guardians, many Straight Arrow investors like index funds as a way to keep up with the stock market. These funds are constructed to mirror the performance of the S&P 500 or the Dow Jones Industrial Average (DJIA).

If your resources are over $1 million, you may want to build your portfolio with individual issues, rather than buying mutual funds. If so, start with a base of blue-chip (better-known, mature, well-established, financially secure) companies.

Another alternative would be to buy conservative income stocks. Income stocks are mature companies that pay larger dividends to their shareholders than growth companies do. The high-income payout affords downside protection for the stock's price. If the stock drops, the yield (dividend/price) goes up, making the issue even more attractive.

After your foundation of blue-chip and income stocks has been purchased, look to add growth stocks in smaller amounts. Growth stocks typically pay little or no dividends. The idea is that money earned by the company is best used by reinvesting in the company to foster more growth. Rather than income, you profit here through appreciation in the stock price as the company grows. Although these issues are more volatile, they offer greater appreciation potential than more mature income-oriented stocks.

---

[5]TY $\times$ (1 − Combined tax rate) = ATY, or, the Taxable yield of the fund multiplied by 100% less your Combined tax rate, equals the After-tax yield. For a more thorough discussion of this formula, refer to page 89, just before the description of the Guardian investor.

International Securities for Straight Arrow Investors

There are two main types of actively traded international securities: stocks and bonds. Treat the stocks as an extension of your domestic stock position. Bonds should be viewed as an extension of your fixed-income portion. But, keep in mind that we recommend diversification into international issues, because of their tendency to fluctuate in somewhat different cycles than domestic markets, either leading or lagging the United States. This loose correlation provides you with downside protection.

For example, on October 19, 1987, the U.S. market, as measured by the DJIA, fell a record 508 points, or 22.6 percent. That was the biggest drop in a single day in history, dwarfing the 12.6 percent crash of October 28, 1929. By the end of October 1987 the New York market was down 32 percent. But the Tokyo market, which many analysts had thought was more vulnerable than the New York market, fell only 17 percent.

The best way for most Straight Arrow investors to take positions in international issues is through an established international mutual fund. Funds that are *global* invest in U.S. issues as well as in foreign stocks. *International* funds invest all their proceeds in foreign stocks.

International bonds have neither the liquidity nor the general acceptance of the American investing public that foreign stock issues enjoy. In the past few years, however, there has been a sharp increase in interest in this market sector.

Here, too, we recommend that you invest through an international or global bond fund. These funds' track records are generally not very long, so we suggest that you stick with the better-known managers who have experience in international markets.

Another alternative to consider, once your assets have increased, is to invest directly in foreign issues through American depository receipts (ADRs). These are marketable certificates confirming that you own a portion of foreign stocks that are deposited with a U.S. bank. The bank handles all currency conversions and passes all dividends through to you. ADRs are traded on the exchanges of many large foreign countries, as well as on U.S. exchanges and the OTC market. With ADRs you can avoid many of the problems inherent in buying stocks directly on foreign exchanges.

Real Estate and Inflation Hedges
for Straight Arrow Investors

Inflation protection is afforded through equity real estate investment trusts (REITs), publicly offered real estate limited partnerships, and gold or silver shares, bullion, and coins.

Also, mutual funds specialize in real estate-oriented investments. They usually are not limited to buying REITs but, instead, invest in other related industries, such as lumber companies, home builders, furniture companies, and other similar issues. As always, the mutual fund approach gives you broad diversification with professional management.

After establishing a base of equity REITs (those REITs that invest directly in properties, rather than issuing or buying mortgages) or a precious metals mutual fund, or both, you may want to add public or private real estate limited partnerships.

These limited partnerships have historically been sold as tax shelters. The 1986 Tax Reform Act culminated a decade of tax code revisions, which discontinued many tax benefits offered by tax shelters. As a result, limited partnerships are now sold mainly for their income-producing capabilities.

Multiple writeoff tax shelters (where you write off two or three times your investment) are things of the past. Because of the limitations on how losses in limited partnerships can be applied, so-called *passive losses* can only be used to offset *passive income*.

The best tax shelters for you will be your own home and any wholly owned income property you run as a landlord and operator.

Many types of precious metals investments are being hawked. "Buy gold at LOW LOW prices from gold mines *before* it is mined" is one such promotion. Gold and silver prices are highly volatile, so you don't have to take any more risk than is inherent in the commodities themselves. A number of mutual funds offer just about every combination you may desire. Those with successful long-term records are run by experienced managers. See Chapters 7 and 8 for a discussion of the possible alternatives offered by precious metals funds.

Take a moment to review any terms that may be unfamiliar to you in Chapter 8 (the last chapter in the book, preceding the Appendix). When you are done, turn to "Making Your Portfolio Work." You will learn the next step in building your portfolio: how you go about identifying those investment vehicles you will want to investigate further.

Building the Individualist's Portfolio

Table 5–4 provides a BB&K Rosetta Stone with a more detailed listing of the investment vehicles that are appropriate for Individualist investors. The first thing you will notice is that more types of potential investment vehicles are listed here than for the other types of investors.

The Individualist's careful, confident, and analytical nature is rewarded with the widest possible variety of investment choices. If you are an Individualist, take a moment to scan the whole chart before concentrating on the portion that applies to your financial physique. Your career and life goals, situation, and resources will change as time passes. It will prove valuable for

TABLE 5–4
Investment Vehicles for the Individualist Investor

Individualist Financial Physique

Assets

Higher

III. Strong and Sturdy

CE —taxable/tax-free money market funds, T-bills, Euro CDs, commercial paper, banker's acceptances, TANs, Swiss bank accounts, S&L/bank CDs.

FI —Treasury notes/bonds, FNMA or GNMA bonds, all muni/corporate bonds, second mortgages, interest rate options, all mutual bond funds and/or unit trusts.

US —all mutual funds, all stock portfolios, options, index funds, convertibles.

INT —mutual funds, ADRs, and listed and OTC stocks.

I/RE—all income-limited partnerships, all REITs, own property, SAMs, oil drilling or development, gold/silver mutual funds and/or bullion and/or coins.

IV. Strong and Quick

CE —taxable/tax-free market funds, T-bills, Euro CDs, commercial paper, acceptances, TANs, Swiss bank accounts.

FI —Treasury notes/bonds, FNMA or GNMA bonds, all muni/corporate bonds, Euro and nondollar bonds, second mortgages, interest-rate options, taxable/tax-free mutual bond funds and/or unit trusts.

US —all mutual funds, ADRs, and listed and OTC stocks.

I/RE—all income limited partnerships, growth REITs, own rental homes and properties, raw land, oil drilling, gold/silver mutual funds and/or bullion and/or coins.

Lower

I. Light and Agile

CE —taxable money market fund.

FI —Treasury notes/bonds, FNMA or GNMA bonds, all munis and corporate bonds, interest-rate options, taxable mutual bond fund or unit trusts, or both.

US —income, growth, aggressive growth mutual funds, individual stocks, options.

INT —mutual funds.

I/RE—public income limited partnerships, income/growth REITs, gold/silver mutual funds and/or bullion and/or coins.

II. Lean and Quick

CE —taxable/tax-free money market funds, T-bills.

FI —Treasury notes/bonds, FNMA or GNMA bonds, taxable/tax-free mutual bond fund, all munis and corporate bonds, interest-rate options.

US —income, growth, aggressive growth mutual funds, individual stocks, options.

INT —mutual funds, ADRs.

I/RE—public income limited partnerships, equity REITs, oil drilling, gold/silver mutual funds and/or bullion and/or coins.

Lower   *Higher*
Income

Key: CE = cash equivalents   US = U.S. equities   I/RE = inflation hedges/real estate
     FI = fixed income   INT = international securities   muni = municipal bond

you to be aware of the various investment options open to you as your assets and income increase.

Cash Equivalents for Individualist Investors

The most convenient cash equivalent vehicles for most investors are money market funds. They are liquid, pay interest, and most of them feature checkwriting privileges (usually at a minimum of $100). Most money market funds are sold without charging commissions, although they all assess a management fee.

When your resources increase, you may want to buy Treasury bills directly from the Federal Reserve. T-bills are the most liquid money market instrument. They are also the most secure, since they are backed by the full faith and credit of the U.S. Treasury. The minimum investment is $10,000, with increments of $5,000.

Since you tend to analyze situations carefully, you should consider other vehicles as your assets expand, including bank and savings and loan CDs, Eurodollar (U.S. dollars deposited abroad) CDs, commercial paper (short-term corporate notes), banker's acceptances (short-term notes secured by goods in trade), and municipal tax anticipation notes (TANs; short-term loans to governments in expectation of tax revenues).

Very sophisticated Individualists who wish to hedge the dollar value of their investments in international markets should look at Swiss bank account deposits. At least one money market fund, International Cash Portfolios, invests solely in short-term paper in foreign markets.

Fixed-Income Vehicles for Individualist Investors

While there are many possible alternatives for fixed-income vehicles, you should set the foundation for this portion of your portfolio with Treasury notes and bonds. Other secure options include Federal National Mortgage Association bonds (Fannie Maes) or Government National Mortgage Association bonds (Ginnie Maes). These two are securities backed by mortgages that are issued by banks and thrift institutions. The government agency pools the mortgages and then "passes through" the interest and principal payments on the underlying mortgages.

As your assets increase, you can secure higher yields at slightly more risk with corporate bonds that are rated AAA, AA, or A by Standard & Poor's (or the equivalent top three rankings by Moody's, or other rating services).

If you are in a high-income tax bracket (combined federal and state), it pays to compare *after-tax* returns for taxable bonds and tax-free munici-

pals. To find the after-tax yield for a taxable bond use the formula:[6] TY ×
(1 − Combined tax rate) = After-tax yield, or, the Taxable yield of the fund
or bond multiplied by 100% less your Combined federal and state tax rate,
equals your After-tax yield. Compare that return with what is being offered
by comparably rated municipal tax-free bonds.

If you are in the Strong and Sturdy category, you may want to consider
Eurodollar bonds (U.S. dollar-denominated bonds issued by foreign authorities). At times the yield on these Eurodollar bonds has been substantially
above that of equivalent U.S. bonds. The Eurodollar bond market presents
greater risk, because it is largely unregulated.

Very well-capitalized and more speculative-oriented Individualists may
even want to investigate interest rate options. Such options are not explicitly
fixed-income investments but, instead, play on the direction of interest rates.
If you expect interest rates to go down, you would buy a "call option." If
you think rates are going up, you would buy a "put option." This market is
very risky. It is also short-term-oriented, since an interest rate option termi-
nates worthless on expiration date.

U.S. Equities for Individualist Investors
Common stock mutual funds are the natural starting point for all Individualist investors, since these can accommodate any investment objective (income, growth, balanced, aggressive growth, and the like) and they are run
by professional managers.

As your resources and experience permit, you may want to purchase a
few well-chosen stocks yourself. If you are interested and have the assets,
you can assemble a portfolio of individual stocks to achieve your long-term
goals.

Options have drawn increasing investor interest since they were first introduced on listed exchanges with the Chicago Board Options Exchange in
the 1970s. You can explore many possible strategies with options, from simple buying and selling to putting together "spreads," "straddles," "sprad-
dles," and "ratio spreads," which are the simultaneous purchase and sale of
various combinations of puts and calls. Like we said, it is complex and suitable only for Individualists with extensive investing experience.

Index mutual funds, which mirror the performance of the S&P 500 or
the Dow Jones Industrial Average, are suitable for all financial physiques.
Strong and Sturdy investors also may want to investigate *convertible bonds*
(bonds that are convertible to stock).

---

[6]For a more detailed discussion of this formula, see page 89, just before the section detailing
the Guardian investor.

Strong and Quick Individualists, those with plenty of assets and cash flow, may want to experiment with venture capital investments. If this appeals to you, consider it only for your longest-term or least-critical goals.

International Securities for Individualist Investors

It is wise for even veteran Individualists to go slowly in this area. Many different factors are involved with international investing. We recommend you begin with established mutual funds that invest in both a variety of foreign stocks traded on the major international exchanges and an assortment of important foreign government bonds.

As your assets and experience increase, you may invest directly in foreign companies through American depository receipts (ADRs). ADRs are marketable certificates of ownership of a portion of foreign stocks held by U.S. banks. The certificates trade like stocks on the exchanges and on the OTC market. The depository bank handles all stock-related transactions, such as dividend collection, currency conversions, and remittances.

Foreign bonds have a number of disparate considerations that make it essential to have the professional services provided by mutual funds. Also, most international bond markets are not as closely followed as stock markets. As a result, obtaining information on foreign bonds is more difficult.

Eventually, well-capitalized and experienced Individualists may add individual foreign stocks or bonds that appeal to them. Many foreign issues offer the benefits stipulated by your stock requirements.

Real Estate and Inflation Hedges
for Individualist Investors

Unless you are already in a top tax bracket (federal and state) you should begin by investing in equity real estate investment trusts (REITs), publicly offered real estate limited partnerships, or gold or silver shares, bullion, or coins.

Some mutual funds specialize in real estate related stocks. In addition to REITs, these funds invest in companies whose business is closely related to real estate, such as housing construction firms, lumber mills, household appliance manufacturers, and others.

A wide range of mutual funds invest in precious metals. These funds invest in South African mines, or North American mines, or all mines except South African, as well as bullion.

As your resources increase, you may want to expand your holdings by buying and operating your own rental property. Other types of real estate investment are also feasible—depending on your interest and experience —including private or public real estate limited partnerships, raw land, or commercial development.

Since some of the terms we've used may be unfamiliar to you, take a moment to review them in Chapter 8. Then turn to "Making Your Portfolio Work for You" and you will learn how to identify investment vehicles you will want to investigate further.

Discovering the Enthusiast's Investment Vehicles

If you are an Enthusiast investor, take a moment to review Table 5–5, the detailed breakdown of the BB&K Rosetta Stone that covers appropriate investments for Enthusiasts. It is a good idea to be familiar with the full range of investment options, since you will be going through changes in your financial resources and goals over time. If any of the terms are unfamiliar to you, look them up in Chapter 8 before going ahead with this section.

Cash Equivalents for Enthusiast Investors

Money market mutual funds, or bank money market deposit accounts, should form the foundation of the cash equivalent portion of your portfolio. Depending on your tax bracket, you may want to buy primarily tax-free funds.

If you are in a high income tax bracket (combined federal and state), it pays to compare *after-tax* returns for taxable versus tax-free money market funds. To find the after-tax yield for a taxable fund use this formula:[7] TY × (1 − Combined tax rate) = ATY, or, the Taxable yield of the money market fund, multiplied by 100% less your Combined federal and state tax rate, equals the After-tax yield of the investment.

Compare that return with what is being offered by comparable tax-free money market funds. To find a "comparable" fund, look at the "average maturity" of the money market instruments held by the fund. The longer the average maturity, the higher the risk.

As your resources and experience increase, you may want to add Treasury bills, the most liquid and most secure money market instrument available. The minimum investment is $10,000, with increments of $5,000 thereafter. T-bills can be purchased directly from the Federal Reserve at regular weekly auctions of three- and six-month bills.

Other vehicles that are appropriate for experienced Enthusiast investors include certificates of deposit (CDs) from banks or savings institutions, commercial paper (short-term corporate notes), banker's acceptances (short-term notes issued by banks which facilitate trading), or tax anticipation

---

[7]For a more detailed discussion on this formula, turn to page 89, just before the Guardian investor section.

TABLE 5–5
Investment Vehicles for the Enthusiast Investor

Enthusiast Financial Physiques

III. Strong and Sturdy

CE —taxable/tax-free money market fund, Euro CDs, commercial paper, acceptances, TANs, Swiss bank accounts, S&L/bank CDs.

FI —Treasury notes/bonds, FNMA or GNMA bonds, all muni/corporate bonds, Euro and nondollar bonds, second mortgages, taxable/tax-free mutual bond funds and/or unit trusts.

US —all mutual funds, all stock portfolios, covered options, index funds, convertibles.

INT —mutual funds, ADRs, and listed and OTC stocks.

I/RE—public/private income limited partnerships, all REITs, own property, raw land, SAMs, oil income, gold/silver mutual funds and/or bullion and/or coins.

IV. Strong and Quick

CE —taxable/tax-free money market funds, Euro CDs, commercial paper, acceptances, TANs, Swiss bank accounts, S&L/bank CDs.

FI —Treasury notes/bonds, FNMA or GNMA bonds, all muni/corporate bonds, Euro and nondollar bonds, second mortgages, taxable/tax-free mutual bond funds.

US —growth/aggressive growth mutual funds and stock portfolios, venture capital, covered options, index funds, convertibles.

INT —Mutual funds, ADRs, and listed and OTC stocks.

I/RE—public/private income limited partnerships, growth REITs, own property, raw land, SAMs, oil, gold/silver mutual funds and/or bullion and/or coins.

I. Light and Agile

CE —taxable money market fund.

FI —Treasury notes/bonds, taxable mutual bond fund and/or unit trust.

US —income, balanced, growth or aggressive growth mutual funds, index funds.

INT —mutual funds.

I/RE—public income limited partnerships, income/growth REITs, gold/silver mutual funds and/or bullion and/or coins.

II. Lean and Quick

CE —taxable/tax-free money market funds, Swiss bank accounts, S&L CDs.

FI —Treasury notes/bonds, FNMA or GNMA bonds, taxable/tax-free mutual bond funds or unit trusts, or both.

US —income, growth, aggressive growth or balanced mutual funds, index funds.

INT —mutual funds.

I/RE—public income limited partnerships, growth REITs, oil drilling, gold/silver mutual funds and/or bullion and/or coins.

Higher

Lower

Assets

Lower   *Higher*
Income

Key: CE = cash equivalents   US = U.S. equities   I/RE = inflation hedges/real estate
FI = fixed income   INT = international securities   muni = municipal bond

notes, TANs, which are issued by state and local governments in expectation of tax revenues.

More sophisticated and well-capitalized Enthusiast investors may want to investigate Eurodollar CDs (U.S. dollar deposits in foreign banks). This market is huge, but largely unregulated. Often the rates offered by these CDs are higher than comparable CDs in the United States.

Enthusiast investors who are concerned about hedging the future value of their dollars may invest in Swiss bank deposit accounts, which operate much the same as U.S. bank accounts, except they are denominated in the currency of your choice. If the dollar is weak, the logical choice would be the Swiss franc, Deutsche mark, or Japanese yen. Typically, the interest rate paid on Swiss deposit accounts is considerably less than that paid on U.S. bank savings accounts. You must decide if the appreciation of the underlying currency is sufficient to make up for the lower interest rate.

Fixed-Income Vehicles for Enthusiast Investors

As with all the other investor personality types, Enthusiast investors should build the foundation of their fixed-income portfolio with Treasury notes and bonds. These are the safest fixed-income vehicles. Try to keep a mix of maturities. The longer the maturity, the higher the risk. You can invest directly in Treasury notes and bonds or buy a mutual fund that invests solely in Treasury issues. This would give you immediate diversification in terms of maturities.

As your assets increase, you may want to purchase unit trusts (professionally selected, but nonmanaged portfolios) of government or corporate bonds, or both. With unit trusts you know the exact makeup of the portfolio.

Depending on your tax bracket (combined state and federal) you may want to buy tax-free municipals for a major portion of your fixed-income position. Use the after-tax yield formula described for cash equivalents to determine whether you should buy taxable or tax-free bonds.

Other fixed-income vehicles with liquid active markets include mortgage-backed *pass-through* bonds: Fannie Maes (issued by the Federal National Mortgage Association) and Ginnie Maes (issued by the Government National Mortgage Association). Other government agencies also issue bonds that you may want to consider if your financial physique is Lean and Quick.

When your assets and sophistication have increased, you may want to add more speculative municipal or corporate bonds, but stay with the top three rankings. Other vehicles that may be of interest include Eurodollar bonds. These bonds are denominated in U.S. dollars and issued by foreign authorities.

U.S. Equities for Enthusiast Investors

This is a problem area for many Enthusiasts. The stock market is probably the single most widely reported investment activity. The strong herd instinct of Enthusiast investors can lead to difficulties, because the most optimistic news reports often appear just when the market is topping. The most pessimistic reports tend to occur near market bottoms. As a result, the Enthusiast is often stimulated to buy at a high price and to sell when prices are low.

One way to avoid making mistakes that you will regret later is to buy a mutual fund whose objectives (growth, income, or a mix) most closely matches your own. One good alternative for many Enthusiast investors is to buy *index funds*. These funds are designed to mirror the movements of the major market indexes, such as the Standard & Poor's 500 or the Dow Jones Industrial Average. With an index fund you have a good idea how your investment is doing, just by knowing the market's performance for the day.

If you have sufficient interest to develop good analytical skills (and can avoid jumping in and out of the market with each new fad), you may want to assemble your own portfolio of individual issues. To do this, your base of assets should be substantial, because you still will need broad diversification within the stock portion of your portfolio. But, before buying any stocks, make sure they match your long-term investment objectives. The latest hot item is not likely to meet this requirement all the time!

Another alternative that appeals to many Enthusiast investors is convertible bonds. This special type of bond is issued by companies with a set "conversion ratio" into the stock of the underlying company. The yield on the bond tends to be less than that of nonconvertible bonds, because of the potential growth offered by the stock "kicker."

Options trading is a high-risk arena that is not appropriate for most Enthusiast investors. However, if you have moved into either the Strong and Sturdy or the Strong and Quick category, you may want to investigate options with a small percentage of your funds from your stock allocation. *Writing covered options* is the most conservative options strategy. This approach can increase the income you receive on individual stocks you own. Even this strategy, though, should be undertaken only if you thoroughly understand all the potential consequences.

International Securities for the Enthusiast Investor

International stocks and bonds offer important diversification benefits for your portfolio. While you can view them as extensions of your domestic stock and fixed-income investments, there are unique problems and considerations when dealing with international issues.

The cornerstone of the international portion of your portfolio should be laid with select mutual funds specializing in foreign stocks and bonds. Buy a different fund for each. The chief advantage of the mutual fund approach is that you have professional management handling details like currency conversion, meeting foreign security regulations, and coping with differing economic environments.

Once you have gained some experience and your assets increase, you may want to invest in American depository receipts (ADRs). ADRs are marketable securities backed by foreign stocks that are on deposit with U.S. banks. There are hundreds of ADRs trading on listed exchanges and the OTC market. The depository bank takes care of currency conversions for dividends and other shareholder activities.

When your resources increase even more, and if you have the interest and desire to cope with the complications, you may want to consider buying individual foreign stocks or bonds directly through an international brokerage firm.

But a word of caution is in order. Many Enthusiasts cannot resist the urge to follow brokers, ads, or friends into currently hot investments, with overconcentration or dangerous risks to their assets as a consequence. If you are one of these doubly enthusiastic investors, you will be better off letting a mutual fund professional handle your international investment decisions.

Real Estate and Inflation Hedges
for Enthusiast Investors

The foundation for this portion of your portfolio should be built with equity real estate investment trusts (REITs). Equity REITs pool investor money that is invested in real estate projects. Some REITs specialize in certain geographical areas or in particular types of projects. There are over 140 REITs trading on listed exchanges or OTC market.

The classic inflation hedge, precious metals, is available in a number of forms. We recommend you buy a mutual fund that specializes in gold or silver investments, or both. These funds typically buy shares in gold and silver mines in South Africa, North America, and the rest of the world. Some funds invest a portion of their assets in gold bullion. You may also want to consider buying gold or silver coins.

As an Enthusiast, you must guard against your tendency to plunge into the latest trendy investments. Just because you've read a lot about something, or your broker is hawking a new investment, doesn't make it any better than tried and true vehicles. This is particularly so in the case of limited partnership investments.

Historically, real estate limited partnerships have been targeted to the tax-shelter audience. However, the 1986 Tax Reform Act culminated a decade of tax code changes that have largely eliminated the tax-writeoff benefits of these investments. Real estate limited partnerships are now designed to generate good cash flow, rather than multiple writeoffs. But you must be careful. The cash flow projections often are not realistic. Keep an eye on the leverage used in the deal. If borrowed money constitutes over 70 percent of the funds for a project, be wary. The highly leveraged real estate syndications suffered most during the severe shakeout in this industry in the 1980s.

Nonetheless, as your income, assets, and experience increase, you should actively investigate publicly offered real estate limited partnerships that offer a good cash flow with growth potential. These partnerships are structured in a variety of ways. They may concentrate all their investments in one territory, or they may diversify into more than one geographical area. Some are more leveraged than others. When looking at cash flow projections, keep in mind that promoters like to sell "best case" scenarios. Ask yourself how realistic the projections on interest costs and occupancy rates are.

By the time you reach the Strong and Sturdy or the Strong and Quick asset level, you may want to investigate oil and gas limited partnerships. These still have some tax benefits, although they have been trimmed back. With energy prices being a major component of inflation, they also offer excellent inflation protection.

One other alternative for the asset-rich person is to buy a wholly owned income property yourself, which you will manage and operate. Some good tax benefits are still available. Carefully selected, conservatively financed deals offer good growth potential with a steady cash flow.

Now turn to the section, "Making Your Portfolio Work for You," and learn how to identify those investments you will want to investigate further.

Uncovering Investments for Adventurer Investors

If you are an Adventurer investor, take a moment to review Table 5–6. This table delineates the portion of the BB&K Rosetta Stone that applies to all four financial physiques for Adventurers. Regardless of your current financial position, look over all the potential investments depicted. Your goals, resources, and needs will change throughout your life. It will be useful to have some idea of what vehicles are appropriate for a variety of financial situations.

New investments are continually popping up. It is impossible for most nonprofessional investors to keep up with all the latest offerings. Look up any unfamiliar terms in Chapter 8.

Cash Equivalents for Adventurer Investors
All Adventurers should invest in money market funds or in bank money market deposit accounts as the base of their cash equivalents, which is the

TABLE 5–6   Investment Vehicles for the Adventurer Investor

Adventurer Financial Physiques

III. Strong and Sturdy

CE —taxable/tax-free money market funds, Euro CDs, commercial paper, acceptances, TANs, Swiss bank accounts, S&L/bank CDs.

FI —Treasury notes/bonds, FNMA or GNMA bonds, all muni/corporate bonds, Euro and nondollar bonds, second mortgages, private convertibles, interest-rate options, all mutual bond funds or unit trusts.

US —all mutual funds and stock portfolios, venture capital, options, convertibles.

INT —mutual funds, ADRs, all stocks, venture capital.

I/RE—public/private income limited partnerships, all REITs, own property, raw land, SAMs, oil, gold/silver mutual funds and/or bullion and/or coins.

IV. Strong and Quick

CE —taxable/tax-free market funds, Euro CDs, commercial paper, acceptances, TANs, Swiss bank accounts, S&L/bank CDs.

FI —Treasury notes/bonds, FNMA or GNMA bonds, all muni/corporate bonds, Euro and nondollar bonds, second mortgages, private convertibles, interest-rate options, taxable/tax-free mutual bond funds or unit trusts.

US —growth or aggressive growth mutual funds and stock portfolios, venture capital, options, convertibles.

INT —Mutual funds, ADRs, listed and OTC stocks, venture capital.

I/RE—public/private income limited partnerships, growth REITs, own properties, raw land, SAMs, oil drilling, gold/silver mutual funds and/or bullion and/or coins.

I. Light and Agile

CE —taxable money market fund.

FI —Treasury notes/bonds, all muni/corporate bonds, taxable mutual bond funds or unit trusts, interest-rate options.

US —all mutual funds, individual stocks, index funds.

INT —mutual funds, ADRs.

I/RE—public income limited partnerships, income/growth REITs, gold/silver mutual funds and/or bullion and/or coins.

II. Lean and Quick

CE —taxable/tax-free money market funds, Swiss bank accounts.

FI —Treasury notes/bonds, FNMA or GNMA bonds, all muni/corporate bonds, interest-rate options, taxable/tax-free mutual bond funds or unit trusts.

US —growth or aggressive growth mutual funds, individual stocks, options, convertibles.

INT —mutual funds, ADRs.

·I/RE—public/private income limited partnerships, growth REITs, oil drilling, gold/silver mutual funds and/or bullion and/or coins.

Higher

Lower

Assets

Lower   *Higher*

Income

Key: CE = cash equivalents   US = U.S. equities   I/RE = inflation hedges/real estate
      FI = fixed income   INT = international securities   muni = municipal bond

most liquid portion of the portfolio. Money market funds generally pay higher interest than passbook savings accounts, are very liquid, and most have check-writing privileges.

If you already have substantial assets, use a portion of the amount allocated to cash equivalents to buy Treasury bills directly from the Federal Reserve. These are the most liquid and secure money market instrument and the interest earned is exempt from state taxes. The minimum initial investment is $10,000, with increments of $5,000.

Other investments to consider as your assets grow include higher-paying vehicles like certificates of deposit (CDs) issued by banks or savings institutions, commercial paper (short-term corporate notes), banker's acceptances (short-term notes secured by goods in trade), and tax anticipation notes, TANs, which are issued by local governments in expectation of tax revenues.

As your sophistication and interest grow, you may want to consider Eurodollar certificates of deposit. These are dollar-denominated CDs issued by foreign banks. They often pay a higher interest rate than domestic CDs.

If you are concerned about maintaining the dollar value of your investments, you could hedge through Swiss bank accounts. These accounts are similar to U.S. bank accounts, except you can specify the currency in which you would like the account to be denominated. If the dollar is weak, you would want to have your account in a strong currency, such as the Swiss franc. Only a small portion of your funds should be allocated to this activity.

Fixed-Income Vehicles for Adventurer Investors
Treasury notes and bonds should form the foundation of the fixed-income sector of your portfolio. Many Adventurers make the mistake of ignoring these lower-yielding investments, because they see them as suitable only for pension funds, senior citizens, or other risk-averse investors. Don't fall prey to the same mistake. The fixed-income portion of your overall portfolio plays a very important role. When the economy is sluggish, stocks will often drop in value. Interest rates fall in a recessionary environment as business demand for money drops. So, while your stocks may be losing, your bond investments will be appreciating (remember, bond prices move inversely to interest rates). Your policy should call for slow but steady gains, letting the power of compounding work for you.

Besides, fixed-income investments are not all that stuffy. There is a broad range of instruments with widely varying degrees of risk and potential return. While the yield may be fixed, your prospects for receiving it vary from instrument to instrument. Low-rated or junk bonds offer high yields, compared to Treasury issues. But the likelihood of junk bonds fulfilling their part of the bargain (i.e., paying you regular interest and redeeming your principal in full) is dependent on the state of the economy.

We strongly recommend that Adventurers ground their fixed-income portfolio in Treasury notes and bonds. Once your assets have grown, move into more speculative areas, including lower-rated corporate and municipal bonds.

If you are in a high income tax bracket (combined federal and state), it pays to compare *after-tax* returns for taxable versus tax-free bonds. To find the after-tax yield for a taxable bond use this formula:[8] TY × (1 − Combined tax rate) = ATY, or the Taxable yield of the bond or fund, multiplied by 100% less the percentage of your Combined federal and state tax rates, is equal to the After-tax yield of the investment.

Compare that with the current yield being offered by similar (in terms of maturity and safety rating) tax-exempt municipal bonds. Don't be afraid to have a mix of taxable and tax-free bonds.

A good way to get broad diversification of your bond portfolio is to buy mutual funds specializing in the instruments you want. For example, buy funds that invest only in Treasury notes and bonds, as the base of your fixed-income segment. Then, purchase bond funds with higher-income and higher-risk objectives. Spread your investment out over time with tax-free funds (if pertinent in your tax situation), junk bond funds, and middle-of-the-road (rated AAA through A) bond funds.

If your assets are substantial, you can assemble your own portfolio of individual issues, as long as you maintain good diversification within the fixed-income asset class. Avoid buying a few hot tips.

Aggressive, experienced Adventurers may want to investigate interest-rate options. These are not the same as fixed-income securities with set yields that return your principal upon maturity. Interest-rate options offer you a very high-risk way to speculate on the direction of interest rates themselves. If you think rates will be going down, you would buy "call options." If you expect rates to go up, you would buy "put options." This area is very complex but, if your curiosity is piqued, and you have sufficient assets to undertake the high risk, you may want to invest a small portion of your money in interest rate options.

Mortgage-backed pass-through bonds, Fannie Maes (issued by the Federal National Mortgage Association) or Ginnie Maes (issued by the Government National Mortgage Association) provide a very large liquid market. Numerous mutual funds and unit trusts also invest in these pass-through bonds.

As your assets and experience grow, many different vehicles may inter-

---

[8]for a more detailed discussion about this formula, see page 89, just before the section discussing the Guardian investor.

est you. As an example, you may want to look into Eurodollar bonds (U.S. dollar-denominated bonds, but issued by foreign companies or governments).

One last fixed-income investment to consider are hybrid investments known as *convertible bonds*, which are convertible into the stock of the underlying company at a set ratio. As a result, they offer some of the features of both stocks and bonds. They pay a fixed interest rate (usually lower than nonconvertible bonds), and they offer the additional kicker of growth potential through their conversion value. When the price of the underlying stock rises to the point that it is economically viable to convert the bond into stock, the convertible will tend to fluctuate with the price of the stock, rather than as a bond. There are many strategies used by professional investors with convertible bonds that may be of interest to Adventurers.

U.S. Stocks for Adventurer Investors
Most Adventurer investors approach investing in the stock market with zeal. Fortunately, this asset class provides plenty of alternatives.

You should start with a mutual fund that has the same objectives you are seeking: income, growth, a combination of the two, or aggressive growth—all of which, and more, are offered by mutual funds.

When your resources have grown and you have become more experienced in the market, you may want to buy individual stocks. This can be an adjunct to the base provided by your mutual fund(s). For example, you may want to invest in a few well-chosen individual speculative issues.

With sufficient resources, you may prefer to assemble a diversified portfolio wholly comprised of individual issues. But, remember, it's as important to diversify within your individual stocks as it is to diversify over all five asset classes.

Well-capitalized Adventurers who are willing to take the time to carefully research proposals may be interested in venture capital investments. These privately placed stock offerings are the start-up capital for very speculative ventures. Although they are very risky, they offer great growth potential in return.

As you gain experience, the options market may appeal to you. This market is also very high risk, and in no case should more than 10 percent of your stock allocation ever be devoted to this area. Many sophisticated and complex strategies are employed by options professionals.

Stock options are a leveraged play on stocks, requiring pinpoint timing skills. When you buy a stock, there is no maturity or expiration date; you can hold the stock for as long as the company is in business. With options, you have a set time period for the underlying stock price to move in the direction you expect. If it does not, you will lose the amount you paid for the option. As you can see, options trading is for savvy traders only!

International Securities for Adventurer Investors

Unless you have had previous experience with international securities, it is best to begin with established mutual funds that invest in the areas you want. There are funds that specialize in stocks or bonds. A number of international stock funds have proven track records of five or more years.

International bond funds are much newer; only a few have been around since 1985. However, you can minimize your risk here by selecting an international bond fund from a family of funds with a proven management record.

Although we recommend that you should consider your international stock and bond positions as extensions of your domestic stocks and bonds, the differences are significant. The international markets tend to lag or, occasionally, lead U.S. markets. These differing cylces are what make them valuable additions to your portfolio.

When it comes time to expand your international investments, you may want to select individual American depository receipts (ADRs). ADRs are marketable certificates, traded like common stock, representing the ownership of a portion of foreign stocks held by a U.S. bank. The depository bank handles all the paperwork associated with ownership, including currency conversions for dividends and notification of other shareholder business. ADRs are traded on U.S. exchanges and the OTC market.

Venture capital opportunities in foreign countries are an opportunity for well-capitalized and knowledgeable Adventurer investors, meant for only a select few. The risks are high and intensified by widely varying regulations in each country. An experienced advisor may be able to help you sort through a proposal to see if it has legitimacy and merit.

Real Estate and Inflation Hedges for Adventurers

The 1986 Tax Reform Act culminated a decade-long move to change the tax code to eliminate most tax-shelter investments. The days of multiple writeoffs (when you could deduct from your taxes two, three, or more times the size of your investment) are gone. This aspect probably affects Adventurers more than other investor personality, because aggressive tax-avoidance schemes would appeal to their impulsive, confident nature. All in all, the tax revision led to a good change. You should be evaluating an investment on its economic merits, not just its tax benefits.

Protection against inflation is still an important goal, though, whether or not you are able to avoid taxes. When your assets are small, look to buy equity real estate investment trusts. REITs pool investor money to buy equity interest in real estate projects. The income passes through in the form of dividends. Theoretically, as the property appreciates, the value of your REIT will go up.

REITs are traded just like stocks. Many are listed on major exchanges while others trade on the OTC market. Equity REITs invest directly in property. Mortgage REITs raise money to be loaned to developers. Their price tends to trade more like bonds—in direct relation to the trend of interest rates—than stocks. Equity REITs are better inflation protection investments.

No inflation protection would be complete without some precious metals. Gold or silver can be purchased through many mutual funds that specialize in buying mining shares. You can also buy bullion or coins for inflation protection. Gold and silver are very volatile, hence are high-risk.

As your income and assets expand, consider buying publicly offered real estate limited partnerships. While these are no longer marketed for their tax benefits, many are being structured to provide generous cash flows. Some privately offered real estate limited partnerships offer similar benefits.

One last area to investigate would be oil and gas limited partnerships. Since energy is a major component in inflation, ownership in a successful oil and gas venture would provide substantial protection. Also, some tax benefits are available to qualified investors. This area is very high-risk, with potential high reward. Such energy investments should only be undertaken once you have put together a firm foundation.

Next you will learn how to identify the investment vehicles you will want to investigate further.

MAKING YOUR PORTFOLIO WORK

When you completed Action Paper No. 7, Your Asset Allocation Plan, referred to in Chapter 4, you assigned a dollar amount to each of the five asset classes. You also devised a tentative plan, beginning with restructuring your current holdings. The next step is to bring that restructuring to its completion. You will survey the specific investment vehicles in each class that you will later want to investigate in depth.

Notes: Making the Most Effective Use of the BB&K Rosetta Stone

Make Sure the Vehicle Pays Money When You Need It

When researching a specific investment vehicle, make sure that it has a distinct and repeatable response to *specific* changes in the economy. Although you can't know in advance what changes the economy will undergo, you do know that changes will occur. Does the investment vehicle you are look-ing at react the same way to specific changes?

These changes do not have to be positive in all cases (*That* would be an ideal investment!). The important consideration here is that the change in reaction to the economy should be *predictable*. Otherwise, it will be impos-sible to judge the role such a vehicle will play in preserving and advancing your portfolio's equity.

For example, a typical common stock or mutual fund *should* follow the general trends of the Business Cycle. The stock or fund should perform well when the economy is expanding, or, at least, when people *expect* the econ-omy to expand. This may occur after a prolonged period of sluggish or neg-ative growth in the economy. These same vehicles *should* do less well when a recession hits.

You may or may not make money with your particular stock or fund, but you should know how it will react under certain economic conditions. Avoid those investments whose value seems to have no apparent relation-ship to the things you can readily measure, such as the CPI, interest rates, or other economic measures.

Make Sure the Vehicle Pays Off in Your Lifetime

If a vehicle interests you, be sure it's either liquid (in case you change your mind), or has a finite life. Bonds and some REITs have specific maturity or expiration dates.

Under most circumstances, it is poor money management to put your assets into an open-ended investment that is both illiquid and has not set a method or time limit for paying you back. Such things as shares in someone else's closely held business don't meet this test.

Make Sure the Vehicles Protect You from Different Risks

In Chapter 2 you learned about the six different kinds of investment risk. If you invest your entire portfolio in vehicles that protect against only one or two of these risks, you defeat the purpose of diversification. When you guard against only some of the potential dangers facing investors, you are almost sure to fall prey to others.

Diversifying over different asset classes is not an absolute guarantee against this danger. For instance, if you buy stock in a financial institution, in speculative bonds, and in real estate, you may benefit from dropping inter-est rates but a sharp rise will hurt all three. Diversification over different as-set classes would not help you at all in this case.

Be certain that the *offsetting* qualities of the asset classes in which you have diversified are not undermined by the *specific* vehicles you select within each class.

The difference between diversification and simply owning different investments is that proper diversification is designed to protect your portfolio from different types of risk. Owning different types of investments that, nonetheless, react in the same manner is no protection.

Using the BB&K Rosetta Stone to Choose the Vehicles for Your Portfolio

Figure 5–1 has been filled in for our Lean and Quick example. Use the blank Action Paper No. 8, Your Investment Vehicles, which you will find in the Appendix at the end of the book. Follow along as we show how the sample action paper was completed to identify the most suitable vehicles for the Lean and Quick investors.

In Chapter 3 we discussed various methods for working out differences between investor personalities. If you are creating your Personal Profit Portfolio as a team, you probably noticed that the BB&K Rosetta Stone prescriptions are based on the needs and perspectives of a *single* investor personality.

To show you how two diverse personalities may be able to work together on a project like this, we will assume that one of our Lean and Quick investors is a Guardian and the other an Enthusiast. This disparate team provides us with broad contrasts. See if our problem-solving approach can help you.

Cash Equivalents

The first thing our Lean and Quick investors looked for were similarities in our recommendations. Since tax-free money market accounts were prescribed for both, this was an easy choice. Note, also, that they have included a memo to check out T-bills further. This was certainly meant more for the Guardian; but, putting a firm foundation in place affords greater potential to utilize additional funds for more speculative purposes, which will please the Enthusiast.

Fixed Income

The allocation for fixed-income vehicles limited them to mutual funds or unit trusts, because they did not have sufficient funds to buy individual issues. Both personalities would be well suited with tax-free bonds, if their after-tax calculations showed that was the way to go.

Again, the Guardian's need for security would be satisfied with Treasury notes. These are also recommended for Enthusiasts, at least in the beginning stages. Bond funds became the latest investment craze when they

FIGURE 5-1
Lean and Quick's Desired Investment Vehicles

Action Paper No. 8

Your Investment Vehicles[*]

Name(s) _Lean and Quick_   Date _December_

Asset Class	Current Target Allocation ($) (from Action Paper No. 7)	List of Current Vehicles	BB&K Rosetta Stone Recommendations	Considerations	Vehicles to Investigate Further[*]
Cash Equivalents	3,500	Passbook savings account	① Should be tax-free? ② May want T-bills later?	Transfer from savings to money market fund?	Ask our bank about tax free money market fund.
Fixed Income	12,000	Bond fund (Special situation)	① Tax free bond fund? ② May want Treasury notes later.	Sell bonds, buy diversified mutual fund?	Investigate "family of funds" advertisement
U.S. Stocks	19,250	High Tech common stocks	① Should get diversified mutual fund?	Sell risky stocks, set-up IRA stock fund?	(see above) Find out about "growth" stock funds
International Equities	—	None	① Should eventually get Int'l stock mutual fund	None right now	Nothing right now
Real Estate/ Inflation Hedges	19,750		① Publicly offered program, maybe later? ② Buy American Eagle and/or REIT's and a Maple Leaf	Buy real estate partnership gold fund	Look into real estate programs

[*] **Important note:** These vehicles must be considered preliminary selections only. More self-evaluation of your financial situation, tax needs, money management skills, and life goals will be necessary before you shop for specific investments.

were aggressively marketed for their high current income in the early 1980s. That satisfied the Enthusiast's impulse to be "with it."

Given this couple's need to diversify over many types of investments, and the growing flexibility that mutual fund "families" give their shareholders for switching between funds, they decided to check out fund families. This approach satisfies the Guardian's desire for working with well-established and proven companies. It also allows the Enthusiast enough elbow room to move around when necessary.

Common Stock
The stock market is destined to cause the most controversy for most couples, because it offers such a wide range of vehicles, each with its own risk/reward parameters. There are very conservative stocks. There are very risky *new issue* stocks. And there is a whole world in between.

Both investors recognized that they did not have sufficient capital to buy individual issues, so they had to decide what type of mutual fund they would buy. The Guardian would be most satisfied with an index fund that is designed to mirror the stock market averages. Of course, the Enthusiast would be disappointed settling for the "average," preferring high volatility where there is potential for high returns. But, it wouldn't be fair to the Guardian to buy an aggressive growth fund.

They decided to compromise. There are many good, solid, conservative long-term growth funds that should meet both their needs. They both agree that their concentrated position in a single high-tech stock is not appropriate. They agree to research the range of growth stock funds to see if there is something that will satisfy both of them.

International Securities
Our Lean and Quick investors did not allocate any funds to international securities. Buying stocks is still very new for them. The international arena scared them off, for now.

But, since established international funds were the recommended starting place for both personalities, they've agreed to research the matter—but not to commit funds as yet. Their investment plan calls for additional money to be added each year. By the time their resources have grown, they will be more comfortable with this asset class.

It's important to feel comfortable with your investment choices. Even though we recommend that you diversify into all five asset classes as soon as you can, it would be self-defeating to force yourself to invest where you are ill at ease. Once our Lean and Quick investors have a little experience with mutual fund investments in stocks and bonds, the transition to international securities should be painless!

Real Estate and Inflation Hedges

When you get past buying your own home, real estate investing takes on a complicated face. Just how safe are those limited partnerships? What about all the scandals revolving around tax-shelter-oriented real estate deals?

We all feel most comfortable with what we know. We know our own area of the country best. We also know that, when oil prices fell sharply in the 1980s, real estate in the "oil patch" region of the country collapsed.

This area left many doubts for both partners. But they agreed that real estate certainly held up well over the long term. They will buy equity REITs, which have broadly diversified portfolios. That way they hope to avoid another oil patch crash.

They also knew that, the closer you are to your real estate investment, the larger the potential reward. The Guardian does not want to invest in a publicly offered limited partnership without more understanding. The Enthusiast wants to investigate this alternative, because it seems to offer greater potential. They agree to research the topic. The key will be to find an established syndicator who can relieve the Guardian's anxiety.

Neither could argue with gold as the classic inflation hedge, but they differed on how to best buy into it. They knew that South Africa had severe political problems and the Guardian didn't want any of that. They settled on trying to find a gold mutual fund that invested primarily in non-South African shares and bullion. But if that isn't possible, they will consider gold coins issued by the United States or Canada that seem to offer some potential.

Now It Is Your Turn

When you have completed Action Paper No. 8, you will have finished your portfolio planning effort. Now you know how much and where you must invest to achieve a balanced, diversified, goal-getting portfolio. But most important, you know which vehicles will *feel right* to you along the way. In the next chapter we will cover how to manage your portfolio.

WRAPPING UP

In this chapter you learned how different investment vehicles suit different investor personalities. What is right for one person is not necessarily correct for another. Remember, investment professionals come in a variety of personalities themselves. Rather than following the advice of some reputed expert, you now have the tools to evaluate what will work for *you*.

Narrowing the choice of investments to those that can play a role in your Personal Profit Planning is no small task. You are already far better prepared for the inevitable surprises than most investors ever will be.

You know that investment success is dependent on organization, planning, knowledge of your own strengths and weaknesses, and discipline. Luck certainly helps, but hoping for it is not going to achieve your financial goals.

CHAPTER 6

GUIDELINES FOR MANAGING YOUR INVESTMENTS

You now have the information and organization to begin building your Personal Profit Portfolio. Next, you will have to develop the skill to *manage* your investments on a continuing basis. Although there are many approaches to investing, we recommend two distinct paths, one of which will be right for your particular style of portfolio management.

If you find the process of investigating economic developments, researching individual investments, and monitoring your portfolio is a chore, you will prefer the passive "fixed-mix" method. But if you enjoy the challenge of the ever changing economic and investment environment, you will want to take the active "dynamic-mix" approach. Whichever you choose, you will have to make your financial decisions in light of varying degrees of risk and uncertainty.

In this chapter we discuss how professional investors deal with the same risk and uncertainty considerations that you face. If the dynamic hands-on approach to portfolio management appeals to you, you will find the ideas we present about compensating for the unknown to be valuable.

THE ADVANTAGES OF MULTIASSET INVESTING

Throughout the book we have presented a detailed plan to help you design and build your own *diversified portfolio*. Before you plunge ahead, however, you should know something about other investment practices. (For more details about the two strategies described below, see "Single Asset Investment Methods: Technical Analysis versus Fundamental Analysis," on page 130.)

Technical analysts generally believe that a *timing* method will enable them to achieve above-average results. Typically, they have developed systems based on price, volume, and sentiment, which signal *when* to buy or sell securities as a whole, or in specific issues.

Fundamental stock analysts, on the other hand, decry timing as unworkable and impractical. They argue that investment success comes through buying "undervalued" companies and waiting for the market to recognize their true worth. Fundamentalists determine an establishment's value, based on their analysis of its current and potential earnings, management, and industry.

Regardless of your "timing" or analytical skills, if you invest in only one asset class there will be wider swings in your portfolio than if you are diversified over slightly correlated asset classes. The diversified asset allocation approach has the benefit of enabling your portfolio's value to be more stable.

Assets might be correlated together or inversely, or there might be no correlation at all. Assets that are correlated respond to a given situation by moving in some predictable way in relation to each other.

Assets that are correlated *together* move in the *same* direction in response to a particular event, declining or rising as the case may be, although not necessarily by the same amount or percentage. Assets that are *inversely* correlated are in a reciprocal relationship (i.e., they respond *differently* to the same event). In other words, whatever causes one to rise in value will also cause the other to decline, and vice versa, but not necessarily to the same degree. Assets that are not correlated have no predictable response to a given situation.

When building your portfolio you will want to invest in assets that have an inverse correlation or none at all. But, because correlation coefficients change in time, it's difficult and time consuming to keep track of what assets are correlated and in what manner. By investing across four or five asset classes you should be well covered on this front. That's one of the beauties of diversification.

As we indicated earlier, a diversified asset allocation strategy can be implemented by taking one of two basic roads: *fixed-mix* or a *dynamic-mix* approach. In the following pages you will learn to identify which is right for you. Both styles of portfolio management have advantages and disadvantages.

Taking the Passive Approach

You have learned a lot about how you relate to money from the exercises and examples in the preceding chapters. You may be very cautious—a Guardian; or, you may be a risk-taker—an Adventurer. But knowing your investor personality and your financial physique is only part of the equation. You also have to ask yourself how *involved* you want to be with your investments. The answer to that question will determine what management style is most appropriate for you.

If you do not wish to, or simply cannot, devote much time to managing your investments, you should consider the "passive" fixed-mix approach. Investors prefer this method for many reasons. You may have business or personal pursuits that require a great deal of your time. Or, you may have neither real interest nor enthusiasm for financial affairs. If you have to force yourself to follow the markets, the odds are that you will not be happy or successful as an involved investor.

However, if you are very interested in the investment markets and have the time to dedicate, you will want to approach your investment portfolio more actively. Taking this route requires more time, more involvement, and more commitment. Later in this chapter we will explore the pros and cons of the "active" approach.

When we refer to the passive approach we do not mean to suggest that you buy a number of different investments, put them away, and forget them. In today's wide-swinging volatile markets, forgetting an investment may prove very costly. Yet, it is possible to achieve above-average investment returns without being involved on a day-to-day basis.

The fixed-mix method requires that you decide what percentage of your funds you want to invest in each asset class, and then select appropriate vehicles in each category (see the guidelines in Chapters 4 and 5). On a regular periodic basis you would so adjust your holdings that your mix would remain constant.

A conservative investor might keep as much as 40 percent in cash equivalents, 20 percent in fixed income, and the balance divided equally among the remaining three asset classes, or even 50 percent in cash equivalents with the rest apportioned among the remaining categories. Conversely, a more aggressive investor might have an amalgam, such as 30 percent stock, 10 percent cash, and 20 percent in each of the other classes. Some investors find it most convenient to divide their investments equally among their chosen asset categories. There is no single correct combination for a fixed-mix portfolio. What matters, of course, is what combination is the right one for *you*.

The actual vehicles you choose for each asset class will depend on what you've done in the previous chapters. Guardian investors will buy primarily blue-chip stocks, Treasury bonds, low-leveraged real estate, well-known international companies, and government-guaranteed cash equivalents. Adventurers will take a different tack—buying more speculative growth issues (e.g., Apple instead of IBM) and lower-rated corporate bonds (even so-called *junk bonds*, with their high potential yields and their concomitant high risk). They may even dabble in international bond funds as well as international stocks.

It's impossible to list all the possible combinations for investor types here, especially when considering that many couples have disparate personalities, which must be reconciled to the mutual satisfaction of both parties. However, even passive investors must do their homework to ferret out investments that meet their needs *and* fit their investor personalities. In the next chapter we provide guidelines for selecting an advisor to help with this step.

The key to a successful fixed-mix approach is that, once you have determined the percentage to be applied, you should keep your assets at the same ratio. Don't switch around. If you find yourself doing so, or wanting to, you may be becoming a more dynamic-mix person than you realize.

How to Reallocate a Fixed-Mix Portfolio

Once you have made your initial investments, you will have to review your portfolio periodically (quarterly or annually) and readjust those asset classes that have changed.

Let's say that at the beginning of the year you have a portfolio of $100,000, which you allocate equally across five asset classes, putting $20,000 in domestic stocks or mutual funds, $20,000 in international stocks or mutual funds, $20,000 in real estate partnerships or REITs, $20,000 in cash equivalents or money market funds, and $20,000 in fixed-income or bond funds.

Six months later you find that you were fortunate to experience an overall increase in your portfolio, made up of gains in several classes and of losses in others. At that time you would readjust your portfolio so each asset class still represented 20 percent of your total.

Look at Table 6–1 to see how you would handle changes in your portfolio in an equally apportioned fixed-mix asset allocation. Beginning in January, the $100,000 portfolio shows resources equally allocated among the five asset classes, at $20,000 each. In June of the same year the values of each asset class changed, bringing the new value of the portfolio to $103,100.

To maintain the fixed mix, you would reallocate the new total of $103,100 in equal amounts to each asset class, dividing the sum by the five classes to come up with $20,620 for each. To accomplish this, you would sell $3,380 in stocks and $1,380 in your international fund, reducing both to the new appropriate level, as in Table 6–2. You would reinvest the $4,760 you've received as a result of the sale as follows: $20 to your money market fund, $1,620 to fixed income, and $3,120 to real estate,

TABLE 6–1
Fixed-Mix Portfolio Reallocation

Asset Classes	January	June	Reallocation
Money-market fund	$ 20,000	$ 20,600	$ 20,620
Stocks (growth fund)	20,000	24,000	20,620
Fixed-income (bond fund)	20,000	19,000	20,620
International (Int'l equity fund)	20,000	22,000	20,620
Real estate (REITs)	20,000	17,500	20,620
Total portfolio	$100,000	$103,100	$103,100

thereby bringing all asset categories to $20,620, or 20 percent each of your new portfolio figure.

Adding to Investments by Dollar Cost Averaging

Passive managers are comfortable adding to their investments by a fixed amount of dollars at set intervals. By doing so, you will put into practice one of the tried and true long-term investment techniques: *dollar cost averaging*, also called *constant dollar plan investing*, which is a buying strategy calling for regular flows of new money.

This system ensures that you buy more when prices are low and less when prices are high, thereby keeping the average price of purchased assets lower. The dollar cost averaging plan, if faithfully adhered to, forces a discipline that can make the difference between long-term investment success and failure.

TABLE 6–2
Adjusting the Fixed-Mix Portfolio

June Portfolio	Amount	Change	Adjustment
Money market	$ 20,600	$ 600	+ $ 20
Stocks	24,000	4,000	– 3,380
Fixed income	19,000	1,000	+ 1,620
International	22,000	2,000	– 1,380
Real estate	17,500	2,500	+ 3,120
Total	$103,100	$10,100	—

The Advantages for the Passive Investor

One of the chief problems that beginning investors face is their tendency to want to do too much, too soon. Short-term trading is a troublesome proposition for even experienced professionals. The fixed-mix approach avoids the mistakes that short-term timing errors create.

The discipline of the fixed-mix strategy forces you to stay with the long-term "secular" trends that make the big money. Since your allocation to U.S. stocks will stay at your predetermined percentage, you will not be tempted to try to "call the top" of the market and sell out early, or, as happens more often, continue buying too heavily right at the top, when most people are overly enthusiastic.[1]

There are other, ancillary benefits for the fixed-mix investor. For one, transactions fees usually will be lower. Instead of making frequent alterations to your portfolio as changes occur in the marketplace, you will make reallocations only at fixed intervals.

For another, this method minimizes investment decision stress. That's a benefit that shouldn't be overlooked in today's high-stress society! As an example, following a fixed-mix investment strategy also allows you to be a contrarian: going against the crowd, which would otherwise be a difficult road to follow psychologically. Managing your investments in this way takes the emotional burden off your shoulders.

Our own studies tell us that a portfolio managed by the fixed-mix method and diversified over the five asset classes, which we have used here, grew at an average annual rate, compounded, of 10.3 percent between 1966 and 1987. That includes reinvestment of interest and dividends. Compare that with the 9.1 percent earned by the S&P 500 in the same time period. Equally important, the diversified portfolio was only about 50 percent as risky as the stock market, when risk is considered a function of volatility.[2] (See Figure 6–1.)

Finally, our research shows that the fixed-mix method, if consistently applied, *will outperform most single-asset approaches, with less risk.* In fact,

---

[1]Many investors made exactly these mistakes in the bull stock market that began in 1982. By 1984 many pundits felt that the market had gone too far, too fast. But, while they were selling and looking for the onset of a bear market, stock prices continued to climb for another two and a half years. By August of 1987 the stock market had already rallied over 40 percent in one of the strongest upmoves in history. Many analysts and traders concluded that the old boom and bust cycle was finally a thing of the past. Prosperity and ever rising prices seemed to be the new "norm." But they learned differently when the stock market plunged over 500 points October 19, 1987, for the largest single-day drop in history.

[2]See Chapter 8 for a discussion on volatility.

FIGURE 6–1
Diversified Portfolio Index

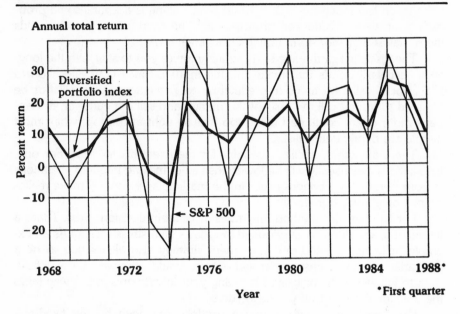

because of the discipline of buying low and selling high that is forced by periodic reallocations, the diversified portfolio does better than simply buying and holding the five separate asset classes. Our analysis shows that the fixed-mix diversified approach adds about 0.5 percent per year over the 20-year period we studied. That translates into $5,562 extra for every $10,000 invested.

Disadvantages of the Fixed-Mix Portfolio

Virtually every investment decision has its pros and cons. Your portfolio management style is no exception. If you are a passive investor and take the fixed-mix approach, you will be settling for a return that is just slightly above average. When you consider that some 60 percent of all professional money managers (they are primarily timers and single-asset managers) underperform the S&P index, that is quite an accomplishment.

But as a passive fixed-mix investor, you will sacrifice potentially large returns for greater safety and stability. For instance, following this strategy you would have constantly trimmed your stock portion back during the period from 1982 to 1987, when the U.S. market underwent a recordbreaking rise, and you would have done well. But if you had reinvested your stock profits (either through increasing your stock allocation, or by letting the stock profits build on themselves), the overall return of your portfolio could have been much higher.

By adopting a fixed-mix approach, you limit your flexibility to take advantage of such unique situations. As an example, consider the gross undervaluations of U.S. bonds in 1982 and again in the summer of 1987. Yields on Treasury bonds went over 10 percent! Obtaining a *U.S. government-guaranteed* double-digit return on your money certainly would have been appealing. But, because of the fixed-mix approach, you would not keep more than your predetermined percentage of your assets in bonds. Remember, the only adjustments made are to realign your allocations and bring each of the five asset classes back to your *fixed*-mix percentages.

No matter how great the temptation to do otherwise, it's important to be consistent in your strategy. You should not take turns with, nor combine, the fixed and dynamic mix.

As we have indicated before, profit is not measured only in terms of dollars. Limited involvement might mean that there will be little *psychic profit* for you. For some investors, the satisfaction of doing it right is a major motivator. In any case, one of the things we hope you develop through reading this book and, more important, putting these lessons into practice, is an excitement and enthusiasm for investing. It is a rewarding, fascinating, ever changing world.

Taking the Active Approach

The alternative to the passive fixed-mix approach is the active *dynamic-mix* approach. When you elect the hands-on method, you will reevaluate your investment holdings regularly in light of the economic environment. Your research and conclusions about future economic trends and developments will influence your allocation decisions.

It is usually best to set regular periodic intervals to reexamine your portfolio and make any significant asset allocation readjustments you feel are necessary. The discussion on forecasting later in this chapter is primarily directed at you, the active investor. The variable recommended ranges for each asset class, as discussed in Chapter 4, provides good guidelines for beginning your own dynamic portfolio.

An active manager will set the allocation levels for each asset class in accord with his or her evaluation of the prospects for each category. At BB&K our entire research staff is involved twice a year in intensive month-long reviews of both the state of the economy and the performance of the investment markets, prior to setting new allocation levels for our managed accounts.

Single-Asset Investment Methods:
Technical Analysis Versus Fundamental Analysis

Making Investment Decisions Using Technical Analysis

Technical Analysis: A Matter of Time

Timing is most closely associated with that branch of investment analysis known as *technical analysis*. Technical analysts examine past price histories for indications of future price movement. They make extensive use of price charts, which plot the daily ranges of each security's price. When their price charts develop certain configurations resembling historical price patterns, they buy or sell in expectation that the pattern will unfold as it did in the past.

They also make use of other price or volume-related data. These analysts carefully monitor price momentum and investor sentiment. For example, when price momentum begins to slow down, they watch for a reversal of a trend. They use a variety of mathemetical formulas for evaluating momentum or rate of change.

Technical analysts also employ a number of widely used sentiment measures. Basically, they try to ascertain what the smart money[1] is doing. They have also developed a number of tools to evaluate what the more impetuous, less-informed "public" traders are doing. Technical traders then try to align themselves on the same side of the market as the smart money.

For example, if their analysis[2] shows that "insiders" (corporate executives with early access to private business information) are buying more heavily than usual, that would be a buy signal. But if their indicators show that there is heavy buying by "odd lotters" (less than 100 shares is considered an odd lot), then they would be more cautious. Odd lotters tend to be less-sophisticated traders prone to trading on emotion, rather than from carefully considered facts.[3]

Timing versus Asset Allocation

Stock market timers may think they are diversified by buying a number of different stocks, but they are still investing in a single asset class. And, when the stock market drops, few issues buck the overall trend.

Timing Methods in a Diversified Portfolio

A diversified portfolio approach does not prevent you from adopting timing techniques for *those asset classes where it works*. If you decide to change your asset allocations, because of fluctuations in the underlying economic picture, you could use timing tools to fine tune your buys and sells.

But stock market timing has an inherent flaw as a portfolio management method: It's impossible to know the future. Regardless of how some method worked in the past, there is no guarantee it will continue to do so in the future. As a result, useful timing techniques are in a constant state of flux.

A Risky Timing Technique: Selling Short

It's possible to make money on falling stock prices by *selling short,* a practice that is the business of professionals only. Selling short goes against the odds. Since the inception of the stock market in the United States, stock prices have tended to rise over time.

A trader who sells short essentially "borrows" stock from the pool of stock held by brokerage firms in "street name."[4] The trader sells the stock, believing that the price will decline and hoping that it can be purchased at a lower price and returned to the pool. Obviously, stock that has been borrowed must be replaced, which it is when the trader buys the stock through the same broker. The short seller only makes money if the price of the stock in question declines after it was borrowed. The difference between the selling price and the buyback price (minus commission) is the short seller's profit.

Short selling is a very high-risk proposition, because the price of the stock might rise. If a short seller has to buy back the stock at a higher price than he or she sold it, there would be a loss. When you buy a stock, the most you can lose would be a drop to zero. But, since a stock price could rise infinitely, theoretically at least, the loss to a trader selling short could be substantial.

Short selling requires a margin[5] account. The broker keeps daily track of the stock that has been sold short because, if the price rises, the broker will require the short seller to either close the position or to post more money as a guarantee that the trader will be able to buy back the stock at higher prices. This is the dreaded "margin call" that is the bane of leveraged speculators.

Making Investment Decisions Using Fundamental Analysis

Fundamental Analysis: Back to Basics

The correct time for fundamental analysts to buy a stock is when the price is below what they feel it is worth, based upon their assessment of the company's business prospects. Fundamental analysts look at such details as the company's book value (assets minus liabilities), cash flow, earnings, the earnings growth rate, and types and level of debt. In addition, they examine the health of the company's industry to discern if there is a growing or decreasing demand for the industry's goods.

Fundamental analysts also look at the price/earnings (P/E) ratio, which is reported in the stock pages of most newspapers. The P/E is simply the price of the stock divided by the earnings per share for the last year. Conventional wisdom says that the higher the P/E, the greater the risk. High P/E stocks tend to be more volatile.

Fundamental analysts do not be-

132   Chapter 6

lieve that anyone can know when substantive price movement will begin. Rather, they are willing to buy and hold—until either the market recognizes the undervaluation or the company's prospects deteriorate.

Fundamental Analysis versus Asset Allocation

The fundamentalist single-asset approach has many of the same problems as the technical timing school. When the stock market goes down, few stocks counter the trend. An undervalued stock may stay undervalued for years. There is no guarantee that the marketplace will put the same price on a stock that an analyst feels is "right."

Inherent Problems in Single-Asset Approaches

There is no way to prevent losses in the inevitable downcycles, which is the major drawback to a single-asset approach. With Murphy's Law in full force, the time when you absolutely *must* have your money is just when you will garner the most disadvantageous prices.

A static approach in either economic or market forecasting will not work. People change all the time; as a result, markets are constantly changing. A key element in successful economic forecasting is flexibility.

---

[1] "Smart money" refers to corporate insiders, Wall Street professionals, and large speculators, the people who allegedly "know."
[2] Since corporate insiders have to file reports on transactions of their stock with the SEC, their activity—at least to some degree—is public, as long as you know what to look for. Technical analysts can keep abreast of some early stock movement by researching these reports.
[3] Technical traders consider odd lotters to be a proxy for the general public. The traders would be inclined to sell when the odd lotters buy in the belief that, by the time the public started buying aggressively, the prices would not represent good values. This theory holds that the public is the last to get in on a good thing.
[4] When you buy stock from a broker who holds the stock for you, instead of issuing certificates to you, the stock is held in "street name."
[5] "Margin" is the security deposited with a broker as a provision against loss on transactions.

Advantages to the Dynamic Approach

Correct "timing" can yield above-average results, although it's a mistake to become overly focused on short-term timing. Nonetheless, recognizing where the economy is in the overall Business Cycle can help you reallocate assets to maximize your returns. For instance, in the summer of 1982 the economy was first showing signs that it was starting to move ahead after being mired in a recession. Since U.S. stocks benefit from economic growth (especially early growth from a recessionary environment), an increase in that allocation would have yielded significant above-average returns.

Our research shows that our active portfolio management style adds about 2 percent per year to the total return that would be achieved from a simple buy and hold strategy. That's a significant payoff over the long term, but it entails substantial effort.

Different asset classes are more or less volatile at different times. In the late 1970s precious metals became very volatile. By 1984 and 1985 precious metals had lapsed into narrow trading range doldrums. In the late 1970s and again in the spring and summer of 1987, the bond markets underwent unprecedented volatility. Because active asset allocation managers are able to take action, they can minimize the risk inherent in such wide-swinging markets by reducing their exposure.

Diversification limits risk by decreasing overall portfolio volatility, particularly compared to the single-asset approach. A flexible manager can take measures to further enhance that benefit. For instance, by combining negatively (inversely) correlated investments in a single portfolio, you can reduce your portfolio's volatility. An example of negatively correlated assets would be gold and bonds. When inflation is picking up, gold prices usually rise. At the same time, fears of inflation—especially since the high-inflation days of the late 1970s—tend to depress bond prices. By altering the ratio of gold to bonds you can "fine tune" the volatility of your portfolio for the economic environment.

An active portfolio manager is in a position to take advantage of short-term aberrations that occur in different markets. The bond and stock markets in 1982 are two cases in point. U.S. Treasury long-term bonds were yielding over 10 percent in 1982. By the end of 1986 long-term Treasury bonds had experienced one of the most powerful bull markets in history. In the summer of 1982 the stock market was at one of the lowest valuation points in history. Dividend yields were at the upper end of historical ranges, and a record number of stocks were selling below book value. Five years later the stock market had increased over 300 percent, to reach a new all-time high of over 2,700. Astute managers responded to one or both of these situations by increasing their respective allocations.

Active involvement in ongoing investment decisions enhances your sense of accomplishment. When you are more directly involved you can appreciate the thrill of victory that much more. That "psychic profit" is a big motivator for many investors.

Disadvantages to Dynamic Allocations

No matter how organized you are, there never seems to be enough time in the day to accomplish what you want, especially when you have to contend with your business and other matters, as well as your investment decisions. When you elect to take a more active role in your financial affairs, it can become very time consuming. As we have demonstrated, there is virtually no limit to the amount of information you can accumulate about the economy and the investment markets. If you allow it, your search for such knowledge and facts can occupy all your free time.

A dynamic asset allocation portfolio will incur greater transaction costs than a fixed mix. Every time you want to change something, there will be a charge. If your activity is significant, those transaction fees can substantially reduce your bottom line.

While good timing decisions can make you feel the thrill of victory, timing errors will bring home the agony of defeat all too clearly. If you had decided in the summer of 1982 that the recession was going to deepen, rather than end, your lower stock allocation could have proven costly. When you take the dynamic approach, you trade the security of median returns for the potential of better returns—but with the equal chance of worse results.

A dynamic portfolio manager must guard against human nature! It's natural for you to tip the scales in areas that are doing well, just when you should be looking elsewhere. In late 1979 you would have been hard pressed to find a gold or real estate investor who wasn't very optimistic about the prospects for even greater profits. But both markets suffered sharp selloffs in the early 1980s.

In August 1987 the stock market reached another all-time high. After bucking all the negatives for the better part of the prior two years, it seemed as though the bull market would go on forever. Many investors who missed the last upleg increased their positions to "make up for missed profits." And, as you know, on October 19, 1987, the stock market suffered the worst single-day fall in history.

A dynamic portfolio manager must use the age-old investment wisdom known as *contrary opinion*. Stated simply, the "crowd" is wrong at major turning points. When everything you read and everyone to whom you talk focuses on making money in stocks, or any other asset class, that's the time to get out.

THINKING ABOUT THE FUTURE

Events in the future—from business cycles to fluctuating interest rates to changeable weather—depend on such a great multitude of interrelated factors that it's impossible to list them all. Forecasting future values with precision is futile.

Some people try to solve complex investment problems using computer power. But, remember the lesson from Chapter 2: People, not numbers, determine economic trends. Individuals, with their varied wants, needs, desires, experiences, and unique knowledge of their own circumstances, cannot be reduced to ciphers.

Others tackle investments as though financial problems can be overcome with sheer willpower. But, those looking for precise answers, regardless of their will, intellect, and technological help, are destined to be disappointed. This frustration drives some people to extreme measures. Astrological projections, tea leaf reading, and investing by the phases of the moon are only a few of the more exotic methods used by some investors.

Then there are the forecasting fatalists. Their sense of futility over the lack of precision results in a "give up" attitude. They don't see the point in trying at all, since there is no way to be *sure* that investments made today will be right for tomorrow.

Let the Markets "Forecast" for You

Once you have made your portfolio allocations in accordance with the guidelines in this book, and you have invested your money, you will find that your investments will fluctuate. Some may go up sharply, while others drop.

Since your portfolio is diversified, the changing dollar values of each asset will probably result in a kind of "mechanical reallocation" of your assets. The "winning" assets will increase their share of your portfolio's total value, while the "losing" assets will decrease their percentage. You now have an important decision to make. Forecasting, like it or not, is part of that decision.

If you decide to hold things as they are (the passive manager's preferred strategy), your portfolio will be heavily weighted toward "yesterday's" winners. When the markets change (and they will), those profits may shrink. More than likely, the previously out-of-favor assets will begin to shine; but these will be the very assets, unfortunately, which are underrepresented in your portfolio! Diversification will still be working in your favor, preserving your initial investments; but you will face a grim period waiting for your "buy and hold" strategy to pay off.

In the investment world, one thing you can be sure of is that big winners can sometimes become big losers. You must take steps to preserve your profits. The simplest form of forecasting is to let the market and your diversification targets do the work for you.

Invest in Out-of-Favor Assets

When an asset's value appreciates to the point where it substantially exceeds its allocation limit, *sell* enough of it to bring that asset back to its target allocation. Take the proceeds and put them into an out-of-favor asset class. When that asset's upcycle occurs, your position will have increased automatically, enhancing your profits. At the same time, this automatic "forced" reallocation helps cut the potential losses you would have incurred in the other now-declining asset class.

This strategy essentially forces you to *buy low and sell high*. That really is the ultimate purpose of all investment forecasts. But it is far easier to talk about selling a high-performing asset to buy others that are "in the dumps" than it is to do it. For some investor types, such as Guardians and Enthusiasts, it is a real struggle. Nonetheless, disciplining yourself to make such moves, while market prices are still in your favor, can often make the difference between just middling through and achieving meaningful returns.

Learn to Be Contrary

With this approach you will become a *contrary investor* (i.e., one who purposely goes against the crowd). The term *crowd* describes the masses of unsophisticated investors who are usually wrong at key turning points. We all know people who are crowd followers, rather than independent actors. They buy stock after a few years of bullish price action, when the stock market is front page news. When the crowd buys, the contrary investor sells. Eventually these buyers will cease buying. No one knows exactly when they will be satiated, but we do know that time will come. And when it does, the contrary investor will buy. Contrary opinion is a highly valued and trusted investing tool employed by professionals.

Everyone Is a Forecaster

Every time you make an investment decision you are making or using some kind of forecast. In Chapter 2 we observed that everyone is an investor. When you decide to keep your money in a passbook savings account or a checking account, you are acting on your own implicit forecasts of the future.

You may not realize it, but a number of your future expectations go into the decision to keep your money in a checking account, which pays no interest. Perhaps you think the stock market is vulnerable. Or, maybe you think money market funds will encounter problems. Or, you may have expectations about how soon you will need the money. The "forecast" certainly doesn't have to be a detailed analysis of the economy! It's a decision you make, based upon your knowledge of your particular circumstances.

Even when it comes to specific investment decisions, based upon your understanding of the economic future, you should not be afraid to forecast just because it's inexact. You should rid yourself of the notion that making economic forecasts is either a task for experts only or something you can decline, like an invitation, because it isn't your cup of tea.

When you do something as straightforward as depositing your paycheck, you are making an economic forecast of sorts and acting on your conclusions. The logic of your decision and the nature of your forecast may have gone something like this:

1. *This paycheck is the only new income I'm going to have for awhile.* You've already made a prediction about your future performance as a money-maker. You *might* lose your job next week. Or, you *could* get an unexpected windfall—an inheritance or bonus. In either case, you've decided that neither of these events will happen and that this paycheck is all the new money you're going to have until your next paycheck. That decision is based, primarily, on your past experience.

2. *This paycheck will be better off in the bank than as cash in my pocket.* Your deposit implies yet another forecast: Your money will be safer in the bank than with you. This doesn't mean that you really fear being robbed, or that you'll lose the money somewhere, or that you'll spend it recklessly. It means you have intuitively assessed the various risks involved of alternative courses of action. You act, of course, based upon the information *you* have about those options. In this case, you decide that depositing your pay was better than cashing the check and putting the money in your pocket.

Every decision you make is predicated on your own forecasts, although you usually don't think of your decision-making process in such terms. *All decisions are made with varying degrees of risk and uncertainty.* As a successful Personal Profit Planner, it's important that you know what these two considerations mean to you. It's equally important to know what your options are for dealing with them. One of our main goals is to provide you with the knowledge, confidence, and ability to deal effectively with both risk and uncertainty in your future investment decisions.

Coping with Risk in Your Decision Making

There are many levels of "risk." The odds for some risks are easy to compute. For example, on the TV show "Let's Make a Deal," contestants choose from among three closed curtains for the grand prize. The risk of penalty or chance of reward is easily determined.

Another level of complexity can be observed in various gambling ventures. In such games as blackjack, professional "card counters" quite accurately figure the odds on what they will be dealt next, based on the distribution of cards that have already been dealt.

Still other risk situations can be narrowed to a mostly mathematical exercise. Auto manufacturers, for example, know how many spare parts to make for any given model, based on the past rates of failure for those parts.

Even more complex questions arise in the area of finance, because of the human element, as we have emphasized in discussing the economy. The probabilities of receiving any particular return on an investment range from "highly probable" (as with the annual interest rate paid on passbook savings accounts) to "almost impossible" (such as quadrupling your money in one year from an aggressive growth stock).

All these decisions involve some level of *risk*. By "risk" we mean the chances you take to receive a specific return on your money.

Coping with Uncertainty

Beyond the risk of receiving a quoted rate of return, the larger and more difficult question is of the probability of receiving a specific *real* (adjusted for inflation) return on a given investment. While at first glance the two may appear to be similar, the factors involved are considerably different.

Look at a typical passbook savings account. If you deposited $100 at 6 percent simple interest, there is a very high probability that you would have $106 in your account at the end of the year. But that does not necessarily mean you would achieve a 6 percent increase in the purchasing power of your original investment.

Without knowing something about the economic forces at work during the year (such as the rate of inflation or deflation), you cannot know what the effective *real* returns will be. If inflation was 5 percent during the year, your real return would be only 1 percent. However, if prices dropped (deflation) during the year by 8 percent, your investment would actually leave you 14 percent ahead economically. Imagine receiving a 14 percent real rate of return from a passbook savings account!

Such decisions, where the various probabilities of alternative outcomes are *not known* in advance, are decisions made under *uncertainty*. Decisions involving future states of the Business Cycle, inflation, and other macroeconomic variables all take place with great uncertainty. It's far different from a gambler assessing the risks of the next card in the draw.

The Dilemma of Real World Decisions

Nearly all financial decisions, from those involving investment selection to those involving portfolio allocations and reallocations, entail elements of risk and uncertainty. Decisions based on known risks are relatively straightforward. The TV game show contestant knows there is a one-in-three chance of winning the grand prize. The card counter knows what the mathematical odds are that the next card dealt will be a 10.

Decisions in the face of economic uncertainties—inflation, deflation, elections, natural disasters, war, peace, and so forth—are infinitely more complex. These judgments depend as much on the decision maker's optimism, pessimism, desire for reward versus desire to avoid regret, and so on. In other words, the human, nonmathematical element plays a major part in the final conclusions.

This, then, is the key question you must address in deciding your approach to portfolio management: Do you want to *try* to make a difference in the final return of your portfolio? Or, do you want to start off on the best footing you can and, within limits, let nature take its course?

We call the difference between these two basic alternatives your *portfolio management style*. Your future financial fitness may depend on just how well you understand it.

WHAT IS YOUR PORTFOLIO MANAGEMENT STYLE?

To assess your basic approach to portfolio management, complete the following Taking Stock questionnaire. Once you (and your partner, if you have one) have finished, read the evaluation to see where your responses fall. As with investor personalities, a range covers most investors. Knowing yourself and your attitudes about such areas as economic forecasting will help extend your investing "comfort zone."

| Taking Stock Number 4 |

What's Your Portfolio Management Style?

As you've learned in this chapter so far, managing a successful portfolio takes more than technical expertise alone. You must make your decisions amid risk and uncertainty in a way that not only works economically but feels right for you as well.

After reading each statement below, decide which number from the following scale best reflects how strongly you agree or disagree with that statement. Here's the scale and a sample question to show you what we mean:

What's Your Portfolio Management Style? (*continued*)

Strongly Agree **5**	Mildly Agree **4**	No Opinion **3**	Mildly Disagree **2**	Strongly Disagree **1**

Partner **A**   Partner **B**

Example: You have to be a genius to be a winner in the stock market. _____ _____

If you agree that exceptionally bright people are the only ones rewarded with big profits in stocks, you would put a 5 in the blank. If you think that brains make no difference at all—perhaps *luck* governs all big returns—then you would put a 1 in the blank. If you suspect that brains don't hurt, but other factors might be equally important, you would probably put a 3. If you feel brains are a bit more important than luck—or some other factor—you might put a 4, and so on.

Remember, this is not a competition, so don't try to "win" with the highest or lowest score. There are no right or wrong answers, only alternate ways of handling similar investment problems. The ways that feel best to you will help determine your most comfortable portfolio management style.

When you have completed the questionnaire, read the evaluation and discussion of your responses.

Partner **A**   Partner **B**

1. When all is said and done, people who put their money in long-term investments and seldom change them get the best returns. _____ _____

2. Some experts will tell you when real estate should outperform stocks or when stocks should outperform bonds, and so forth. If I took their advice, and shifted my assets accordingly, I would come out ahead. _____ _____

3. Broker commissions and other "buy and sell" transaction fees usually eat up any profits you might make from shifting your assets. _____ _____

4. Although it's pointless to try to forecast short-term fluctuations in the markets, you can make money by forecasting longer-term business cycles and trends. _____ _____

5. Because your capital gains and losses must be reported to the IRS, keeping track of your "buy and sell" transactions is just too much trouble for the average investor. _____ _____

6. If an investment expert told me what to do and when to do it, I wouldn't mind shifting my assets and handling the paperwork. _____ _____

What's Your Portfolio Management Style? (*concluded*)

	Partner A	Partner B

7. My portfolio is so small that, even if I would get good investment advice for a couple of hundred dollars a year, I couldn't afford to take it. _____ _____

8. No matter how busy I am, I always find time to read the business and financial news. _____ _____

Now transfer your answers to the tally below, and then add them as indicated for yourself and your partner.

Odd-numbered Questions			*Even-numbered Questions*		
Question	Partner A	Partner B	Question	Partner A	Partner B
No. 1	_____	_____	No. 2	_____	_____
3	_____	_____	4	_____	_____
5	_____	_____	6	_____	_____
7	_____	_____	8	_____	_____
Total	_____	_____	Total	_____	_____

Evaluating Your Portfolio Management Style

The questionnaire you have just completed measured several basic attitudes relating to investment management. When these attitudes are applied to real world investment decisions, they form what we call your *portfolio management style*. Here's the way you'll score your answers.

First, add your answers for the even-numbered statements (**2, 4, 6,** and **8**) on the questionnaire and enter that subtotal at the top of page 142. Second, add your answers for the odd-numbered statements (**1, 3, 5,** and **7**) and enter that subtotal below the first. Next, subtract the second subtotal from the first (retaining the minus sign if your second total was larger than the first). Repeat these steps for your partner.

Figure 6–2 shows the scale we use to classify your total portfolio management score according to the many investors we have observed.

The Active Portfolio Manager

If your net score was anything greater than zero, you tend to favor the *active* portfolio management style. You believe that the power of economic and market forecasting will add value to your portfolio, and you are pre-

	Partner A	Partner B
Subtotal for even-numbered items	————	————
subtract (−)		
Subtotal for odd-numbered items	————	————
Net portfolio management score	(+ or −) ————	(+ or −) ————

pared to implement the expert advice you receive. Just how far you're willing to go in pursuit of these beliefs, however, measures just how *active* an active manager you really are. It's worth a closer look to see how the two subcategories of active managers really operate.

FIGURE 6–2
The Basic Portfolio Management Styles

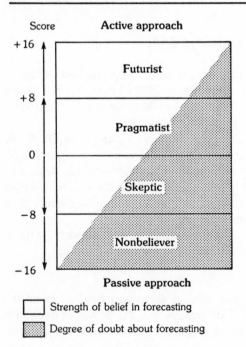

The Futurist.   If your net score was +9 to +16, you believe so strongly in the power of forecasting that you're willing to stake a good deal of money and prestige on what you judge to be good advice. You are willing to seek and pay for the best expertise available and to restructure your portfolio as necessary to implement the recommendations. We call this most zealous of all forecasting true believers, the *Futurist* portfolio manager.

The Pragmatist.   If your net score was 0 to +8, you're a *Pragmatist* portfolio manager. You believe that it's possible to forecast economic events with reasonable accuracy; but, you're not sure that anyone (or any organization) can do it consistently, nor that their advice can always be implemented in a practical or profitable way. Pragmatists tend to make their own judgments about forecasting advice and are hesitant to change their allocations or investments unless they are strongly convinced about the reliability of the suggested advice.

The Passive Portfolio Manager

If your net score was between 0 and −16, you favor the *Passive* portfolio management style. But don't let the name fool you into thinking that this is a lazy person's or a low-return sort of strategy. Many professional money-managers believe, as these people do, that more money is *lost* trying to second-guess the markets than most people *ever* make when their "prognostications" turn out to be true. As with the active approach, the passive style can vary in degree of passivity, depending on the views of the individual managers. Here are the two subcategories of this style as we've observed them.

The Skeptic.   If your net score was between 0 and −8, you tend to doubt that economic forecasting can be done reliably, and you suspect that people who pretend to do so owe their good fortune more to luck than to their skills and methods. This doesn't mean, however, that all *Skeptics* inevitably adopt a "buy and hold" investment strategy for all their vehicles, or that they never check the economic trends and reallocate their resources. Skeptics still know the value of diversification. As their investments achieve rewards at varying rates, Skeptics are willing to restructure their portfolios to keep that diversification within our suggested ranges.

The Nonbelievers.   If your net score was between −9 and −16, you favor the *Nonbeliever's* portfolio management style, which truly espouses the buy-and-hold investment philosophy. You are sure that economic forecasting is, at best, an activity conducted "by the self-deluding as a guide for the misled," and that most financial soothsayers deserve the bad press they eventually get. You *do believe*, however, that a portfolio of well-chosen investments—selected for their fundamental value and held even when the going gets tough—will eventually pay handsome returns to any investor who has the ability (and nerve!) to wait out the markets. In this respect, Nonbelievers think the only forecast that makes sense is the one that reflects, optimistically, "No matter how bad things seem to be right now, they'll eventually get better."

MAKING DECISIONS ABOUT YOUR PERSONAL PROFIT PORTFOLIO

The Taking Stock evaluation depicts variations in approaches to portfolio management. Passive portfolio managers prefer to buy and hold their investments, letting economic nature take its course.

Those people who search for and use economic forecasting information to help them make investment decisions are active portfolio managers. Much of our discussion in this chapter has been directed to them. If you are an active portfolio manager, the following examination of your use of forecasting information can help to enhance your portfolio. Your first step will be to focus on your investor personality.

Forecasting and the Investor Personalities

As we discussed in the Portfolio Management Style Evaluation, not all active portfolio managers are equally active. Even among Futurists and Pragmatists there's room for each investor personality to exert its own strengths and weaknesses on your decisions. Here are some guidelines for each personality type.

Adventurers as Portfolio Managers
Adventurer investors think any market and any system can be beaten—and most are willing to give it a try. There are more Futurist portfolio managers among Adventurers than any other type. They are energetic readers and users of investment journals and newsletters. When they engage professional planners or brokers, they still tend to take an active interest, with frequent questions and suggestions. Commissioned salespeople don't complain, though, because Futurist Adventurers trade frequently. After all, salespeople are paid, whether the trades make money or not.

Futurist Adventurers believe their money should be invested where the action is, and they're willing to switch quickly from one hot item to another. They're never satisfied with the returns they get, which could always have been higher. That fact alone disturbs them.

If anything, Adventurers tend to ask too much from their forecasters. They try to apply the advice of their experts to specific short-term trading. Very few people achieve investment success with that strategy.

Guardians as Portfolio Managers

When Guardians fall into the active part of the management-style scale, they are usually Pragmatists. They tend to be secure only with the longest view of economic trends and cycles. As a result, they make reallocations in their portfolio infrequently. Unfortunately, the accuracy of economic forecasts dwindles as they stretch further into the future. Guardians have difficulty making changes when conditions change.

Guardians are suspicious by nature. Constant change and frequent scandals reinforce their reasons for staying put. Among investor types, Guardians are most likely to measure a forecaster's past predictions against how things actually developed. They want to see whether their advisors' computers are really performing meaningful analyses, or if the forecasts are just an attempt to dazzle with mounds of numbers. They are suspicious, wisely enough, of even the latest thing—computerized forecasting models.

Enthusiasts as Portfolio Managers

Most Enthusiast investors are active portfolio managers in the Futurist mold. They seek information from virtually every source, consulting print and electronic media. Some Enthusiasts carry these impulses too far and fit in with those forecasters who are not necessarily the most astute or responsible (i.e., those who are too often in fashion or currently in the news).

Enthusiasts tend to agree with any firmly stated forecast. Too frequently they change horses merely to be active, instead of taking carefully considered action to improve their position.

Individualists as Portfolio Managers

Active Individualists tend to find and use sophisticated forecasting newsletters and advisors. They often trust the technical expertise and high-tech tools of the trade—computer models, econometrics—more than is warranted. Aggressive Individualists are always battling their frequent temptation to second-guess the experts.

When Individualists act on those decisions, they run the risk of not only wasting the money paid for such services; but, they also end up paying a price for undoing a consistent investment strategy through inconsistent excursions into their own reallocations.

Individualists believe strongly in forecasting. They tend to be more impressed by the more technical approach. Individualists will frequently suspend their own common sense if it seems that their own conclusions are in conflict with an elegant technical solution. Such tendencies make for pleasant mental exercises, but technical models don't make the investment markets run. Individualists should guard against suppressing their intuitive side.

The Straight Arrow as Portfolio Manager

Straight Arrow active investors tend to view economic forecasts as just one more bit of datum in the overall equation of their success. They are open to all sides of a question, which sometimes makes it difficult for them to arrive at a decision in the face of conflicting evidence.

Because of this indecisiveness, Straight Arrows run the risk of delaying their portfolio reallocations or reinvestment choices until the best opportunities pass. Active Straight Arrows also have trouble sticking with one investment strategy for the long term. They tend to shop around for advisors continually, even when the advice they are following is doing the job it should.

Economic Forecasting: How It's Done

You probably have little or no interest in becoming an economic forecaster. Nonetheless, you should know enough about how such forecasts are made to recognize a well-thought out, thoroughly researched forecast when you see it. The following is a brief synopsis on the science and art of financial forecasting.

The Past Is Prologue

Few things stay the way they are forever, whether they are economic guidelines, market timing signals, or just about anything else! Change is a fact of life. Things change at different rates and at different times. Big fundamental changes usually take longer periods to occur.

Accepting the fact of ongoing change will prove very helpful in the art of forecasting. It simply means that, if something is the way it is today because of an event that happened yesterday, it very likely will continue down the same road tomorrow, unless there's a new event that "impacts" it. Or, you could consider it the social sciences' corollary to the law of inertia: An object in motion will tend to stay in motion in the same direction unless affected by some outside force.

This tendency to follow an established track is called a *trend*. Trends are an important and, in many cases, a primary tool used by economic forecasters. This is particularly so for near-term predictions.

Notice in Figure 6–3 there are several trend lines that emerge from historical data. Projecting future events from historical facts by extending the trend lines is called *extrapolation*. Such extrapolations, though, become increasingly inaccurate the further they are extended from the historical data.

FIGURE 6-3
Trend Line Extrapolations: Telling the Future from the Past

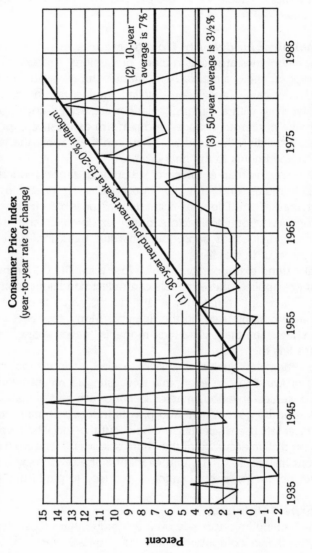

Consumer Price Index
(year-to-year rate of change)

(1) 30-year trend puts next peak at 15-20% inflation!

(2) 10-year average is 7%

(3) 50-year average is 3½%

The actual forecast depends greatly on which method the analyst chooses. Those who look at 50-year cycles think we're headed back to the 0% inflation rates of the 1930s, while those with a shorter perspective see only higher and higher prices. Which forecast do you believe?

Trends are more reliable if they are derived from many facts measured over a longer time.

How Analytical Models Are Constructed

Modeling techniques are used in many professions. Architects prepare models of proposed new projects. Auto manufacturers build mockups of their projected new cars. These very detailed models are far more than fancy toys. By working with a dimensionally correct, scaled-down model, designers can make numerous changes and perform exhaustive experiments without actually building the product. They can then apply the results of their modeling experiments to the final design.

Economic and market forecasters work with similar models, made up of numbers, formulas, and, critically, assumptions. By describing known economic or market conditions as accurately as possible on paper, forecasters then *substitute* hypothetical factors for key existing elements. Thus, they can make predictions about subsequent market behavior, were those same changes to occur in real life.

Unlike trend extrapolations, which lose reliability the further into the future they are applied, these models can reflect conditions many years, even decades, away. Unfortunately they are only as accurate as the data, formulas, and assumptions used by the analysts. Many economists, with tongue firmly in cheek, say that, while their model is "never wrong," the real world sometimes lets them down!

This particular analytical system, called *econometric modeling*, has played a growing role in economic forecasting in recent years. Computer-generated studies of various market scenarios are part of many sophisticated forecasts used by government and private industry. It may seem that econometric forecasts use a scientific method, but the social sciences cannot provide the predictive accuracy of the "hard sciences." As we have emphasized throughout this book, the human element is the predominant factor in economic developments, and it cannot be reduced to pure numbers.

Using Expert Opinions

In contrast, many investors rely on a technique that utilizes the subtlest and most authoritative computer of all—the human brain. "Expert opinion" provides a *qualitative* assessment of the future, as opposed to the *quantitative* approach of econometricians.

Experts make forecasts in a variety of ways. At times they deal with responses to formal surveys conducted by research firms. Some experts prefer to analyze trends, current events, and econometric models prepared by others, making effective use of the information produced by "number mills."

Experts provide the indispensable human link in interpreting forecast information.

Changing Forecasts in a Changing World
There is some truth to the argument that an almost "self-fulfilling prophecy" is inherent in the forecasts made by some prominent economists or institutions, such as federal agencies. As an example, if the U.S. Labor Department and a number of respected private economists were to predict a rise in the level of employment (i.e., a drop in the unemployment rate), the business community might respond optimistically by hiring more workers. Because economics is so influenced by human attitudes and emotions, it is easy to see how such forecasts can affect the very events they try to predict.

Of course, even the most detailed mathematical model or the most astute forecaster will be wrong. Economic forecasts must take into account uncontrollable, unanticipated factors. The usefulness of such forecasts is connected to the speed with which they can be revised. Of course, *what you do* with the forecast information is often as important as the forecast itself.

Become Your Own Forecaster
You may want to make your own economic forecasts, depending largely on your own interest and the time you have to devote to the project. You can avail yourself of numerous books and magazines devoted to various schools of thought on investing; but, before you charge into the field on your own, a note of caution.

While some individuals have been successful as independent forecasters, our own experience shows that results are usually better if the forecasting is conducted in a group atmosphere. Perhaps the best way to show you what we mean is to briefly explain how we do that job ourselves.

Gather the Data and Organize Your Facts. Biographer James Boswell once observed, "Knowledge is of two kinds: we know a subject ourselves, or we know where we can find information on it." His observation is particularly applicable to economic forecasting. This multidisciplinary research generates mounds of raw data that need to be processed. The further removed you get from raw statistical data, the more you rely on other experts to synthesize and decode this information for you; but, their opinion of what is important may not be the same as yours.

We have found it essential to spend many thousands of dollars annually to subscribe to the multitude of necessary statistical and quantitative information sources (the raw data). But that's only part of our information-gathering expense. Our company and our employees spend many more thousands of dollars traveling to meet with other money management experts, attend professional conferences, and otherwise keep abreast of developments in the investment field.

Be Prepared to Pay For the Help You Need.   We are convinced that a group of highly skilled, well-qualified, experienced analysts can reach better decisions than one individual working alone. We have committed significant resources in salaries and benefits to attract and keep the cream of the crop in market analysts. But economic and organizational inducements are not the only consideration. There are also subtle psychological rewards that such individuals need.

Professionals, relying on brainpower and judgment to earn their living, must be given room to learn, grow, make mistakes, and change their minds. If you want to use the services, perspectives, and analyses of similar professionals, you have to be prepared to meet both their financial and psychological needs. In the next chapter we provide guidelines for selecting and working with investment professionals.

WRAPPING UP

In this chapter you've discovered what your portfolio management style is and that your portfolio can be custom-designed to suit your temperament. If you are a passive manager, you will follow a fixed-mix method that will force you to practice a discipline of sound investment principles without requiring excessive involvement. If you are an active manager, you have learned a variety of hands-on approaches you might pursue.

It is fitting in this chapter on forecasting you should once again be reminded that it is people, not cold, unemotional numbers, that make the real difference in the economy.

You have seen that, no matter how thoroughly something is researched, you simply cannot know the future with certainty. As a result, it is important for you to diversify your investment portfolio over the five asset classes to minimize the risk of disaster while still retaining the potential for good returns.

You have been reminded that all investors "forecast" whenever they make a financial decision. You've learned that:

1. Passive portfolio managers prefer to make one forecast only—when they initially allocate their resources. They seldom, if ever, change their allocations, or their individual investment vehicles. They favor the buy-and-hold strategy for their investments.

Ode to the Half-Brained Investor

For years, scientists have known that the human brain—like the earth itself—is divided into two hemispheres, each with its own characteristics and functions. The brain's left side (which controls the right side of the body) seems to be the seat of linguistic, rational, intellectual, and deductive processes—in short, our quantitative and analytical capability. The brain's right side, however, is the location of musical, artistic, intuitive, imaginative, and inductive processes—all those things we usually regard as the opposite of, and extraneous to, logical activities.

Which side should you develop as an active portfolio manager? If history is any guide, *both* are needed if you hope to match (let alone beat) the markets in which you have invested. As an anonymous poet once wrote:

Predicting the future with half of your brain
Is like washing pure gold dust right down the drain.
Figures and tables and graphs—they are good.
And computers much better than knocking on wood.
But man minus feeling is like day without night:
With just numbers behind you, you *won't* get it right!

2. Active portfolio managers use economic forecasts both to avoid *negative* returns and to seek higher returns by anticipating market changes.

The primary concern for either type of portfolio manager is to choose the strategy that will best meet their financial goals. Obviously, some investors have more of a need for reliable forecasting information than others. Adventurers and Enthusiasts tend to seek more aggressive growth than the norm, so they have a greater need for forecasting acumen.

You had a glance at how economic forecasts are made. With a caveat, we gave you some insight to help you decide if you'd rather be your own forecaster, or if you'd prefer to find advisors to help you make your investment decisions.

In the next chapter we cover how to evaluate investment advisors and what you should know before taking anyone's advice. Remember, it is most important that your advisor fits your style and personality. Don't try to be something you are not for the sake of following a recommended advisor. We also take a look at the world of mutual funds. Taking charge of your financial life means making informed decisions about how to best employ your resources to achieve your goals.

CHAPTER 7

SELECTING PROFESSIONAL
MANAGEMENT FOR YOUR
INVESTMENTS

THE NEED TO TAKE CHARGE OF
YOUR FINANCIAL AFFAIRS

You have learned a great deal so far about the forces that affect the investment markets. You found that the *Business Cycle* has very real meaning to you and your family. What happens in the United States and international economy is not just grist for the financial press and a game for rich Wall Street investors; it directly affects *your* standard of living. You can simply accept your financial condition as is, governed by the vagaries of the economy, or you can exert positive influence over your financial well-being by taking charge.

Being responsible for the state of your financial life is not unlike taking care of your physical health. In recent years, a great deal of attention has focused on physical fitness and health. As a result, people are taking charge of their physical well-being with increasing frequency. To live a long and fulfilling life, you have to do what you can to stay healthy and fit; no one can do it for you. If you postpone dealing with your physical well-being until it becomes necessary to see a doctor, it could be too late.

Preventive medicine is the byword in modern health care. Similarly, preventive financial care plays an important role in assuring you a rewarding life. That care starts as soon as you begin to take control of your own financial affairs. You'd never expect to be guided through a diet and exercise program without your participation. After all, for you to get the benefit, you have to do the work, "no pain, no gain."

In the same way, no one can help put your financial house in order without your effort. You have already begun to practice preventive financial

152

care by using this book. You'll be well on your way to attaining financial well-being by putting what you've learned here into practice.

Taking charge may seem difficult at first. The investment world is increasingly complex and in constant flux. It can, indeed, seem overwhelming. But, rest assured, our approach works! The five basic asset classes will provide you with the diversification necessary to minimize the volatility of your investments, while affording you the opportunity of seeing those assets grow.

By now you should recognize that, for investments to fit into your world, you have to know where you are (your financial physique), and who you are (your investor personality). You then have to define your goals in *specific* terms.[1] And you have to select suitable investment vehicles that will help you reach your desired goals within your stated time frame. Then you have to elect a portfolio management style that suits you, be it a "passive" fixed-mix or an "active" dynamic-mix approach.

In this chapter you're going to learn how to select a professional to help you manage your own investments, or to manage them for you. You'll also read about a booming part of the investment industry that may provide the single best method for you to execute what you've learned in these pages. You won't have to become an analyst, researching 50,000 domestic stocks, thousands of bond issues, thousands of foreign stocks and bonds, or even hundreds of real estate projects. But, you can have the benefit of such analyses by using outside advisors or by investing through *mutual funds*. Mutual funds are run by professional money managers who decide what and when to hold, buy, or sell to best meet the investment objectives of their funds.

FORECASTING SHOULD FIT YOUR NEEDS

Below are our observations on how investors of any type can acquire and put to use the kind of forecasting that is most appropriate for their needs.

Let Your Advisor Know Your Biases

Many people think they can't make worthwhile forecasts if they are prejudiced by a specific investment philosophy. As you've seen through the evaluation of your own investor personality and portfolio management style, these biases are with you, whether you attempt to disguise them or not. We

---

[1] Of course, all your goals will not be financial; but, achieving your financial goals can bring you a long way toward realizing the nonfinancial objectives in your life as well.

recommend that you make your philosophy an integral part of the formal forecasting process.

At BB&K we strongly believe in the value of diversification, risk assessment and control, and an active portfolio management style. Our forecasting effort takes each of these elements into consideration. By recognizing and dealing with our biases, our investment performance is enhanced. Total objectivity is impossible. Everyone copes with life from a certain unique perspective. Just as you have learned to work with, not against, your particular investor personality, so should your forecasting endeavors increase your comfort level, not add additional stress.

Use Multiple Strategies

There is no single best approach to forecasting. In fact, it's important to avoid overreliance on any one tool. At BB&K we use three basic technical and qualitative strategies in our economic forecasting.

First, we work out potential economic scenarios for the next four years. We examine how the different investment markets have reacted to similar environments in the past. We then project how they may react in the future. We estimate the probability of each scenario actually happening.

Next we research the fundamental value of various asset classes. We compute the anticipated yields for representative investment vehicles in each class. Finally, we calculate after-tax returns based on these yield projections. These are adjusted for the probability of realizing each scenario. We then reallocate our clients' assets in accord with our findings.

Our conclusions are often different from what we expected at the beginning of the process. Just as often, we reach our final decisions in opposition to what our computers and competitive forecasters recommend. By designing and implementing this consistent procedure, we have added a significant premium over the normal market rate of return that might have been expected.

This may sound a bit overwhelming for you to undertake yourself. Don't worry. That's both understandable and common. We do this for a living. The assets we manage for other people are substantial and it's worth our time and effort as *money-makers* to go to this detail.

If you have the curiosity, time, and drive to pursue the management of your assets by yourself, it would be foolish to pay someone to do it. But you may decide that your time is better spent increasing *your own money-making* skills. This will enhance the income you receive in your chosen profession. "Cross-training" to a very specialized and difficult career just to eke out an extra percentage point or two from your investments may not be a good investment decision. There *is* an alternative, though. That is the subject of the balance of this chapter.

FINDING A GOOD FORECASTER: TRAITS TO LOOK FOR

As we've indicated earlier, forecasting is as much an art as it is a science. Better forecasters allow for an intuitive element in their analyses. To find a forecaster with whom you feel comfortable, you will have to consider more than background and credentials. Through our years as professional money managers we have identified the characteristics that would help qualify a good forecaster. You should look for these traits when seeking such assistance with your investment decisions.

1. No Substitute for Experience

A degreed, seasoned economist is not necessarily the right person to rely on for stock market forecasts. Although appropriate academic credentials are important to consider, they certainly are not enough. Most successful forecasting organizations assemble teams of specialists from many fields. Their forecasts, thus, are supported with input from a number of disciplines; ranging from economics and finance to liberal arts.

More significant than academic background and organizational structure is the *experience* of individual forecasters. Look for actual application in the markets they analyze. Practical experience in the markets is necessary to ensure that the forecaster is aware of the many psychological, political, and economic factors, the regulations and other real-world ingredients that affect the way things are done. Your forecaster must be familiar with the more subtle naunces that distinguish each market, which are often overlooked in purely quantitative analyses.

Experience is so very important that you should not rely on forecasts from people or institutions who have not weathered at least one complete Business Cycle, which takes about three to six years, at a minimum.

2. Forecasts Should Come from More Than Just Number-Crunching

A forecaster should have a balanced point of view. This "whole-brained" way of looking at the world takes into consideration the indefinable human element that distinguishes useful forecasts from simplistic, numerical extrapolations of trends. Your advisor should know when to look past the quantitative data and rely on *qualitative* factors. As you know by now, instinct and intuition play an important part in a good forecaster's analyses.

As we mentioned earlier, most forecasting organizations work with a team concept. If you decide to put together your own advisory team, one member should be a *generalist*, familiar with history, psychology, politics, and other elements that make economics a *social* science.

Your personal advisors should understand that investing is a goal-related activity. You aren't just looking for mathematical maximization of returns but a way to achieve your goals within your comfort zone of risk and uncertainty. Some investors are interested primarily in growth, while others seek current income. The forecasts and advice you use must address *your needs*.

3.   Good Advisors Learn from Their Mistakes

The most consistently high-quality forecasts, logically enough, come from people who make them for a living. Full-time forecasters are dedicated to research and to the development of their skills. They also take the time to analyze their own mistakes. The ability to acknowledge and learn from mistakes is a critically important trait.

Your advisors should have enough seasoning to not only monitor the economic and market landscape but also to measure the *effectiveness* of their own advice. Making mistakes isn't bad. Failing to acknowledge and profit from them is.

4.   Make Sure Your Advisor Is in Sync with You

We've been arguing that nonquantifiable factors, such as human judgment and personal perspective, make a big difference in forecasting. For you to make the best use of independent advisors, you should make sure they think and feel the same way you do about investments. Don't force yourself to accept the advice of someone who has a good reputation or has been referred to you by friends. What works for someone else may not work for you.

For example, an Enthusiast investor would probably have trouble following the advice of a forecaster who is not well known. Similarly, Adventurers might have difficulty with a forecaster whose advice is directed at pension funds and other risk-averse institutional investors. Adventurers would feel equally uncomfortable with advisors who deal only in very long-term projections.

This doesn't mean there is a different reality for each investor personality. Individual investors do not necessarily share the same concerns about risk and return contingencies, although all investors consider such matters important. You should find those advisors who share your beliefs.

5. Finding an Expert Who Is Right for You

We have already discussed a mechanical approach that portfolio managers can take. You adopt a fixed reallocation scheme based on the increasing and decreasing values of the various asset classes in your portfolio. With this method, you periodically realign your portfolio to your targeted allocation levels by selling a portion of assets that have appreciated. You then invest the proceeds from your sales in other, out-of-favor asset classes.

If you decide you do not want to take that approach, yet the idea of becoming a grass roots forecaster doesn't appeal to you, either, then, as an alternative, buy the best forecasting advice you can and follow it. The advice may be from an individual advisor, such as a broker or financial planner. Or, more likely, it will come from one or more of the many newsletters published specifically for this purpose. The following is a brief survey of the kinds of information and services that are available.

Newspapers and Magazines

Unfortunately, periodicals that profess to give forecasts and other useful investment advice usually provide neither. The articles are generally written by financial journalists, not by practicing investment managers. Such publications tend to give more space to popular issues, rather than to fundamental portfolio management concerns. Even worse, they offer a variety of viewpoints and feature various "experts" at different times.

For instance, when famous investment advisors are asked about their views on recommended allocation strategies in one issue of a magazine, they are rarely asked to update their advice at a later date. As a result, they can seldom correct their mistakes or offer new ways to implement their recommended strategies in differing economic environments. Even articles by acknowledged leaders in the field tend to be too general or, conversely, focused too narrowly on a single field of interest. We're intimately familiar with this problem, having contributed our share over the years!

What you need, and should be seeking, is a *consistent* perspective. A diversity of forecasts will compound your forecasting problems. What it boils down to is this: We think you should read periodicals like *The Wall Street Journal, Fortune, Business Week*, and *Barron's* (to name only a few) for their news and objective data. But we think it's unwise for you to rely on their articles for reallocation advice.

Brokerage and Bank Advice

Brokerage firms and banks, for the most part, sell financial products, rather than advice. Although many publish economic newsletters, they typically do so as promotion or as a sideline to their product-marketing efforts. And just as typically, the actions they recommend are usually satisfied by one or more of the various products or services they sell.

Some of these publications are interesting, but few are really worth the fees charged for them. Many newsletter-type advisories are offered free by brokers and banks. Read them for the factual information, but don't expect to get top-flight objective investment advice from them. Remember that old Wall Street adage about pricing: "If it's free, that's probably the right price for the advice."

Government Publications

The Government Printing Office generates hundreds of books and pamphlets on subjects related to economics. We have found that the only government publications that are really useful for our economic research are the Commerce Department's *Business Conditions Digest* and the *Federal Reserve Bulletin*. They contain important statistical information, although they may be too technical for many investors.

Investment Advisory Newsletters

Our advice for most active portfolio managers is to subscribe to an advisory newsletter published *specifically* to help multiasset portfolio managers. They range in price from $40 to $1,000 per year. From the variety, price, coverage, and perspective of what's published, there is bound to be at least one advisory newsletter that fits both your investor personality and your economic circumstances.

BB&K publishes a monthly newsletter, *Economic Analysis and Investment Outlook*. In it we present our current economic outlook and asset allocation guidelines. For a sample issue and subscription information, write us at 2755 Campus Drive, San Mateo, California 94403.

Investment Services

You can combine advice and management by putting your assets with a money management service. Full-service brokers often perform this management task for clients. They are usually compensated by a portion of the commissions charged on each transaction. There is a conflict of interest inherent in this arrangement, though, since the manager is compensated for the number of transactions made, not for the outcome achieved.

Some financial planners, who receive a commission from products they sell, might also find it difficult to retain their objectivity. We certainly do not mean to condemn either brokers or financial planners. You should, however, understand how fees are assessed and how your money manager is paid.

Mutual fund switching services are one popular option for many investors. These firms not only give you advice but actually will shift assets for you. They will move your assets among growth, bond, money market, precious metals, or other funds, depending on their expectations. Naturally, they assess a fee for this service.

MUTUAL FUNDS

Mutual funds came on the scene in 1924, in Boston. In the 1970s the industry experienced dramatic growth as a result of the development of money market funds. The dramatic growth continued into the mid-1980s with the introduction of long- and short-term, tax-free municipal bond funds, GNMA funds, Treasury bond funds, and corporate high-yield bond funds. In just one decade, from 1977 to 1987, the number of funds more than quintupled, from 427 in 1977 to 2,324 at the end of 1987.[2] In 1986 the sales of stock, bond, and income funds rose sharply. The assets and number of accounts under mutual fund management hit new highs. Consumers redirected resources from savings and other investments into mutual funds. The financial market was favorable, and the mutual fund industry responded with innovation and effective marketing. But, in October of 1987, the stock market took a dramatic turn. Mutual fund sales reacted quickly to the changed market climate.

The chart[3] of Table 7–1 shows the escalation in the number of mutual funds of all kinds and the impact of the introduction of money market and short-term municipal bond funds.

What Are Mutual Funds?

Mutual funds are investment companies that pool the funds of many investors to make sizable purchases of investment vehicles. Since 1940 the industry has been closely regulated by federal (and state) legislation, designed to prevent self-dealing and other conflicts of interest, to maintain the integrity of fund assets, and to protect its shareholders from paying excessive fees and charges. The federal and state laws are meant to ensure that mutual

---

[2] *1988 Mutual Fund Fact Book: Industry Trends and Statistics for 1987* (Washington, D.C.: Investment Company Institute, 1988).

[3] This chart and much of the information about the history, description, and regulations in the mutual fund industry come from the *1988 Mutual Fund Fact Book.* Used with permission.

TABLE 7–1
Mutual Fund Growth

Year	Total Number of Funds	Number of Stock, Bond, and Income Funds	Number of Money Market and Short-term Municipal Bond Funds
1940	68	68	none
1950	98	98	none
1960	161	161	none
1970	361	361	none
1975	426	390	36
1980	564	458	106
1981	665	486	179
1982	857	539	318
1983	1,026	653	373
1984	1,246	820	426
1985	1,531	1,071	460
1986	1,843	1,356	487
1987	2,324	1,781	543

funds are operated and managed in the interests of their shareholders. Mutual fund companies must register with the United States Securities and Exchange Commission and must file full information regarding each fund. The activities of investment managers are limited by law. The SEC also limits the types of advertising that a mutual fund can use. As with all securities, mutual fund sales are subject to antifraud provisions.

Every mutual fund is required to provide you with a prospectus detailing the fund's operations, its history, performance record, fee structure, services, and the background on its management team. It's important to read this information carefully *before* investing. Not all funds are created equal. If you take the time at the start to look beyond the sales hype, you may preclude a big mistake.

Funds are sold to the public in two basic ways. Many are sold through a salesforce, including brokers, financial planners, and insurance agents, who are recompensed through a sales commission included in the price of shares (called a *load fund*) or through a distribution fee paid by the fund, or in both ways. Others sell directly through advertising and direct response, with little or no sales commission, although, in some cases, the fund's directors may authorize use of a small percentage of the fund's assets to support sales efforts. Open-end mutual funds are required by law to redeem outstanding shares at their current net asset value each day, regardless of their sales method.

Historically, mutual funds have invested in common stock; but, with the industry's explosive growth in recent years, funds now invest in everything, including U.S. common stocks, bonds, international securities, options, futures, gold, money market instruments, real estate, and more. Mutual fund companies have two basic operating structures: "open end" and "closed end."

Open-End Funds

The investment company of an open-end fund offers shares to the public continuously. Investors buy shares at the fund's *net asset value (NAV)*, which equals the amount of all the fund's holdings minus its liabilities, divided by the number of outstanding shares.

If the mutual fund is a *load* fund, it assesses a percentage of your investment as a sales charge. For example, if there is an 8 percent load charge and you invest $1,000, you actually buy $920 of the stock in the fund. The 8 percent load charge is paid to the salesperson or organization who sold the shares to the fund.

No-load funds have gained wide popularity among investors. Because they do not assess any *front-end load* charge, your full investment is put to work in the fund's asset pool. Your profit or loss depends solely on how well the fund's assets perform. If the fund's manager does a good job, then the shares purchased by the fund appreciate, and the NAV of the fund increases. When you sell your shares in the fund, you make or lose money, depending on how well the fund's manager performed.

But the no-load concept has become clouded somewhat in recent years, because mutual funds have devised a number of other ways to charge fees. One of the most common is to impose a fee when you sell your shares in the fund, tied to how long you held the fund. The longer the holding period, the lower the redemption fee.

Load funds face substantial competition from a product which, essentially, charges no front-end fees. Why would someone buy a load fund? Since most no-load funds are marketed through the mails, you never get to meet a salesperson who can answer your questions and service your account; nor would one be assigned to you. And, in all likelihood, each time you phoned the fund, someone else would take the call. Such impersonal arrangements are not conducive to building relationships. Many investors prefer to conduct business through a broker with whom they've developed a good working affiliation. The fee, in such cases, is offset by the convenience of having someone they trust handle any problems that may arise.

Purveyors of load funds contend that the funds will be less susceptible to wide swings in the assets under management. They argue that, if the asset base is more stable, it redounds to the benefit of the fund's investors.[4] Second, they claim that the very existence of a professional salesforce will keep money flowing into the fund more steadily than will the direct mail and magazine advertising, which are relied on by no-loads.

While the arguments seem logical, there is no evidence that load funds outperform no-load funds. Either the fear of massive redemptions does not adversely affect the management of no-load funds or there are enough other factors impacting on total performance that it becomes a negligible factor.

Before buying a fund you should carefully check a fund's *expense ratio* (i.e., the ratio between a fund's assets and the annual operating expenses incurred for managing them). This often overlooked measure is certainly not the most critical element in selecting a fund, but, nonetheless, it's an important point to consider. These annual operating expenses are deducted from the fund's investment income (e.g., dividends and interest).

Beyond load charges (which may range from 4 percent to 8.5 percent) and redemption fees, mutual fund companies incur a number of annual operating costs. The money manager (or investment advisor) is paid a fee for managing the fund and selecting its portfolio, usually about one half of 1 percent of the total value of assets managed, annually. Other fund operating expenses are usually in the same range, for a total of about 1 percent per year for all the fund's costs of operations.[5] Some funds use a predetermined percentage of fund assets to help cover these costs. Some funds may charge an annual fee of 1 percent or so.

You can find a fund or group of funds to satisfy virtually any type of financial service you desire. Like most businesses, mutual fund companies want to attract new clients and retain current customers. They are continually offering shareholders new and varied services and features, many of which have come about in response to customer need, new legislation, or

---

[4] A load fund's asset base would be less volatile because the front-end load discourages impulsive short-term switching (not a good idea for an amateur investor, anyway).

[5] The fund's operating costs include fees to the investment manager for handling the assets, to the custodian agent who holds the shares, to the transfer agent who keeps track of shareholder records, and to payments to others for a variety of services and housekeeping chores, including the fund accountant, attorneys, auditors, and the board of directors. Charges also cover insurance and brokerage costs for buying and selling. Some funds charge these costs as "12b-1" fees, named after the 1980 SEC rule that permits them. The 12b-1 charges should be detailed in the fund's prospectus.

competition from other funds, as well as from other segments of the financial industry.

Several investment management firms offer a number of mutual funds, known as *families*, which provide added benefits to shareholders. Some of these organizations offer such a broad range of funds that investors can easily achieve diversification among the five asset classes within one family of funds.

While legal regulations require that you complete and sign forms to open an account, most funds allow investors to conduct further business by telephone. Fund groups typically allow their shareholders to switch between different funds in the family by telephone. Even groups selling load funds usually offer substantial discounts on the load fees for shareholders who want to switch between funds within the same family.

Not only can you switch between funds by phone but most funds also allow you to redeem your fund shares by telephone. Most money market funds also offer check-writing privileges to their shareholders, with the minimum amount as low as $100.

Other services offered by mutual fund companies include: special IRA accounts, which usually require a smaller minimum amount than for other investments; automatic investment programs, which routinely deduct prearranged sums from your bank account to add to your investment fund; and fixed (or variable) remittances to be made from the fund on a regular basis.

Closed-End Funds
A closed-end mutual fund has a fixed number of outstanding shares. Rather than continuously offering new shares to the public at its net asset value, as open-end funds do, closed-end funds raise money for a set time period. The fund is then closed to new money. The shares of a closed-end fund then trade in the after-market,[6] just like the shares of any common stock. Their price is determined by supply and demand in the marketplace, rather than by an objectively set net asset value. Most closed-end funds sell at a discount to their NAV. However, some funds occasionally sell at premiums, when their investment specialty is in vogue.

For example, ASA is a closed-end fund that invests in South African gold shares. When gold fever is running high, as it was in the late 1970s, ASA would sell at substantial premiums over its net asset value. When inflation turns down, as it did in the early 1980s, ASA would then sell at a discount.

---

[6] *After-market* refers to trading on all exchanges or OTC.

You purchase a closed-end fund through a broker, just like stock, and you pay a commission to buy or sell. Many closed-end funds are listed on the major exchanges; others are traded on the OTC market.

Proponents of closed-end funds claim that, since the managers do not have to worry about fluctuating money under management, they can concentrate their efforts on making the best use of the set sum they have. They argue that the constant fear of redemptions hanging over an open-end fund inhibits performance.

Statistics do not bear out the argument that closed-end funds will perform better, though. In fact, there are good and bad performing open-end and closed-end funds, load and no-load. A fund's structure is not a very good indicator of its future performance.

The fact that most closed-end funds sell at discounts to their NAV attracts value-oriented investors, who are lured by the opportunity of buying something that is demonstrably undervalued. There is always the chance the fund will move from a discount to a premium, without a substantial change in the market as a whole. Such value-oriented investors buy when funds trade at discounts and sell when they move to premiums.

Categories of Mutual Funds

Table 7–2 describes the 22 categories of mutual funds as defined by the Investment Company Institute, and it shows the median purchase amount for the particular category of fund. The number of mutual funds is noted in the left column. At the far right, the source of sales is given as a percentage of total sales, either through direct marketing (no-load) or through a salesperson (load).[7]

Cash and Equivalents: Money Market Mutual Funds
It wasn't until the 1970s that average consumers became concerned about protecting the purchasing power of their money. The inflationary surge in those years demonstrated that the passbook savings route taken by most savers was a losing proposition. At that time, the maximum interest rate that banks and thrift institutions could charge was fixed by law. Interest of 5.25 percent for banks and 5.5 percent for thrift accounts was acceptable when inflation was virtually nonexistent. But, when inflation began to run into double-digit numbers, consumers demanded an alternative.

---

[7] Money market and limited maturity municipals offer liquidity, safety, and modest returns. Bond and income funds offer higher returns, somewhat greater risk. Equity funds offer higher returns, longer-term but high risk for short-term investment.

TABLE 7–2
Mutual Fund Types

Mutual fund types:
As of 12/31/87 there were:
  2,324 mutual funds in 22 categories;
  54.5 million accounts;
  $769.9 billion assets
  ($180.7 equity funds;
   $273.2 bond and income funds;
   $254.7 money market mutual funds
   $ 61.4 short-term municipal bonds).

Categories of mutual funds:

No.	Fund Type; Description	Source of Sale Sales-force (%)	Source of Sale Direct Mktg. (%)
186	**Aggressive growth funds (equity).** (Goal: maximum capital gains.) Some invest in nonmainstream stocks (e.g., new industries or companies, or those out of favor). May use specialized techniques, such as option underwriting. High risks; potentially great reward. (Median purchase amount: $1,300.)	35.8	64.2
308	**Growth funds (equity).** (Goal: growth through capital gains.) Invest in common stock of more settled companies. (Median purchase amount: $830.)	64.7	35.2
188	**Growth and income funds (equity).** (Goal: dividends.) Invest mainly in common stock of companies with longer track record, expectation of higher share value, and solid record of paying dividends. (Median purchase amount: $730.)	60.3	39.7
22	**Precious metals funds (equity).** (Goal: diversification.) Invest in stocks of gold mining and other precious metals companies. (Median purchase amount: $830.)	40.2	59.8
47	**International funds (equity).** (Goal: diversification.) Invest in securities of foreign companies. (Median purchase amount: $830.)	47.6	52.4
34	**Global equity funds (equity).** (Goal: diversification.) Invest in stocks of both U.S. and foreign companies.	98.4	1.6

TABLE 7–2 (*continued*)

		Source of Sale	
No.	**Fund Type;** Description	*Sales-force (%)*	*Direct Mktg. (%)*
28	**Flexible portfolio funds (bond and income).** (Goal: diversification.) Invest in common stocks, bonds, money market securities, and other types of debt securities. May hold up to 100% of any one of these types of securities or any combination. Change easily.	91.8	8.2
31	**Balanced funds (bond and income).** (Goals: conservation of investors' principal; current income; increase both principal and income.) Own a mixture of bonds, preferred stocks, and common stocks. (Median purchase amount: $730.)	66.7	33.3
43	**Income equity funds (equity).** (Goal: dividends.) Invest in stocks of companies with good dividend-paying records.	47.0	53.0
88	**Income mixed funds (bond and income).** (Goal: high level of current income.) Invest in common stock of companies with good dividend-paying records, often including corporate and government bonds as part of the portfolio. (Median purchase amount: $1,100.)	80.9	19.1
88	**Income bond funds (bond and income).** (Goal: generation of income.) Invest in a combination of government and corporate bonds.	73.1	26.9
19	**Option/income funds (equity).** (Goal: high current return.) Invest in dividend-paying common stocks on which call options are traded on national securities exchanges. Current return generally consists of dividends, premiums from call options, net short-term gains from sales of portfolio securities on exercises of options or otherwise, and any profits from closing purchase transactions. (Median purchase amount: $1,100.)	85.1	14.9
148	**U.S. Government income funds (bond and income).** (Goal: safety.) Invest in a variety of government securities: U.S. Treasury bonds, federally guaranteed mortgage-backed securities, and other government issues. (Median purchase amount: $730.)	96.1	3.9

TABLE 7–2 (*continued*)

		Source of Sale	
No.	**Fund Type;** Description	*Sales-force (%)*	*Direct Mktg. (%)*
55	**GNMA or Ginnie Mae funds (bond and income).** (Government National Mortgage Assoc.) (Goal: safety.) Invest in government-backed mortgage securities for majority of portfolio. (Median purchase amount: $1,200.)	74.6	25.4
16	**Global bond funds (bond and income).** (Goal: diversification.) Invest in bonds issued by companies or countries worldwide, including United States.	69.3%	30.7
42	**Corporate bond funds (bond and income).** (Goal: high level of income.) Buy bonds of corporations for majority of fund's portfolio, balance in U.S. Treasury and other government entities' bonds. (Median purchase amount: $1,100.)	83.2	16.8
70	**High-yield bond funds (bond and income).** (Goal: high yield.) Invest in corporate bond funds mostly rated below investment grade. Higher yield potential; greater degree of risk.	72.9	27.1
150	**Long-term municipal bond funds (bond and income).** (Goal: tax saving.) Invest in bonds issued by local governments (cities and states) to build schools, highways, libraries, etc. Income earned is usually federally tax-exempt. (Median purchase amount: $1,600.)	57.6	42.4
218	**Long-term state municipal bond funds (bond and income).** (Goal: tax saving.) Same as above, predominantly in municipal bonds which are exempt from federal income tax as well as exempt from state taxes for residents of the state specified.	67.0	33.0
112	**Short-term national municipal bond funds (bond and income).** (Goal: tax saving.) Invest in municipal securities with relatively short maturities, also known as *tax-exempt money market funds.*	n. a.	n. a.
42	**Short-term state municipal bond funds (bond and income).** (Goal: tax saving.) Invest in only one state's	n.a.	n.a.

TABLE 7-2 (concluded)

| | | Source of Sale | |
		Sales-force (%)	Direct Mktg. (%)
No.	**Fund Type;** Description		
	municipal securities with relatively short maturities. Exempt from state taxes for residents of that state.		
389	**Money market mutual funds.** (Goal: safety, stability.) Invest in short-term securities sold in the money market (e.g., Treasury bills, certificates of deposit of large banks, and commercial paper—short-term IOUs of large U.S. corporations). (Median purchase amount: $970.)	n.a.	n.a.
	Note: There are three broad types of money market funds offering shares: (1) general purpose and (2) broker.dealer funds sell to both individuals and institutions (individuals represent about 75% of the fund's assets), and (3) institutional funds concentrate on institutional investors, such as businesses and bank trust departments with fewer funds and larger amounts to invest.		
	Broker/dealer: 45%, $103.3 billion; General purpose: 28%, $64.3 billion; Institutional: 27%, $61.7 billion		

Note: n.a. means not available.

The response to the new need was the creation of money market funds (see Table 7-1). These funds pool money from many investors to purchase money market instruments that otherwise would be outside the range and experience of most people. For example, money market funds can buy the highest-paying CDs, which require deposits of $100,000 or more. Or they buy other instruments, such as commercial paper, banker's acceptances, or repurchase agreements, which are traded in such large size or in such very specialized markets that they are beyond the scope of the average consumer.

When you buy a money market fund you are buying shares of the pool of assets under management. Each share is priced at $1. With $1,000 you buy 1,000 shares. When interest is credited to your account, it is in additional $1 shares. Most funds accrue interest daily and credit it monthly. Just as the balance of your savings account will not go below your original sum unless you withdraw funds, neither will the balance of your money market account decrease.

The money market fund revolution has made it possible for small investors to move beyond passbook savings accounts and achieve returns comparable to what has been available only to a select and wealthy few. Actually, you will not receive exactly the same return as those who invest directly in these instruments, because you will have to compensate the professional manager who selects and monitors the investments. Money market funds do not charge fees to buy or sell. Their investment management fees are assessed on the total assets under management and are, typically, quite modest.

Operating expenses vary widely, however. These should be considered when you evaluate different money market funds. An important advantage of money market funds is their ability to compound your return. But, the higher the expense ratio,[8] the more you are paying for management, which leaves you less in the pool to be compounded.

In summary, money market funds offer many advantages for the average investor. They are very liquid; your shares can be redeemed by writing a check or phoning in your request. They offer you the chance to buy sophisticated instruments that you couldn't or wouldn't want to buy yourself. Since their portfolios are diversified, you have much less risk than if you were dependent on a single issuer. For example, if you bought $20,000 in commercial paper issued by a private corporation and that company then defaulted (or had financial difficulties), you could lose your entire investment. However, if you had purchased a fund, the default of a single issuer would only affect 1 percent or 2 percent of the total portfolio, so your proportionate risk is considerably lessened.

Following all the various complications and fluctuations of the money markets is a full-time job in itself. A money market fund with a good track record affords you professional management at a very low average cost. And, keeping track of the value of your investment is as easy as keeping track of your passbook balance. All shares are priced at $1.

This doesn't mean that there are no disadvantages. When interest rates fell in the 1980s, many investors pulled out of the funds and reverted to savings accounts. In an effort to hold their shareholders, some of these funds elected a risky strategy: They extended the average maturity of their portfolio. In other words, instead of buying only vehicles with maturities of one year or less, they bought notes with maturities of as much as five years.[9] This tactic enabled the funds to earn a higher interest rate for their

---

[8] This is the ratio between a fund's assets and the expenses involved in managing them.
[9] The longer the maturity, as a rule, the higher the yield, but the higher the risk as well.

shareholders; but, at the same time, it exposed the funds to additional risk if interest rates were to rise.

One of the main advantages of a money market fund is supposed to be that, when rates go up, so will the rates paid by the fund, because the short-term instruments in the fund's portfolio will mature. When new instruments are purchased to replace the maturing ones, it will be at higher rates. Hence, the yield of the fund will fluctuate with market interest rates.

But, if the fund buys longer-term vehicles, it will not rise and fall in tandem with market rates quite so well. If the fund buys notes as much as five years out, when interest rates rise there will be fewer instruments maturing in the fund's portfolio. With fewer investments maturing, the fund will not be able to buy as many new, higher-yielding investments. At some point, the average yield of the fund will fall below other funds that have shorter average maturities.

On the one hand, professional management is a plus. On the other, it can prove costly if management takes such a risk. The competition for investor funds is fierce. As an investor you have to be on your guard. Remember, what looks good today may be because the fund has sacrificed flexibility for the future. We strongly recommend that the *average maturity* of your selected money market fund should be six months or less to avoid this problem.

Types of Money Market Funds.   There are many types of money market funds available to the public. Once you know your objectives and investor personality (you *do* have that well in hand by now!) it's a matter of selecting a fund that meets those requirements.

The safest funds are those that invest solely in 90-day T-bills, since the shorter the maturity the lower the risk. Obviously, Treasury bills are the most secure; but, if you are willing to take slightly more risk, non-Treasury securities offer higher yields. The diversification offered by money market funds affords some protection against loss.

Money market funds cover a full range of products. There are funds that invest only in overnight repurchase agreements (repos). You can't keep maturity shorter than that! They are not as secure as Treasury bills, though. There is a legal question about who owns the securities that back repos, because of a problem arising in the 1980s when a number of government securities dealers failed. But, the fact that a fund is diversified over many issuers limits the damage from the failure of any one.

Many money market funds are tax free. These funds invest in short-term municipal securities, which pay interest exempt from federal taxes, and, often, state taxation. For example, funds offer residents of the larger states double-tax-free returns (exempt from both state and federal taxes, advertised sometimes as "double-tax free"). New York City even offers triple-tax-free returns, exempt from city, state, and federal taxes. A number of fund families offer tax-free funds for residents of California, New York, New Jersey, and other large states. They invest in municipal securities issued by local governments and the state itself.

Checklist for Selecting Money Market Funds. The following are important items that should be checked prior to buying a money market mutual fund:

1. *Track record.* How long has the fund, or its parent company, been in business? A company should have at least five years' experience managing funds.

2. *Type of securities in portfolio.* What types of securities is the fund allowed to buy? What are the restrictions? What is the normal distribution between Treasury bills and notes and those issued by private concerns? The higher the percentage of Treasury securities, the safer the fund—but, also, the lower the average yield.

3. *Average maturities.* What is the average maturity of the securities held in the portfolio? Are there any restrictions on the length of maturity of allowable vehicles in the prospectus? How readily available is this information?

4. *Shareholder services.* What services are offered by the fund? Does the fund have a toll-free 800 number? Does it offer check-writing capability? What are the fees for writing checks? What is the minimum check that may be written on the account? Does the fund belong to a family of funds that allows telephone transfers? Does it offer IRAs? Does the fund offer telephone redemption privileges?

5. *Fees.* What is the average expense ratio? Although money market funds do not assess any load or redemption fees, the expenses for management vary. You should find a fund that matches your other criteria and has an expense ratio of less than 0.75 percent (75 cents per $100).

Fixed Income: Finding a Bond Fund

Bond funds have been the fastest-growing segment of the mutual fund industry. They became popular when yields on Treasury bonds were over 10 percent in the late 1970s as a result of high inflation.[10] At the same time, the stock market had been in the doldrums since its peak in 1966. No won-

---

[10] To give you an idea of how significant that number is, refer to the discussion covering the power of compounding in Chapter 3. Using the "Rule of 72," you can see that at 10 percent interest compounded, you would double your investment in only 7.2 years!

der many investors decided to go with the very high return that was available on the safest bonds you could buy.

But, the smallest practical amount you can invest in bonds is $5,000 or $10,000. The mutual fund industry recognized that many people wanting those same returns were not in a position to invest that much at one time.

Mutual funds specializing in bond investments have grown into a huge and diverse industry. You can buy both load or no-load bond funds, which invest in a wide variety of fixed-income instruments ranging from conservative T-bills to junk bonds. For example, there are bond funds that buy only short- or intermediate-term Treasury and/or *investment grade*[11] corporate bonds. Other funds buy long-term Treasury and/or investment grade corporate securities.

That is only the tip of the iceberg. The corporate takeover mania in the 1980s generated increased interest and trading activity in low-grade *junk* bonds, which were issued to finance multibillion-dollar mergers. Because these buyouts were usually highly leveraged, the remaining company was left in a precarious position by classic accounting standards. They simply had too much debt relative to liquid assets. The independent rating agencies rated these junk bonds at various ratings below the coveted "A" rating.

The lower the rating, the higher the interest rate the bond must pay to attract buyers. Many bond funds specialize in these controversial instruments. "Instant diversification" is an important advantage that these funds have for most investors. You won't have to research 50 different issues to select 5. When you buy a well-managed fund, you are buying a diversified portfolio. If a single issuer, or even more than one issuer, defaults, the damage to your portfolio is minimized.

Even if you are able to buy five different issues in equal amounts, the default of a single issuer will mean a loss of 20 percent for you. Purchasing a bond fund that invests in a diversified portfolio minimizes such risk.

In Chapter 5 we briefly touched on mortgage-backed pass-through securities. This market experienced explosive growth from 1982 to 1986. The yields on conventional bonds were dropping. Investors, who had become used to higher yields, searched for other vehicles to satisfy their desire for higher returns. Pass-through securities issued by agencies of the federal government generated a great deal of attention.

The two most popular pass-through certificates were those issued by the Federal National Mortgage Association (Fannie Maes) and the Government National Mortgage Association (Ginnie Maes). These multibillion-

---

[11] Investment grade means A-rated, or better, corporate securities.

dollar markets attracted huge sums when yields dropped on conventional bonds.

The mutual fund industry did not miss the opportunity for another ideal vehicle to be "mutual fund-ized." As a result, Ginnie Mae and Fannie Mae funds represent billions of dollars of investor money.

And last, but certainly not least, is the municipal sector. The problems experienced by some issuers of municipal bonds—New York City and Cleveland are two prominent examples—brought home the benefits of diversification to many investors. If New York City could default on its bonds, what local issues are safe?

Diversification in bonds through mutual funds represents a safe and logical alternative for most investors. You can buy funds specializing in different lengths of maturities as well as ratings. Municipal bonds carry ratings just like corporate issues, for example. You can buy funds that invest solely in short-, intermediate-, or long-term municipal debt, with ratings of A or above, BBB or above, and so on, all the way down to bonds that are in default.

Checklist for Buying Bond Funds.   The following is a brief checklist of items you should know before investing in a bond fund:

1. *Track record.* How long has the fund or its parent company been in business? The fixed-income market has proven treacherous in recent years, so it's no place to experiment with an unproven manager.

2. *Maturities.* One of the most important factors in the volatility of bond prices is the length to maturity. The longer the length, the higher the volatility—and the greater the risk. Check the prospectus to see what restrictions, if any, the fund manager has in terms of the average maturity for the portfolio. If there is no information, assume that the manager is not restricted and can do whatever he or she feels is best for the fund. This is *not* the fund for you! You want a fund that will be predictable and help you attain your goals, which you have determined from the exercises we've gone through up to this point.

3. *Size of positions.* Is there any restriction on the size of a position the fund can take in the debt of a single issuer? One reason you buy a mutual fund is to get diversification, so you want to make sure the fund cannot become overexposed to any single issuer. If there are no restrictions spelled out in the prospectus, find another fund.

4. *Bond ratings.* What are the fund's objectives in terms of the ratings of the bonds it buys? Must it buy A-rated bonds and above? Or, does the manager have complete leeway in the mix of the bonds the fund buys? If you are a Guardian investor, you certainly don't want to buy a fund where the manager can sell out the Treasury issues and buy junk bonds! Remember, you are buying funds to meet *your* financial objectives. Make sure the fund's rules and objectives match yours.

5. *Fees.* Does the fund have an upfront load charge? How much is it? What are the management fees? What is the average expense ratio? You should be able to find funds that have an expense ratio of 0.75 percent, or less, which also meet your other objectives. Don't automatically dismiss load funds, especially if you have a good working relationship with a broker. A broker is entitled to compensation for doing a good job. If you have confidence in your own ability, though, you can take advantage of no-load funds, thus putting that much more of your money to work for you.

Stock Funds: Locating the Right Fund or Funds

This is where the mutual fund industry began. Stocks (or equity) funds have been the bread and butter of most investment companies until relatively recently. But, that doesn't mean this segment of the indsutry has been static. In fact, just the opposite is true; there have been massive changes in this market.

Perhaps the most remarkable change has been the development of *sector* funds. Sector funds are mutual funds that specialize in certain groups of common stocks. Some sector funds concentrate in industry groups, such as technology, electronics, basic industry, energy, healthcare, drugs, computers, or almost any other industry category.

You can buy sector funds that invest only in new companies, or in "turnaround" situations (bankruptcies or severely depressed companies), or just in the 30 stocks of the Dow Jones Industrial Average. Some sector funds invest in geographic regions of the country. There are even funds that invest in "socially conscientious" companies.

As you can see, you can invest in virtually any area of stocks through mutual funds, giving you the advantage of "instant diversification" as well as professional management.

Narrowing the Field by Objective.   It used to be that, to choose your investment vehicles, all you had to know was whether you were seeking growth, income, or a combination of the two. Although these broad classifications still apply, the range of choices has expanded.

If you are looking for steady and long-term growth, you will want to buy a growth fund that invests primarily in blue-chip, well-established companies. The upside potential may not be as exciting, but the downside is certainly less grim. This type of fund will usually have a long track record, so you can get an idea of risk and volatility before you buy. It's usually a good place to start.

If you are an Individualist, Adventurer, or Enthusiast investor, you are likely to become bored with a single growth fund. The Enthusiast will want to seek those investments that are the "talk of the industry." With mutual funds, you can zero in on the industry group that is of most interest to you with the immediate advantage of a diversified entry into the field. Even the "most Enthusiastic," thus, can guard against stepping over the cliff with the latest trendy investment.

An Adventurer may prefer to seek new issues, commonly referred to as *initial public offerings* (IPOs). After all, you probably want to catch the next IBM or Xerox before everyone else knows about it.

An Individualist may want to design a portfolio that balances various industry groups in accord with research showing the "normal" performance of each group through an entire Business Cycle.

The point here isn't to focus on specific alternatives for each investor type; but, rather, to show there are many different ways to employ mutual funds to satisfy the objectives of the stock portion of your portfolio. It's easier to research and monitor hundreds of funds than it is to analyze over 50,000 individual issues.

Stock funds can generally be classified by four investment objectives: growth, income, balanced (a combination of growth and income), and aggressive growth.

Growth and aggressive growth funds offer the potential for greater returns over the long term, but they also carry larger risk in the short term.

Income funds tend to be more stable over time. Although they don't have the great upside potential that growth funds offer, they are normally less volatile and, therefore, less risky.

Balanced funds try to work the line between these two. They trade off some upside potential for the greater stability afforded by the income portion of their portfolios.

Checklist for Buying Stock Funds.   The following is a brief checklist of items you should know before investing in stock funds:

1. *Objective.* Are the fund's objectives compatible with your needs and objectives? *Growth* encompasses a wide range of funds. If you are a Guardian investor, you will want to buy funds that stick with blue-chip or better-known companies. A good way to measure the relative risk of growth funds is by the average P/E (price/earnings) ratio of the stocks in the portfolio.[12] Compare it to the average P/E of the S&P 500. The higher the P/E,

---

[12] The fund will give you this information if you request it.

the greater the risk, as a rule. Conservative investors stay with funds whose average P/E stocks is close to that of the S&P.

2. *Experience.* New funds are launched every year. The life of the fund is not as important as the experience of the fund manager. Has the manager been around long enough to have experienced at least one full market cycle—bull market through bear market and back? Bull markets can make geniuses out of dart throwers. The real test of money managers is how well they do in the inevitable bad times. *Forbes* magazine's annual mutual fund issue rates mutual fund performance in both up and down markets. Find those that do well in up markets without getting clobbered in down markets.

3. *Services.* What services does the fund offer its shareholders? Is it part of a family of funds, with money market, bond, international, and gold funds? Can you switch between the funds at no, or low, cost? Can you handle transactions by telephone? Does it offer IRA accounts?

4. *Fees.* Is the fund load or no-load? If it is a load fund, what service can you expect from the salesperson? Is there a redemption charge? What are the management fees? You should be able to find a fund matching your other criteria that has an expense ratio of less than 1 percent. If it's a no-load fund, does it charge its shareholders for the expense of acquiring new investors via 12b-1 distribution plans (which can run as much as 1.25 percent per year)?

5. *Volatility.* Beta is a common measure of a fund's volatility relative to the S&P 500. The S&P's beta is 1. If a fund's beta is 1.10 it means that the fund is 10 percent more volatile than the market. If the S&P moved 10 percent, the fund with a beta of 1.10 would be expected to move 11 percent (10 percent more). For conservative investors, a beta of 1.10 is the maximum. If you buy more than one fund, it's a good idea to try to balance the relative volatility among the funds to 1.10 or less. This means, of course, that you could invest in a higher beta fund (for the potentially greater rewards) and balance the risk with a more stable fund for your "foundation" stocks.[13]

6. *Track record.* In addition to the considerations about the fund-manager's experience, you should have some idea of the fund's actual performance. The S&P has earned approximately 13 percent per year over a period of 10 years. A growth fund should do better than that. An index fund should match it.

---

[13] The beta for a particular fund is not readily obtained and is continually subject to change. One source for betas of no-load funds is *The Handbook for No-Load Fund Investors*, by Sheldon Jacobs (Homewood, Ill.: Dow Jones-Irwin, 1988). This reference work contains past performance data, information on fees, and other valuable information.

International Securities: Funds to Fit Most Objectives

As technology has brought the securities markets of the world closer together, interest in international investment markets has climbed. In the 1970s high inflation in the United States brought about severe dollar weakness. As the dollar fell against foreign currencies, especially the German mark and the Swiss franc, U.S. investors started looking beyond their own shores for investment opportunities. Even during the 1980s, when the U.S. stock market was embarked on a record-breaking bull market, there was always at least one, and often many, foreign stock markets that did even better.

The world stock markets have grown increasingly sophisticated. Today the New York Stock Exchange is the second largest exchange in the world, Tokyo having surpassed it in total capitalization of stocks being traded in 1986.

Every year, a new international fund would be introduced in the United States to capitalize on the hot market from *last year's* performance. Unfortunately, investing doesn't work that way. Last year's returns are just exactly that—last year's. As we have pointed out earlier, there is great danger in being the last to jump on an investment bandwagon.

Don't lose sight of the real value that international investing lends to your portfolio: diversification (i.e., minimizing your risk). Indeed, the world's markets are all related, but that doesn't mean they all move exactly the same. For example, for all of 1987 the U.S. market was flat after posting a near-record 40 percent plus gain in the first seven months. The October crash erased profits and reverberated throughout the world's markets. Five foreign markets outperformed the U.S. market in terms of their own currency and market indices for 1987: Mexico, Spain, Japan, Canada, and Great Britain.

The weak dollar helped improve the returns that U.S. investors received in other markets. To illustrate the point, although the Swiss market was down 30 percent, the Swiss franc gained 27.4 percent against the dollar in the same time period. West Germany's market was off 39.7 percent in D-mark terms, but the D-mark gained 22.9 percent versus the dollar. Even more dramatically, Japan's market posted an 8.2 percent gain for the year, and the yen gained another 31.6 percent that year against the dollar.

Currency exchange fluctuations played an even bigger part in returns for international bond portfolios. When currency changes are factored in, the total return for a diversified portfolio of international bonds[14] was greater than that for U.S. bonds.

---

[14] We included Japan, Germany, the United Kingdom, Switzerland, and Holland.

Our research shows there is a low correlation between foreign bond markets and that of the United States. This means adverse price action in U.S. bonds does not necessarily carry into other markets. International bonds, like stocks, can play a meaningful part in hedging risk for the portfolio as a whole. At the same time, our research shows that the lower risk does not necessarily translate into lower returns.

Types of International Funds. There are load and no-load open-end mutual funds that specialize in foreign stocks and bonds. There are also closed-end funds for foreign stocks. The best-known closed-end funds concentrate their investments in one country or region of the world. These include the Korea Fund, the Mexico Fund, the Asia Pacific Fund, the Italy Fund, the Scandinavia Fund, and the Taiwan Fund; there are more.

Among open-end funds, *global* funds invest in U.S. stocks as well as in foreign issues. When a fund is designated *international*, it invests solely in foreign issues.

You can customize your international portfolio with many specialized funds. Included are sector funds, which invest only in European, Pacific Basin, Asian, or specifically Japanese issues, or funds that invest only in certain types of foreign industry, such as high-technology companies; but investing in foreign bonds is a much newer proposition than investing in foreign stock, with relatively few international bond funds.

Checklist for Buying International Funds. The following is a checklist to consult before investing in international funds:

1. *Experience.* A number of international and global stock funds have five-year and longer track records. But, since international bond funds are much newer, few have track records of any length. If you have sufficient assets to include an international bond fund (and your investor personality allows for the exposure), stay with those funds offered and managed by companies with experience also in foreign stock funds.

2. *Diversification.* If you want to invest in a fund specializing in a specific region (e.g., the Pacific Basin), you should have sufficient assets to buy another fund to give your portfolio geographic diversity. You can literally cover the world by putting together a number of funds that concentrate in either countries or regions.

3. *Fees.* International funds are among the most expensive to run, because of the additional work entailed in currency exchange transactions, worldwide custodial arrangements, foreign regulations, and so forth. If you are buying a load fund, be sure you will be receiving sufficient services to compensate for the load charges. If no-load, keep an eye on the expense ratio. You should be able to buy a fund with an expense ratio below 1.20 percent that meets your other criteria.

4. *Portfolio.* Does the fund's prospectus define any diversification rules? Are there limits on how much of the fund's assets can be invested in a single company? If the fund is not a "sector" fund specializing in a single country or region, does the prospectus spell out any limits on how much can be invested in any one country? You should look for funds whose objective is diversification over many different markets and stocks.

5. *Services.* What services does the fund offer? Is it part of a family of funds, which offer money market, stock, bond and gold funds? Can transactions be handled by telephone? Are IRAs available?

Real Estate and Inflation Hedges

Relatively few mutual funds specialize in the real estate market. The most liquid method for investing in real estate is through real estate investment trusts (REITs). REITs trade like stocks on the exchanges or in the OTC market.

Many fund alternatives offer pure inflation protection. The inflationary 1970s focused investor interest on gold and silver, and the mutual fund industry responded quickly. Today, many different funds offer various approaches to precious metals investing.

When gold funds first came on the scene, they invested primarily in South African mining shares. As political tensions over apartheid mounted, both in that country and around the world, a number of funds reacted with non-South African alternatives.

Checklist for Buying Inflation Hedge Funds. The following items are what you should know before investing in any inflation hedge funds:

1. *Portfolio.* In exactly what does the fund invest? Some funds buy gold and silver bullion and coins, as well as shares of mining companies. If you are one of our more conservative investor types, stay away from funds that invest primarily in South African shares. Some funds invest solely in non-South African mining shares.

2. *Fees.* Is the fund load or no-load? If a load charge is assessed, what services can you expect in return from the broker? What are the management fees? Expense ratios vary widely among gold funds. You should be able to find funds with an expense ratio of less than 1.40 percent that meet your other requirements.

3. *Experience.* When fears of resurgent inflation rose again in 1985–86, a number of new gold funds were launched. Experience in managing funds through up and down cycles is particularly important in gold funds, because of the great volatility involved. It is not unusual for gold shares to lose as much as 80 percent to 90 percent of their value in a down market. In up markets, gold shares often appreciate at startling rates. Shares can double or triple in price in short order. The length of time that a particular fund has been around is not as important as the experience of the management company. For example, a new fund can retain an experienced investment manager to handle investment decisions. Although the investment company is new, management can have long-term experience.

One-Stop Shopping: Diversified Funds

In recent years, as market volatility has increased, a few investment management companies have launched funds specifically designed to give their shareholders broad diversification over different asset classes. The exact makeup and philosophy of each of these funds varies, but the basic concept is the same: Diversification over different asset categories provides downside protection while still offering good prospects for returns. (Where have you heard that philosophy before?)

There are three distinct approaches to diversified or *asset allocation* funds. *Fixed-mix* funds take a permanent portfolio approach. They select four or five asset groups for their portfolios and invest equally among them. In this way, the fixed-mix funds replace the more volatile ups and downs that the average growth fund undergoes with a steadier, more secure return. By diversifying over asset groups that have low correlations (i.e., each class is affected differently by economic developments), they hope to achieve good returns during most economic environments. The percentage allocated to each class stays constant, although the individual vehicles within each class may change.

Limited-mix asset allocation funds invest in only three asset classes: stocks, bonds, and cash equivalents. They usually have the flexibility to have as much as 90 percent to 100 percent of their assets in any one asset. That would be an extreme case, and unlikely in most circumstances.

Some investors believe that, by purchasing *balanced* funds, they are diversifying. But, balanced funds just combine objectives of growth and income, usually a mix of stocks and bonds, or of preferred and common stock.

A few funds take a more diversified approach. Full-fledged *dynamic* asset allocation funds realign their allocations in response to their perceptions of changes in economic trends—varying not only the individual vehicles but also the percentages allocated to each asset class. Dynamic funds are actively monitored and managed, usually by one institution, or, in some cases, by a different manager overseeing each asset class.[15]

Diversified funds may not do as well as the stock market in upside markets; but, they should do well when the market is down. Remember, anyone can do well when the market is performing well. What really matters is how you do when the market takes a down turn. Although you may not get the "very-highs" in diversification, you should still gain decent returns and be protected from risk.

In the previous chapter, we gave you a few guidelines for managing your own diversified portfolio using either the fixed-mix or the dynamic asset allocation method. There is no single *correct* approach. As we have said throughout this book, only *you* can know the right way because only you can know what will feel comfortable to you.

As with any fund, you should read the prospectus. Make sure the objectives of the fund coincide with your own. If you prefer minimal involvement in making your own investment decisions, buying a well-managed diversified fund may be the best approach for you.

Sources of Information for Mutual Funds

The explosive growth of the mutual fund industry has precipitated comparable growth in information and in price data for the industry. Most daily newspapers carry price information for leading mutual funds. Many investment advisory newsletters focus their advice solely on what funds to buy or sell.

If you want more detailed information, *The Wall Street Journal* and *Investor's Daily* carry price quotes for virtually all actively traded mutual funds on a daily basis. Both financial newspapers feature a weekly column on mutual fund investing. The columns range over many subjects, including performance information,[16] updates on services being offered by major fund families, the problems fund managers are facing, tax questions, instructions on how to select a fund, and the like.

Investor's Daily features a list of the 25 top-performing mutual funds for the year in each day's table. It also shows the percentage change for the year and the last four weeks for each fund.

---

[15] For more information on dynamic asset allocation funds, write BB&K at 2755 Campus Drive, San Mateo, California 94403.

[16] The quarterly performance results are widely reported and heavily used by funds in their advertising.

Daily price quotations provide you with little real help in making intelligent mutual fund selections. Fortunately, many sources are there to help you review, analyze, and select the funds that will be right for you.

Forbes magazine publishes a special mutual funds edition every year, usually at the end of August, which features a roundup of the past year's developments for stock, bond, money market, international, and gold funds. Each year *Forbes* honors 20 funds that meet the editors' stringent tests for performance over an 11-year span. This honor roll selection process is heavily weighted to how well each fund performs in both up and down market cycles. They also look at each fund's efficiency and carefully examine each fund's expense ratio. Two funds, with roughly equivalent performance over 10 years, may actually show a large disparity in the bottom line for their investors, because of expenses charged to the fund. Remember, over time, even a difference of 1 percent or 2 percent in the expense ratio can significantly reduce your net return.

The *Forbes* performance listing is unique. It isolates how each fund behaved in both up and down markets, and it assigns a letter rating, A through F, for each fund's performance in each type of market. If you are a Guardian investor, or cannot tolerate the large price swings that characterize today's markets, this information can prove invaluable in your selection process.

Other finance and investment-related magazines feature mutual fund performance data and regular articles describing how to make the most of your fund investing. *Money* includes a monthly "Fund Watch" section, which carries news about changes occurring in the industry. *Money* also lists, on a monthly basis, the "Best-Performing Diversified Mutual Funds" and the "Best-Performing International and Global Funds." Detailed performance data on over 700 mutual funds is included quarterly.

Kiplinger's *Changing Times* also has extensive coverage of the mutual fund industry. Its monthly "Mutual Fund Update" typically focuses on one aspect of the industry. For example, it has featured articles on selecting sector funds, finding the best gold funds, and how to evaluate international funds. It often includes unique performance comparisons among different types of funds (e.g., large aggressive growth versus small aggressive growth versus long-term growth funds). It also runs periodic ratings tables of most funds offered to the public.

Even *Business Week* has an annual mutual fund issue, which appears in February, and includes a creative rating system that shows, at a glance, the relative performance of most funds in both up and down markets over the past five years. The issue also tells you how each fund ranked, relative to other funds with the same objective. For example, let's say that you are exploring growth funds, and there is a universe of over 200 funds that list "growth" as their objective. *Business Week*'s performance tables will let you compare how any of the growth funds did relative to the universe. Each fund is also rated for "risk," based on volatility and performance in excess of the *riskless* return you could earn by investing in T-bills.

Computerized Help for Fund Investors

For those of you who own, or have access to, an IBM PC or compatible, you can take advantage of many computer programs that enable you to do detailed analyses of most mutual funds.

If you like *Business Week*'s annual rundown on mutual funds, with its special volatility and risk rankings, the *Business Week Mutual Fund Scoreboard* provides an extensive database. The equity fund disks carry data on over 700 stock funds. The fixed-income disks cover over 500 bond funds. With this program, you are able to set up such parameters as net annual return, size, beta, and so forth. The program will then sort through the entire database to find those funds that meet your predetermined specifications.

The various performance factors that *Business Week* lists in its annual mutual fund issue are the same items included in the *Scoreboard*. For example, you can easily ask the program to find all the stock funds meeting these criteria:

1. No sales charge.
2. Low volatility (e.g., a beta of less than 1.10).
3. Average annual return over the last five years of 15 percent.
4. Average annual return over the last 10 years of 12 percent.
5. Assets under management of at least $250,000,000.

The program will then sort through the entire stock fund database and print out the names of those funds that meet, or exceed, your criteria. Over 25 separate performance factors can be used in this winnowing process.

For more information on the stock or the fixed-income databases and the analysis program, write: Business Week Mutual Fund Scoreboard, PO Box 621, Elk Grove, IL 60009–0621.

Another program that offers slightly different features is *Fund Wise* by Financial Services. Fund Wise emphasizes its ability to compare fund performance graphically. Its diversification feature calculates how a combination of funds may perform in various market environments. For example, you may want to diversify your holdings by buying a fund that has above-average performance in bull markets with one that does exceptionally well in bear markets. The program also has a "what-if" feature, which enables you to see how a specific fund would have fared in different economic environments. Fund Wise's database includes both stock and fixed-income funds.

For more information write: Financial Services, 261 Hamilton Avenue, Suite 215, Palo Alto, CA 94301, or call (800) 323-9822.

WRAPPING UP

Selecting professional help for your investments should not be approached lightly. An extensive assortment of advisors offer their services to the public. To find the right one, you have to do more than simply check academic credentials. You should take the same care in selecting an investment advisor as you would making investment decisions on your own.

One of the fastest-growing areas in the investment world is mutual funds. There are so many different kinds of mutual funds that almost any type of investor, seeking almost any investment objective, can find one or more that will suit his or her objectives. If you have less than $1 million to invest, we recommend that you look for a number of mutual funds that meet your requirements.

Funds provide many advantages for most investors. Mutual funds offer good liquidity and instant diversification. Through funds, you are able to have the benefits of professional management at a fraction of the cost to hire such management individually.

Funds offer many conveniences for investors. There are funds that allow you to trade on a short-term basis. Most transactions can be conducted by telephone. And most important, mutual fund prices are readily accessible in most daily newspapers as well as in the financial press.

The growth of the mutual fund industry has resulted in improved services, lower costs, and healthy competition. Buying funds is an excellent way to avail yourself of professional management *and* begin to get an insight into the practice of investing.

CHAPTER 8

THE BB&K GUIDE TO INVESTMENT VEHICLES

Chapter 5 presented the BB&K Rosetta Stone—your key to deciphering the complex and sometimes confusing language of investments, investment advertising, and financial services. In this last chapter, we will look more closely at the investment vehicles in each asset class and give you a concise, yet complete, definition of what they are and how you can put them to work for you. To help you find the vehicles you are looking for quickly, we have alphabetized the list within each asset class. You will also see some vehicles within those classes that are not listed on the Rosetta Stone. Although we have not recommended them for your Personal Profit Portfolio, you may currently hold them, or run across them in financial advertisements. We think you should understand what they do—or fail to do—as investment opportunities.

CASH EQUIVALENTS: THE NEXT BEST THING TO MONEY

As you already know, cash equivalents are those most liquid assets that many people consider to be the next best thing to cash. This means they can be readily converted into spendable money (to meet emergencies or to take advantage of new opportunities) without any loss to their current market value.

Bank Certificates of Deposit

Bank and savings and loan CDs are *fixed-term savings accounts*. Maturities on CDs vary from 90 days to as long as eight years. They pay higher interest rates than passbook savings accounts, but they require higher minimum balances. Minimums run from as little as $1,000 to as much as $10,000.

Even though the federal law requiring penalties for early withdrawal expired in 1987, most institutions still assess penalties if you cash in your CD before its maturity date. CDs are insured by an agency of the federal government for up to $100,000, but you should confirm that at the institutions with whom you invest. The interest is fully taxable by both state and federal authorities.

Banker's Acceptances

When a bank acts as intermediary between two trading partners, the draft or bill of exchange used to pay for the goods is a marketable investment. This is because (1) the bank guarantees payment and (2) the draft or bill is secured by the merchandise it finances. In this respect, banker's acceptances resemble commercial paper or Treasury bills. They are short-term notes purchased at a discount—the amount of that discount being proportional to the time and risks involved. Your profit as an investor comes not from interest payments but from the spread between the discounted price of the note and its face value (if you hold it to maturity).

Commercial Paper

Corporations sometimes need to borrow money to pay their short-term cash obligations. The notes they issue for this purpose are called *commercial paper* and, as debt instruments, they are technically classified as unsecured promissory notes with a fixed value and stated maturity date (up to 270 days, but most are for 30 days or less). Although they are usually purchased at par (face) value, some may be bought at a discount—the amount of which is proportional to the borrowing company's creditworthiness. Since they are riskier than comparable notes issued by the Treasury Department, their yields are usually higher.

Eurodollar Certificates of Deposit

Eurodollars are U.S. dollar deposits held in banks outside U.S. jurisdiction. Since, for the most part, they are held by institutions that are not obliged to follow American laws, the interest paid on them and the forms of investment available to such funds are sometimes different from comparable U.S. investments. Euro CDs, then, are Eurodollar time deposits issued by a U.S. bank branch or foreign bank located outside the United States. Because they fall outside the U.S. statutes regarding CD investments, they frequently pay higher interest, have stiffer penalties for early withdrawal, and are generally riskier, owing to a lack of insurance and their dependence on less-stable foreign economies.

Governmental Paper

When state or local governments experience a temporary gap between expected tax revenues and their cash obligations, they sometimes issue *tax-anticipation notes*, or TANs, to make up the difference. TANs are tax-free instruments, like most other government debt, and are reasonably safe investments, since they are backed not only by a public agency but also by revenues from general tax receipts. *Revenue anticipation notes*, or RANs, are similar to TANs, except that the revenues to redeem them must come from sources other than the general tax pool, such as user fees, which can be a little less predictable. *Bond anticipation notes*, or BANs, are sold by local governmental agencies that wish to begin, or sustain, operations to be funded later by public bonds. The only true arbiter of risk associated with any of these instruments is the general creditworthiness of the agency or municipality issuing them. Unlike the federal government, which is the only agency in the country that can manufacture money to repay its debts, the states, counties, and cities—like any other going concern—must rely on their own revenue potential to make ends meet.

Insurance Cash Value Programs

Certain life insurance policies have a cash value associated with them, depending on the age of the policy and the amount of the premiums paid against it. You should know that returns from such pseudo investments are roughly comparable to money market yields, although they are far from guaranteed. Furthermore, the cash reserve (funded by your premiums) used in making these payments is not refunded when you die but is available only as requested by the policyholder during the life of the policy. As a result, these programs do little more than make your insurance more expensive and your investment dollars less productive. Most people would do better to avoid these programs altogether.

Money Market (and Bank Money Market) Funds

Mutual fund companies (and banks) that invest in bank CDs, short-term government bonds, and other relatively liquid vehicles are called *money market funds*. If the funds are invested in vehicles that are taxable, your returns from them will be taxable, also. If the fund invests in tax-free instruments, such as short-term municipal bonds, the returns you earn will be tax free. Many money market funds offer check-writing privileges for your account, but usually for a limited number of checks per month or for amounts over a specified minimum. A minimum deposit is required to open and maintain such accounts, so a portion of your funds will have to be committed to this vehicle indefinitely, even though you could invest that money in other higher-yielding instruments. Finally, since the fund itself invests in a number of vehicles, adding the relative safety of diversification, the different rates of return of each will cause the yield on your market account to fluctuate over time. These programs have grown in popularity since bank deregulation, and they certainly are better alternatives than keeping a comparable amount in a low-interest passbook or no-interest checking account.

Passbook Savings Accounts

The basic interest-bearing account at any commercial bank or savings and loan association (S&L) is the so-called *passbook savings account,* named for the little book that is used to log your deposits, withdrawals, and interest payments. Since you can withdraw the money from such accounts without penalty simply by presenting your passbook, they are almost as liquid as demand deposit (or checking) accounts. They are also very safe investments, insured by the federal government for up to $100,000.

Unfortunately, these investments are taxable, and the after-tax rate of return (even the *pre-tax* rate of return in recent years) is often less than the rate of inflation. Because there are so many other higher-yielding and comparably safe investments open to Personal Profit Planners, we don't recommend passbook savings accounts for anyone.

Savings Bonds

The U.S. government's analogue to the passbook savings account is the U.S. *savings bond* —and it represents nearly as bad an investment in inflationary times. A savings bond is actually a savings certificate (exempt from state taxes) sold at a discount from its ultimate face value. Although it is redeemable upon presentation at a bank or other approved redemption facility, the longer you hold the bond the more it will be worth. Savings bonds held to maturity pay about the same as a commercial bank's passbook savings account (actually, their rate is connected by law to other Treasury Department debt instruments). Because the yield is relatively low, we do not recommend them for your portfolio.

Small Savings and Loan Certificates of Deposit

Because of the competitive nature of retail financial services, thrift institutions with modest reserves (lower dollar deposits) sometimes offer interest on their CDs that is as high as the law allows—and certainly higher than the larger, more conservative S&Ls. Although these CDs can be very attractive to prospective investors, other economic factors (such as the failure rate of small S&Ls) can make them fairly risky (see the definition and discussion of CDs in general under "Bank Certificates of Deposit").

Swiss Bank Accounts

Switzerland's unique and stringent banking secrecy laws has enabled that country to become the center for many international banking practices. Swiss commercial banks usually pay considerably lower interest rates to foreign savers than most domestic or foreign banks. Nonetheless, individuals and businesses around the world choose to do most of their banking through Swiss banks.

The banks offer the full range of financial services, from investment advice to money management to acting as the broker for many different investments. While *secret Swiss numbered bank accounts* still exist, most major Swiss banks no longer offer that service to American depositors. The only reason we know to invest in a Swiss bank account is that there is always the potential to profit from currency exchange rate changes. If your savings were denominated in Swiss francs when the dollar was going down, you would earn not only the interest but also a capital gain from the increase in value of your francs relative to the dollar. Yes, it does sound complicated. Currency exchange speculation is not within the purview of most Personal Profit Planners.

Treasury Bills

T-bills are negotiable federal debt instruments with fairly short maturities, usually of 3, 6, or 12 months. They have a minimum face value of $10,000 and are discounted by competitive bidding among a large number of prospective buyers. The return on T-bills is not a stated rate of interest but the difference between the price you pay and the face value of the bill. Since they are backed by the full faith and credit of the U.S. government, T-bills are considered among the safest and most liquid forms of investment.

FIXED-INCOME INVESTMENTS: TAKING AN INTEREST IN LONG-TERM DEBT

Fixed-income investments include a wide range of interest-bearing debt vehicles, with an equally wide range of risks and returns available from each. Although most people assume such vehicles will (or must) be held to maturity to realize the stated return, novice investors often overlook the active secondary market that exists for many of these instruments—thus giving them not only their fixed return but liquidity quality as well.

A/AAA Municipal and Corporate Bonds

As you learned in earlier chapters, the highest rating any bond from any agency (corporate or governmental) can achieve from the impartial analysts who review them is Aaa (Moody's) or AAA (Standard & Poor's). When you purchase such investments, you are promised the return of your principal plus regular income payments, based on the "coupon" rate of interest. From a total portfolio viewpoint, bonds purchased at a given interest rate actually appreciate in value when interest rates on *new* bonds fall, although you also risk a loss in price if interest rates go up. Since interest rates usually drop during times of economic recession, such investments can be a formidable hedge against a stagnant or depressed economy. Of course, the chief distinction between corporate bonds and municipal bonds (the so-called *munis*) is that the latter's interest payments are tax-free—although capital gains realized on the sale of a muni are taxed at the same rate as similar gains realized on corporate bonds. If you own state-issued bonds and live in that state as well, the income you receive will be "dual exempt" (i.e., free from both state and federal taxes).

As you will see later, bonds rated A, AA, or AAA are only the highest of the several "grades" awarded to such long-term debt instruments. Generally speaking, the lower the grade, the higher the interest (or discount) available on the bond, and the greater the risk.

Baa/BBB Municipal and Corporate Bonds

These bonds are similar to A through AAA bonds, described above, but with a slightly higher risk of default by the issuing agency. Because of this added risk, B (lowest), BB, or BBB bonds usually pay a moderately to substantially higher return, all other factors being equal.

Bond Mutual Funds and Unit Trusts

Any investment company or program that pools investor capital to purchase other securities is technically a *mutual fund*. In the case of bond mutual funds, the securities are corporate or municipal bonds, or both. Thus, the value of the shares you might purchase in such funds depends on the prevailing rate of interest.

Unit trusts are portfolios of corporate or municipal bonds that, once purchased, are not traded except to be redeemed at maturity and, therefore, have lower fees or costs than actively managed mutual funds. The unit shares usually pay returns that are competitive with current interest rates, and the holders of those shares also participate in capital gains if the bonds in the portfolio rise in price. These unit trusts are eventually "self-liquidating" and can be a good vehicle for investors who want both income and possible capital gains from a diversified low-risk investment. If you wish to sell your shares before maturity, you must conduct the transaction through the brokerage firm that formed the trust. Mutual fund shares, however, may be redeemed directly from the fund itself.

C/CCC and D/DDD Municipal and Corporate Bonds

You've probably heard (or experienced!) the joke that goes: "Banks only lend money to people who don't need it!" Bonds issued by organizations (private or governmental) that *really* need the cash (e.g., those on the edge of bankruptcy or have other adverse business or funding problems) are rated Caa (lowest), CC, or CCC and are considered the province of only the most speculative investors. C/D rated bonds (C is the lowest rating by Moody's; D is the lowest by Standard & Poor's) are usually already in default; and, although they are almost always poor investments, some speculators have made money with such instruments when the corporate managers or politicians issuing them managed either to turn the institutions around or liquidate them efficiently—returning at least some portion of the bondholder's principal.

Eurodollar Bonds

As you learned in the discussion of cash equivalent investments, a Eurodollar is any U.S. dollar-denominated account held outside the United States. Eurodollar bonds are similar to the other bonds we've discussed; but, they are issued by foreign agencies and, because of that, tend to respond to foreign (rather than domestic) economic developments. They are redeemed (or annual interest payments are received) in U.S. dollars.

First Mortgage Pools

When someone borrows money to buy real property (a house or office building, for example), the loan is called a *mortgage*, and the oldest (most senior) debt secured by that property is called a *first* mortgage. Naturally, the value of such an investment to a lender is not only dependent on the interest received but also on the likelihood that the borrower will be able to continue making those payments. The market value of first mortgages depends on both the interest they bear and the creditworthiness of the borrower. To spread the risks of default over many investors and many borrowers, investment companies were created to buy these mortgages in pools, paying out a single composite rate of interest, based on the weighted averages of the interest rates of the various mortgages in the portfolio. Since first mortgages are senior (first in line for collection in case of foreclosure) to other loans secured by the same property, they are considered the lowest-risk vehicle for such investments.

Government Agency Bonds

A number of the agencies of the federal government issue debt securities within guidelines set by Congress. Maturities range from as little as 30 days to as much as 25 years. Minimum denominations vary from $1,000 to $5,000. Agencies that issue bonds include the Export-Import Bank of the United States, Farmers Home Administration, the Federal Housing Administration, the World Bank, the Tennessee Valley Authority, the Postal Service, and many others. The market for agencies is liquid, though not as actively traded as that for Treasuries. They generally yield slightly more than Treasury issues with the same maturity.

Interest Rate Options

Options of any kind are rights to buy or sell a specific security at a specific price in the future. Obviously, people agree to buy and sell options because they think the market for the securities involved will change in their favor during the time before the transaction. Interest rate options involve speculating on the future prices of T-bills, bonds, and various other interest-bearing vehicles. Because of their speculative nature, they are always higher-risk vehicles than the basic investment they seek to secure. For example, you might guess the direction of the interest rate change correctly, but that change might occur *after* your option period had expired.

Mortgage-Backed Pass-Throughs:
Freddie Macs, Fannie Maes, and Ginnie Maes

Mortgage-backed certificates are securities issued by agencies of the federal government. Three main government agencies, the Federal Home Loan Bank (FHLB), the Federal National Mortgage Association (FNMA), and the

Government National Mortgage Association (GNMA), buy mortgage loans from savings institutions. They then package these mortgages into pools and sell interests in the pools to individual and institutional investors. They are called *pass-through* because, as the homeowner makes payments of interest and principal on the mortgage, they are "passed through" to the owners of the certificates in proportion to their interest in the pool. The securities issued by these agencies are, in order: Freddie Macs, Fannie Maes, and Ginnie Maes. These instruments can be quite volatile, because the underlying asset of each certificate, the mortgage, may be paid off early. If investors are paid off early (i.e., before the expected maturity), they must find another investment for their money. There is always the risk that interest rates will be lower then. That added risk makes the yield on pass-throughs quite competitive. Ginnie Maes are the most liquid and heavily traded of the three securities.

Private Placement Convertible Debt

Any "convertible" investment is one that can be switched from one vehicle (such as debt) to another (such as equity). A "private placement" simply means that the buyer and seller of the investment get together outside regular market channels. It usually means, too, that the buyer qualifies for such an opportunity by virtue of his or her investment knowledge and wealth, and that the seller does not have to register the offering with the Securities and Exchange Commission—although many other state and federal regulations may be applicable to the transaction.

A *convertible debt* vehicle, then, is one that begins as a loan (bond) and may be redeemed later as stock in the issuing company. Because it is privately placed, it means that the buyer is a sophisticated investor demanding higher returns (lots of stock or higher-than-market interest payments) in exchange for the original cash. Naturally, these types of fixed-income investments are only for Personal Profit Planners who meet these (at times) very stringent investor qualifications.

Second Mortgage Investments

As you know, a mortgage is any loan secured by real property. Since property owners sometimes need to "go to the well" more than once for cash to keep or operate their property, mortgages can be first, second, or even third in line as claims against these assets. A *second mortgage* is just as marketable as a first and, because of its slightly riskier nature (the borrower needed to go to the well at least twice—and a superior, senior mortgage has first rights in case of foreclosure), it usually pays higher returns. Unfortunately, the returns on pools consisting of these investments can fluctuate widely, based on the interest rates used at the time the second mortgages were made.

Treasury Bonds

Treasury bonds are similar to Treasury bills but are of longer duration (over 10 years) and usually have higher yields. They are sold with a minimum face value of $1,000 and enjoy excellent liquidity in a very active secondary market.

Treasury Notes

Treasury notes resemble Treasury bonds, except that their maturities run from 1 to 10 years. Also, like Treasury bonds and bills, they are backed by the full faith and credit of the U.S. government and are considered virtually risk-free. Their values, however, can fluctuate with the levels of competing interest rates.

U.S. STOCKS (DOMESTIC EQUITIES): MAKING THE MARKET WORK FOR YOU

Investments in the domestic stock (equity) market have many unique characteristics. Unlike cash equivalents, which contain vehicles that are more "products" than "procedures," equity investments sometimes depend as much on the *techinque* of the investor as on the form. For example, as you'll see later, investing in "options" (trading so-called *puts* and *calls*) is significantly different from investing in the stocks the options are exercised against. You will encounter this important difference again and again in this section, so be sure that vehicles recommended for you on the BB&K Rosetta Stone are, in reality, *techniques* you can manage.

Blue-Chip Stocks

In poker, the betting chips that have the highest value are always blue—a tradition that is carried into the terminology of the "biggest game in town" (i.e., the U.S. stock market). Blue chips are the stocks of the largest and most stable companies, known for their established management and solid financial strength. In terms of market performance, they usually have a history of consistent earnings (if not dividends) and are frequently categorized as long-term, demonstrated growth investments. Some people consider blue chips to be dull, dull, dull—but for many Guardians, they are the only safe harbor in a sea of turbulent stocks.

Convertible Bonds

As you learned previously, convertible investments are those that switch from one vehicle form to another during their investment life. *Convertible bonds* are one such hybrid instrument, since they begin as interest-based investments (usually paying a lower rate of interest than conventional bonds) only to change later (usually at the buyer's option) to ownership or to stock in the corporation that issued them. Because the real payoff of such vehicles depends on the equity (rather than on the debt) side of the investment, they are listed under this asset class.

Covered and Naked Options

Options are contracts (or rights) to buy or sell a security at a given price, before a specific time in the future. "Puts" are options to sell a given stock at a predetermined price—a "bet" by shareholders that the market value of that stock will go down. "Calls" are options to buy a stock at a predetermined price—a "bet" that the value of that stock will go up. The money paid (or simply pledged, called the *premium*) between parties in this arrangement is forfeited if the option is not exercised within the time allowed. A *covered* option is one wherein the seller of the put owns the stock in question.

This technique, called *hedging*, greatly lowers the seller's risk of loss. A *naked* option requires the seller not only to make good on the price the option stipulates but also to buy the underlying stock (not already owned) for resale at the going market price. Naturally, this is a particularly risky business, and we recommend it only for the most daring stock market pros.

Hedge Funds

"Hedging" in stockmarketese means any maneuver that seeks to protect or improve your position through fancy footwork, rather than (or in addition to) normal market forces (see "Covered Options" discussed earlier). A mutual fund that specializes in puts and calls, short selling, and other short-term trading techniques to come out ahead is called a *hedge fund.* Most hedge funds try to multiply their potential for gain even further by using these techniques on more aggressive growth stocks. Hedge funds, as you would suspect, are suitable only for investors who can tolerate great volatility and uncertainty from that part of their portfolios.

Index Funds

One of the reasons people buy mutual funds at all is to overcome market volatility and to use the law of averages to increase, rather than diminish, their chances for success. Since history has shown that only a handful of money managers can consistently beat the market (gain returns higher than those stocks measured by the major indexes, such as the Dow Jones Industrials or Standard & Poor's 500), a unique breed of mutual funds has evolved, called *index funds*. The objective of these funds, quite simply, is to do no worse than the indexes against which they are compared. They buy the same stocks in about the same quantities as those that comprise a major index and are thereby assured that their fund will "follow the market" accordingly. When the market is bullish, these funds tend to do well. When times are bearish, they take their licks. Because of the long-term growth of the U.S. economy, index funds are likely to be profitable over the span of many years or decades.

Mutual Funds, Unit Trusts, and Other Pooled Vehicles

If you have read our discussion about bond mutual funds and unit trusts under the fixed-income asset class, you already know a good deal about how these programs work with common stocks. Of course, stocks are generally more volatile than bonds, and even the most conservative common stock mutual fund is riskier than its debt-based counterpart in the fixed-income asset class. Stock mutual funds have a number of advantages over individual stocks, however, and you should be aware of at least the most important ones. First, since they are, by and large, well-diversified investments, they are almost always safer than a portfolio with comparable objectives invested in a few (or even as many as 10 or 12) common stocks. Second, they offer specific investment objectives that may be similar to your own, such as current income (through dividends), capital gains (through growth in market value), or aggressive growth (potential for "supermoney" through high-potential stocks). And, because they are run by professional money managers, you are generally assured of reasonable portfolio management, although that is by no means synonymous with success!

Purchased Options (see: Covered and Naked Options)

Venture Capital

You have learned that companies often get money to start (or to continue) operations by issuing new stock. Obviously, if the company has no track record (nothing but a good idea whose time may have come), the value of this stock will be low. This was the case with Digital Equipment Corporation (DEC) in the 1960s and with Intel in the 1970s. Since then, many people have invested lots of money in lots of companies, hoping to discover the DEC or Intel of the future. Investment firms that fund these higher-risk enterprises are called *venture capital* companies. They usually take their profits in the form of equity, hoping that the relatively modest amounts they invest early on will result in stupendous share values a few years down the road. Of course, as the saying goes, "You have to kiss a lot of frogs before you find a prince." Few of these new ventures ever break even, let alone pay the kind of returns that venture capitalists desire, so diversification over many companies becomes a very important strategy.

INTERNATIONAL SECURITIES: IMPORTING YOUR PERSONAL PROFIT

Few ecologies are as curiously independent—yet interdependent—as the environment of international economics. It's no surprise, then, that more and more investors are turning to this arena to broaden and deepen their portfolios. Here are a few of the more important vehicles you'll find available in this expanding asset class.

American Depository Receipts (ADRs)

One way to participate in the international equity market is through an intermediate certificate (and service) called an *ADR*, traded conveniently on the New York or American Stock Exchanges or on the over-the-counter (OTC) market. ADRs are certificates showing that you own a portion of certain international stocks held by U.S. bank branches in other parts of the world. These certificates are made possible by larger foreign companies that empower an American bank to act as an intermediary in the sale of their stock to U.S. citizens. ADRs, which can be held and transferred in lieu of holding and transferring the foreign stocks themselves, help both domestic investors and foreign companies make a market that, otherwise, would be very difficult for either of the parties to establish by itself. In terms of price change, ADRs provide the same gain or loss you would experience if you owned the foreign stocks outright.

Foreign Listed Stocks

A *foreign stock* is one that is registered on a major foreign exchange (such as the London, Paris, Tokyo, or Hong Kong Exchanges) and not on a domestic exchange. These foreign stock exchanges are similar to our own, although the regulatory devices vary enormously from country to country. Although information about the security and the company behind it can be obtained, the offering does not have to meet the disclosure requirements of the American SEC. As a result, this area demands considerably more investor astuteness in assessing the value of the investment.

Foreign Over-the-Counter Stocks

Even in the United States, firms that do not meet the operational or financial criteria to have their stocks listed on the major exchanges may be sold "over-the-counter" by most brokers, although, at least domestically, they must still follow SEC regulations for financial disclosure. Obviously, companies trading stock on the foreign OTC markets do not have to follow American SEC requirements, and so they are considered riskier than their domestic counterparts. As it was with the foreign listed stocks, we consider these vehicles suitable only for the most experienced investment professionals.

Foreign Venture Capital

As risky as venture capital is in the United States, the stronghold of the free enterprise system (see also "Venture Capital" under the domestic equities asset class), it can be even riskier in foreign markets. Participate in these vehicles only if you know exactly what you're getting into.

Managed Swiss Portfolio Accounts

Not to be confused with Swiss bank accounts (see the entry, "Swiss Bank Accounts" under the cash equivalents asset class), these professionally managed accounts are set up by Swiss banks for foreign stock portfolios of greater than $50,000. The Swiss money managers take commissions both on buying and selling transactions, like regular brokers, and collect, in addition, on the spread between high and low prices experienced by your stock during the trading day. Since these accounts trade almost exclusively among themselves in a closed, miniature market, they seem to be a better deal for Swiss bankers than foreign investors, and we don't recommend them for even the best-heeled Personal Profit Planner.

Mutual Funds of International Bonds

A relatively recent development in the mutual fund industry has been the rise of funds devoted specifically to international fixed-income investing. Like their stock brethren, international bond funds can help lessen the volatility of your domestic fixed-income portfolio. Foreign bond markets, though, are not as seasoned as stock markets. There are some distinctions that make investing in foreign bonds more challenging. Each country has its own laws and procedures for defaults or bankruptcies. There are wide disparities in how bondholders fare.

The mutual fund approach to foreign bond investing gives you the advantage of (1) instant diversification over bonds denominated in various currencies issued in a variety of countries and (2) professional management in not only buying the bonds but also in handling all bondholder communication and currency exchange matters.

Mutual Funds of International Stocks

You can now buy shares in mutual funds (registered with the SEC) that invest in foreign stocks listed on the major foreign exchanges. Although these funds work, in principle, like any other mutual funds, there are differences. First, the stocks comprising these international funds are (more than half of the time) out of phase with the U.S. economy and, thus, can lessen the volatility of your domestic equity portfolio. Second, these funds often invest in several different countries and so further dampen the fluctuations you might experience if you held stock in only one or two foreign countries.

REAL ESTATE/INFLATION HEDGES: PROTECTING YOURSELF AGAINST INFLATION

Our final asset class is a "catch all" category that includes a wide variety of investment vehicles in a number of different markets. They do have one thing in common, though: They all have a unique role in counteracting that most dangerous and costly economic phenomenon—inflation.

We have also included brief discussions of a few tax-shelter investments. Tax law changes throughout the 1980s have steadily reduced the number of legitimate tax shelters. As tax rates have dropped, the appeal of tax shelters has also subsided for most people; nonetheless, you may still hear a sales pitch for such an investment. We have one inviolable rule when it comes to evaluating investments that may have beneficial tax consequences: *All such investments* (whether called "shelters" or "hedges") *must pay their own way, first as investments and second as the promised tax or inflation benefits.*

Collectibles

As you know by now, tangible *things*, if they otherwise have marketable value, tend to do well in inflationary times. Items commonly purchased as investments include rare stamps, coins, jewelry, books, antiques, dolls, classic automobiles, art, nostalgia artifacts, and other articles with demonstrated market value. Unfortunately, some people confuse things that are merely old or expensive with collectibles. The two are *not* the same. Be sure you know what you're doing before you purchase such items with investment objectives in mind. Consult an expert and at least one of the many reference books on the particular collectible area that interests you. Finally, you should be aware that, often, there is an unfavorable spread between the retail purchase price and the wholesale (resale) price of some collectibles, so it may be very difficult to achieve the kind of real profits you'd like to see.

Commodity Futures

Historically, a "futures contract" was a promise to deliver a specified good at a specified price at a specified time in the future. Such goods included corn, wheat, soybeans, hogs, and the ultimate commodity, pork bellies (bacon). But the futures industry has undergone a revolution in the last 10 years. Now the most heavily traded futures contracts are those for financial products, like the S&P 500 Index, interest rates futures on Treasury bonds, notes, bills, and corporate and municipal bonds, and many others. Futures are legal contracts between the buyer and seller of the specified item. They are traded on federally licensed commodity exchanges.

Futures contracts can be made with very little money relative to the value of the contract. This high *leverage* means that volatile price fluctuations translate into great swings in portfolio value. Some people have made great fortunes investing in futures.

However, we certainly do *not* recommend them. Repeated studies have shown that most futures traders lose money. The odds of success are *not* in your favor. The estimates of losing traders ranges from 75 percent to 95 percent. You can get all the upside potential you want in the domestic stock market, which is also more orderly and less risky.

Currency Futures and Arbitrage

Arbitrage is the purchase of something in one market for resale in another market to take advantage of the price differential between the two markets. Since international businesspeople need foreign currencies for their operations, they must buy them somewhere, and many investors have made foreign currency futures and arbitrage a lucrative business all its own. Unfortunately, like any future transaction, arbitrage has risks that go beyond those associated with the basic "product" in which it deals. For example, an American business may want to buy a foreign currency "future" to guarantee a set exchange rate for an anticipated sale of merchandise to a firm in another country. An investor might volunteer to supply that future contract, betting that the actual exchange rate on the date the contract is honored will be more favorable than expected. Unfortunately, as currencies become more unstable, the market for futures transactions increases and so do the risks from political, economic, and business sources. Frankly, even experienced currency traders have trouble attaining consistently successful arbitrage, particularly when it takes the form of exchange rate futures.

Farms

We have a general maxim about investing in farms: If you understand farming as a business and want to put some of your resources into it for noneconomic reasons, go right ahead. But, as a general investment for Personal Profit Planners, we think there is far more fertile ground to plow.

Gold and Silver Bullion and Coins

There is only so much precious metal in the earth, and, among all precious metals, gold and silver have been valued and venerated by most cultures around the world. In stable times, they are admired for their esthetic beauty and for the substance bestowed on their owners. In times of uncertainty and crisis, their portable, concealable, and tangible (marketable) nature has reassured their owners of a more hopeful future. You can invest in gold and silver through the purchase of individual stocks, mutual funds, limited partnership mining ventures, or by buying bars, bullion (wafers), or gold and silver coins directly. Although there are times when a liquid inflation hedge like this is appropriate for investors, other factors are to be considered: Such investments pay no income and have poor prospects for price appreciation, which usually indicates that your money would be better invested elsewhere.

Oil Drilling Ventures

Oil and gas exploration and development are conducted by existing energy corporations and often are offered to investors through limited partnerships that finance *ad hoc* energy projects. When the investment is *privately placed*, it means each investor is highly "qualified" (knowledgeable, and with a high net worth). When the investment is *public*, it is often larger and better diversified, although the "front end" fees and commissions can reduce the profit many people seek from equipment depreciation and oil depletion tax benefits. We sometimes recommend oil drilling ventures for qualified Adventurers, or for people with a Strong and Quick financial physique, provided they find out all about the ventures before they invest. More than one large-scale investor has seen his or her oil investment disappear into one dry hole after another.

Oil Income Partnerships

Less speculative, but still containing energy-related risks, are oil income ventures (usually limited partnerships), which acquire oil and gas producing properties that are currently generating income. In the early years of such ventures, that income may be partly sheltered from taxes. For the longer term, if the oil resources are good for the price you had to pay, the price of energy products may keep the return of your investment even with, or ahead of, inflation.

Precious Metals Mutual Funds

Gold and silver mining shares offer the advantage of leverage over straight purchases of bullion or coins. If the price of gold were to rise from $400 to $500, bullion and coins would appreciate 25 percent. It would not be unusual for a portfolio of mining shares to increase at three or four times that rate. Of course, it works both ways. Typically, gold mining stocks will fall much worse than bullion or coins.

Mutual funds offer some benefits to precious metals investors. First, given the political problems of South Africa, mine prices may be moved by wholly unpredictable developments that have nothing to do with economic forces. There are funds that do not invest in South Africa at all; other funds limit their South African investments. The funds provide diversification over the remaining mines.

Some funds also invest in bullion and coins. These funds offer the added plus of slightly less overall volatility. Just as with bullion and coins, your investments in precious metals stocks should be limited to a small portion of your portfolio. They are highly volatile high-risk investments.

Publicly and Privately Offered Real Estate Income Limited Partnerships

A real estate *syndication* is something like a mutual fund for real estate, in that a general partner (entrepreneur and manager) assembles a pool of investor dollars and purchases specific (or a portfolio of diversified) properties. When the objective of such a syndication is income, most of the investor funds are used to finance the purchase of properties, keeping mortgages and debt-service payments to a minimum. This enables the general partner to pay higher cash distributions to the limited partners than would be possible if the properties were highly leveraged. Our rule of thumb states that if total investor capital is more than one third of the purchase price for the properties, it qualifies as a "low-leverage" syndication, with a correspondingly good income potential, assuming the properties and the managers are worth their salt.

Raw (Unimproved) Land

Land that features no useful structures, or is unemployed for agricultural purposes, is called *raw* land, and its economic value lies entirely in the future. Obviously, such land tends to be less expensive the further it lies from the beaten track (i.e., from current developments, urban centers, or other desirable areas). Since land cannot be depreciated (it doesn't "wear out," like a building), your dollars will simply sit there until someone comes along who wants to improve it, with houses or commercial buildings, for example. Unfortunately, state and local authorities can tax your raw land while you wait; and, even though nobody's using it for anything, it can require some cash to keep it in its pristine state, as well as in your possession. We consider most raw land deals to be reasonably speculative, and suggest that you should consider them only if you have a true Adventurer's spirit and plenty of time to wait for the developers to come to you.

Real Estate Investment Trusts (REITs)

REITs (pronounced "reets") are companies that pool investor money to invest in real estate properties or mortgage loans. Like mutual funds, they are professionally managed. When you buy shares in a REIT you are buying proportionate ownership in its assets. REITs trade like stock on exchanges and in the OTC market. Their value is determined by the interplay of supply and demand, rather than by a net asset value like mutual funds.

Equity REITs invest directly in real estate projects. They hope to benefit from appreciation of the value of the project. They typically pay a lower dividend than income-oriented REITs.

Mortgage REITs invest primarily in mortgages on real estate projects. They trade the potential of higher growth for the more certain higher current income. Mortgage REIT holders receive a higher current income, since most cash flow is paid through to shareholders.

There are also *hybrid* REITs, which combine the features of equity and mortgage REITs. This is similar to the way "balanced" mutual funds combine income and growth stocks for a "middle of the road" approach.

REITs offer many benefits, ranging from high current income to growth to inflation hedge. They are good investment choices for almost every Personal Profit Planner.

Single-Family Homes

Most people are well aware of the tax and wealth-building benefits of personal home ownership. Unfortunately, many of these same people reason that, if owning one home is good, owning two (or three or four) of them, and renting them out, is even better. Sadly, this does not often stand up to the realities of practical investing. Although a rental home in a decent neighborhood often will appreciate in price and continue to provide tax deductions as long as you own it, it can become a "cash parasite" instead of the "cash cow" many investors dream about. First, a decent rental property must be well maintained if it is to attract a worthy tenant. But, at the same time, there is usually a limit to how high the rents can be raised in any given neighborhood. Second, since real estate is, by definition, an illiquid investment, it might be difficult to sell your property exactly when you want to, especially if it is too expensive, or if it has been neglected through shoddy landlordship or destructive tenants. All in all, we feel there are better vehicles for personal profit in real estate; and, unless you make your living as a landlord, we suggest you leave such enterprises to the experts.

Wholly Owned Income Property

Some investors decide to cut out the middleman (such as the general partner in a syndicate or the advisor in a trust) and locate, buy, and operate a commercial property themselves. These investments can cover any kind of property, from condominiums and duplexes to multiunit apartment buildings, and, even, to smaller office buildings and neighborhood retail shopping centers. While it may seem like good economic sense (who wants to pay an intermediary for things you can do yourself?), we have found that the opposite is usually the case. Often, those who are attracted to wholly owned property management as a part-time "hobby" are the least suitable to run it. Because their primary motivation is to *save* money as well as to make it, they frequently scrimp on necessary tenant benefits, try to drive too hard a bargain on their leases, and wind up with ill-repaired properties and low-caliber tenants. Even if you are a conscientious and businesslike landlord, your reach may quickly exceed your grasp (both in time and money) when you have several properties to pay for, manage, and operate. Finally, real estate is a business like any other. Those who do well in it understand how to market their product—in this case, living or working space—and, when it's time to take a capital gain, how to sell the property itself. If you can afford the financial burden and emotional stress of many years with negative cash flow, temperamental tenants, unreliable vendors, and large-scale economic uncertainty, real estate operations may be for you. Otherwise, we recommend that you leave such activities to the pros and put your real estate dollars into programs that will deliver the benefits you want, while you concentrate your energies on your own money-making profession.

APPENDIX

ACTION PAPERS

Action Paper No. 1

kypmex

Your Current Asset Mix

Name(s) _____ S + E _____

Date _____ May '92 _____

Asset Class and Name	Market Value or Amount ($)	Totals ($)	% of Total Investable Assets
Cash Equivalents:			
T Rowe Pne Prme Res	17,800		
SIRA CSC ⊄	7,600	36.8 k	_____
SIRA PRA Bank	6,600		
E IRA Bank	4,800		
Fixed Income:			
_____	_____		
_____	_____		
_____	_____	_____	_____
Domestic Equities:			
Evergreen	8,400		
_____	_____	8.4k	
_____	_____	_____	_____
International Equities:			
_____	_____		
_____	_____		
_____	_____	_____	_____
Real Estate and Inflation Hedges			
Town house	45 K	45	
_____	_____	_____	_____
Total Portfolio Value:		_____	100%

Action Paper No. 1

Your Current Asset Mix

Name(s) _____

Date _____

Asset Class and Name	Market Value or Amount ($)	Totals ($)	% of Total Investable Assets
Cash Equivalents:			
_____	_____		
_____	_____		
_____	_____	_____	_____
Fixed Income:			
_____	_____		
_____	_____		
_____	_____	_____	_____
Domestic Equities:			
_____	_____		
_____	_____		
_____	_____	_____	_____
International Equities:			
_____	_____		
_____	_____		
_____	_____	_____	_____
Real Estate and Inflation Hedges			
_____	_____		
_____	_____		
_____	_____	_____	_____
Total Portfolio Value:		_____	100% _____

Action Paper No. 2

Your Personal Balance Sheet

Name

Date

ASSETS		LIABILITIES	
Monetary Assets		**Short-Term Liabilities**	
1. Cash and Equivalents			
		14. Unpaid Bills	
Cash/checking/savings	_____	Taxes	_____
Money market funds	_____	Insurance premiums	_____
Certificates of Deposit	_____	Rent	_____
Bonds (< 1 yr. maturity)	_____	Utilities	_____
		Charge accounts	_____
Total Cash and Equivalents	_____	Credit cards	_____
		Other_____	_____
2. Notes Receivable	_____		
		Total Unpaid Bills	_____
3. Investments			
		15. Installment Loans	
Stocks	_____	(balance due)	
Bonds (>1 yr. maturity)	_____	Automobile	_____
Real estate (REITs,		Other_____	_____
partnerships)	_____		
Cash value of life		Total Installment Loans	_____
insurance	_____		
Cash value of annuities	_____	16. Total Short-Term Liabilities	_____
Retirement plans	_____	(14 + 15)	
Total Investments	_____	**Long-Term Liabilities**	
4. Total Monetary Assets			
(1 + 2 + 3)	_____	17. Non-mortgage Loans	
		(balance due)	
Fixed Assets		Bank	_____
		Educational	_____
5. Home and property	_____	Other_____	_____
6. Automobiles/vehicles	_____		
7. Other personal property	_____	Total Non-mortgage Loans	_____
8. Total Personal Assets		18. Mortgage Loans (bal. due)	
(5 + 6 + 7)	_____	Home	_____
		Other_____	_____
9. Other real estate	_____		
10. Ownership in small business	_____	Total Mortgage Loans	_____
11. Total Fixed Investment		19. Total Long-Term Liabilities	_____
Assets (9 + 10)	_____	(17 + 18)	
12. Total Fixed Assets (8 + 11)	_____	20. Total Liabilities (16 + 19)	_____
13. Total Assets (4 + 12)	_____	21. Net Worth (13 minus 20)	_____
		22. Balance (21 + 20)	_____

Action Paper No. 2

Your Personal Balance Sheet

Name

Date

ASSETS		LIABILITIES	
Monetary Assets		**Short-Term Liabilities**	
1. Cash and Equivalents		**14.** Unpaid Bills	
Cash/checking/savings	_____	Taxes	_____
Money market funds	_____	Insurance premiums	_____
Certificates of Deposit	_____	Rent	_____
Bonds (< 1 yr. maturity)	_____	Utilities	_____
		Charge accounts	_____
Total Cash and Equivalents	_____	Credit cards	_____
		Other_____	_____
2. Notes Receivable	_____		
		Total Unpaid Bills	_____
3. Investments			
		15. Installment Loans	
Stocks	_____	(balance due)	
Bonds (>1 yr. maturity)	_____	Automobile	_____
Real estate (REITs,		Other_____	_____
partnerships)	_____		
Cash value of life		Total Installment Loans	_____
insurance	_____		
Cash value of annuities	_____	**16.** Total Short-Term Liabilities	_____
Retirement plans	_____	(14 + 15)	
Total Investments	_____	**Long-Term Liabilities**	
4. Total Monetary Assets		**17.** Non-mortgage Loans	
(1 + 2 + 3)	_____	(balance due)	
		Bank	_____
Fixed Assets		Educational	_____
		Other_____	_____
5. Home and property	_____		
6. Automobiles/vehicles	_____	Total Non-mortgage Loans	_____
7. Other personal property	_____		
		18. Mortgage Loans (bal. due)	
8. Total Personal Assets		Home	_____
(5 + 6 + 7)	_____	Other_____	_____
9. Other real estate	_____	Total Mortgage Loans	_____
10. Ownership in small business	_____		
		19. Total Long-Term Liabilities	_____
11. Total Fixed Investment		(17 + 18)	
Assets (9 + 10)	_____		
		20. Total Liabilities (16 + 19)	_____
12. Total Fixed Assets (8 + 11)	_____		
		21. Net Worth (13 minus 20)	_____
13. Total Assets (4 + 12)	_____		
		22. Balance (21 + 20)	_____

Action Paper No. 3

Your Personal Income Statement

Name

For the Year Beginning January 1, 19_____ and ending December 31, 19_____

1. **Income**
   - Spouse or Partner A _____
   - Spouse or Partner B _____
   - Total wages or salaries _____
   - Dividends and interest _____
   - Rents _____
   - Other _____ _____
2. **Total Income** _____
3. **Taxes**
   - Personal income taxes _____
   - Social Security and disability taxes _____
4. **Total Taxes** _____
5. **Amount Remaining for Living Expenses, Savings and Investments** _____

6. **Living Expenses**	Fixed	Variable
Housing		
Utilities		
Repairs	___	___
Insurance	___	___
Taxes	___	___
Rent or mortgage payments	___	___
Other _____	___	___
Food	___	
Clothing (including laundry, dry cleaning, repairs, and personal effects)	___	___
Transportation		
Gas, tolls, parking	___	___
Repairs	___	___
Licenses	___	___
Insurance	___	___
Auto payments or purchase	___	___
Fares	___	___
Recreation, entertainment, and vacations	___	___
Medical		
Doctor	___	___
Dentist	___	___
Medicines	___	___
Insurance	___	___
Personal	___	___
Life insurance (term)	___	___
Outlays for fixed assets	___	___
Other expenses _____	___	___
Subtotal	___	___

7. **Total Annual Living Expenses** _____
8. **Amount Remaining for Savings and Investment** _____

Action Paper No. 3

Your Personal Income Statement

Name

For the Year Beginning January 1, 19_____ and ending December 31, 19_____

1. **Income**
   - Spouse or Partner A
   - Spouse or Partner B
   - Total wages or salaries
   - Dividends and interest
   - Rents
   - Other _____
2. **Total Income**
3. **Taxes**
   - Personal income taxes
   - Social Security and disability taxes
4. **Total Taxes**
5. **Amount Remaining for Living Expenses, Savings and Investments**

6. Living Expenses	Fixed	Variable
Housing		
Utilities		
Repairs		
Insurance		
Taxes		
Rent or mortgage payments		
Other _____		
Food		
Clothing (including laundry, dry cleaning, repairs, and personal effects)		
Transportation		
Gas, tolls, parking		
Repairs		
Licenses		
Insurance		
Auto payments or purchase		
Fares		
Recreation, entertainment, and vacations		
Medical		
Doctor		
Dentist		
Medicines		
Insurance		
Personal		
Life insurance (term)		
Outlays for fixed assets		
Other expenses _____		
Subtotal		

7. **Total Annual Living Expenses**

8. **Amount Remaining for Savings and Investment**

Action Paper No. 4

Your Investment Specifications

Name _____

Date _____

Goals (in Priority)	Future Value (at ___ %)	Year Needed	Present Value of Goals for Various After-Tax Rates of Return (factor from Table 4-1 or 4-2 Present Value Table)					Final Investment Objectives (selected from left)	
			6%	8%	10%	12%	14%	Present Value Sum	Percent Return

High Priority, Near Term

High Priority, Long-Term

Low Priority, Near Term

Low Priority, Long-Term

(A) Total Present Value of Goals: _____

(B) Total Investment Resources PLUS Present Value of Projected Savings _____

(C) Final Goals Achievement Surplus (or Shortfall) (B) − (A) above: _____

Action Paper No. 4

Your Investment Specifications

Name _____ Date _____

Goals (in Priority)	Future Value (at ___%)	Year Needed

Present Value of Goals for Various After-Tax Rates of Return (factor from Table 4-1 or 4-2 Present Value Table)

	High Priority, Near Term		High Priority, Long-Term	
	6%	8%	10%	12%	14%
High Priority, Near Term					
Low Priority, Near Term					
					Low Priority, Long-Term

Final Investment Objectives (selected from left)

Present Value Sum	Percent Return

(A) Total Present Value of Goals: _____

(B) Total Investment Resources PLUS Present Value of Projected Savings _____

(C) Final Goals Achievement Surplus (or Shortfall) (B) — (A) above: _____

215

Action Paper No. 5

Your Group I Goal Allocations

Name(s) _____

Date _____

Group I Allocation Costs:
(Short-Term [Less Than Five Years] Needs)

Emergency Reserve _____

Goal Costs, Next Five Years + _____

Total Group I Allocation _____

Group I Allocation Targets

Asset Classes	BB&K Recommended Target Mix Range (percent)	Your Target Allocation Dollars	Percent
Cash Equivalents	20-80	_____	_____
Fixed Income	10-30	_____	_____
U.S. Stocks	10-30	_____	_____
International Stocks	0-10	_____	_____
Real Estate/ Inflation Hedges	0-10 (REITs only)	_____	_____
Total		_____	_____

Action Paper No. 5

Your Group I Goal Allocations

Name(s) _____

Date _____

Group I Allocation Costs:
(Short-Term [Less Than Five Years] Needs)

Emergency Reserve   _____

Goal Costs, Next Five Years   + _____

Total Group I Allocation   _____

Group I Allocation Targets

Asset Classes	BB&K Recommended Target Mix Range (percent)	Your Target Allocation Dollars	Percent
Cash Equivalents	20-80	_____	_____
Fixed Income	10-30	_____	_____
U.S. Stocks	10-30	_____	_____
International Stocks	0-10	_____	_____
Real Estate/ Inflation Hedges	0-10 (REITs only)	_____	_____
Total		_____	_____

Action Paper No. 6

Your Group II Goal Allocations

Name(s) _____   Date _____

Current investable resources
(Balance Sheet Items 4 + 11 PLUS
Income Statement item 8)   _____

Less Group I needs   −
(From Action Paper No. 5)   _____

Group II assets   _____

Group II Allocation Targets
(Long-Term Needs)

**BB&K Recommended
Target Mix Range**
(percent)

Asset Classes	(See Table 4–3 for Your Financial Physique)	Your Target Allocations Dollars	Percent
Cash Equivalents[1]	_____	_____	_____
Fixed Income[2]	_____	_____	_____
U.S. Stocks[3]	_____	_____	_____
International Stocks[3]	_____	_____	_____
Real Estate/ Inflation Hedges[4]	_____	_____	_____
Totals		_____	**100**

Footnotes:

1. If your Group I goals are equal to or greater than one third of your Group II goals, put no more than 5% of your Group II amounts in cash equivalents.
2. If you are an income-oriented investor, use the upper end of the fixed-income range.
3. Although U.S. and foreign stocks can follow different market cycles, you should consider them as a single equity class for the long term. Their total should not exceed 60-65% of your total Group II assets.
4. Precious metals tend to be very volatile. A mix between gold mining shares and gold bullion or coins offers greater stability than shares alone. In any case limit your precious metals position to 12% or less. Your gold investments should not exceed your real estate position.

Action Paper No. 6

Your Group II Goal Allocations

Name(s) _____   Date _____

Current investable resources
(Balance Sheet Items 4 + 11 PLUS
Income Statement item 8)   _____

Less Group I needs   –   _____
(From Action Paper No. 5)

Group II assets   _____

Group II Allocation Targets
(Long-Term Needs)

**BB&K Recommended
Target Mix Range**
(percent)

Asset Classes	(See Table 4–3 for Your Financial Physique)	Your Target Allocations Dollars	Percent
Cash Equivalents[1]	_____	_____	_____
Fixed Income[2]	_____	_____	_____
U.S. Stocks[3]	_____	_____	_____
International Stocks[3]	_____	_____	_____
Real Estate/ Inflation Hedges[4]	_____	_____	_____
Totals		_____	**100**

Footnotes:

1. If your Group I goals are equal to or greater than one third of your Group II goals, put no more than 5% of your Group II amounts in cash equivalents.
2. If you are an income-oriented investor, use the upper end of the fixed-income range.
3. Although U.S. and foreign stocks can follow different market cycles, you should consider them as a single equity class for the long term. Their total should not exceed 60-65% of your total Group II assets.
4. Precious metals tend to be very volatile. A mix between gold mining shares and gold bullion or coins offers greater stability than shares alone. In any case limit your precious metals position to 12% or less. Your gold investments should not exceed your real estate position.

Your Asset Allocation Plan

Name(s) _____

Date _____

Asset Classes	Group I Allocations (from Action Paper No. 5) Dollars		Group II Allocations (from Action Paper No. 6) Dollars		Current Target Allocations Dollars	Percent	Current Holdings Dollars	Percent	Current Adjustments Needed
Cash Equivalents	_____	+	_____	=	_____	_____	_____	_____	_____
Fixed Income	_____	+	_____	=	_____	_____	_____	_____	_____
U.S. Stocks	_____	+	_____	=	_____	_____	_____	_____	_____
International Stocks	_____	+	_____	=	_____	_____	_____	_____	_____
Real Estate/ Inflation Hedges	_____	+	_____	=	_____	_____	_____	_____	_____
Totals	_____	+	_____	=	_____				

Future Adjustments Needed?

Year	Action
_____	_____
_____	_____
_____	_____
_____	_____

Action Paper No. 7

Your Asset Allocation Plan

Name(s) _____

Date _____

Asset Classes	Group I Allocations (from Action Paper No. 5) Dollars		Group II Allocations (from Action Paper No. 6) Dollars		Current Target Allocations Dollars	Percent	Current Holdings Dollars	Percent	Current Adjustments Needed
Cash Equivalents	_____	+	_____	=	_____	_____	_____	_____	_____
Fixed Income	_____	+	_____	=	_____	_____	_____	_____	_____
U.S. Stocks	_____	+	_____	=	_____	_____	_____	_____	_____
International Stocks	_____	+	_____	=	_____	_____	_____	_____	_____
Real Estate/ Inflation Hedges	_____	+	_____	=	_____	_____	_____	_____	_____
Totals	_____	+	_____	=	_____	_____	_____	_____	_____

Future Adjustments Needed?

Year	Action
_____	_____
_____	_____
_____	_____
_____	_____
_____	_____

Action Paper No. 8

Your Investment Vehicles*

Name(s) _____ Date _____

Asset Class	Current Target Allocation ($) (from Action Paper No. 7)	List of Current Vehicles	BB&K Rosetta Stone Recommendations	Considerations	Vehicles to Investigate Further*
Cash Equivalents					
Fixed Income					
U.S. Stocks					
International Equities					
Real Estate/ Inflation Hedges					

*Important note: These vehicles must be considered preliminary selections only. More self evaluation of your financial situation, tax needs, money management skills, and life goals will be necessary before you shop for specific investments.

Action Paper No. 8

Your Investment Vehicles *

Name(s) _____ Date _____

Asset Class	Current Target Allocation ($) (from Action Paper No. 7)	List of Current Vehicles	BB&K Rosetta Stone Recommendations	Considerations	Vehicles to Investigate Further*
Cash Equivalents					
Fixed Income					
U.S. Stocks					
International Equities					
Real Estate/ Inflation Hedges					

*Important note: These vehicles must be considered preliminary selections only. More self evaluation of your financial situation, tax needs, money management skills, and life goals will be necessary before you shop for specific investments.

INDEX